Spiritual Competency
in Psychotherapy

Philip Brownell, MDiv, PsyD, is a clinical psychologist licensed in the United States and registered in the British Colony of Bermuda. He is a practicing gestalt therapist who is certified by the European Association for Gestalt Therapy (EAGT). Dr. Brownell is a member of the Scientific Board of the Research Committee of the EAGT that oversees Gestalt Research Press, and he is an independent scholar. He is the author of *Gestalt Therapy: A Guide to Contemporary Practice* and *Gestalt Therapy for Addictive and Self-Medicating Behaviors*. He teaches and trains internationally and has contributed to numerous books and reviewed journals. Dr. Brownell is also an ordained clergyman and has spent 13 years in full-time Christian ministry.

Spiritual Competency in Psychotherapy

Philip Brownell, MDiv, PsyD

SPRINGER PUBLISHING COMPANY
NEW YORK

Springer Publishing Company, LLC
11 West 42nd Street
New York, NY 10036
www.springerpub.com

Acquisitions Editor: Nancy S. Hale
Production Editor: Shelby Peak
Composition: S4Carlisle Publishing Services

ISBN: 978-0-8261-9933-1
e-book ISBN: 978-0-8261-9934-8

14 15 16 17 / 5 4 3 2 1

The author and the publisher of this Work have made every effort to use sources believed to be reliable to provide information that is accurate and compatible with the standards generally accepted at the time of publication. The author and publisher shall not be liable for any special, consequential, or exemplary damages resulting, in whole or in part, from the readers' use of, or reliance on, the information contained in this book. The publisher has no responsibility for the persistence or accuracy of URLs for external or third-party Internet websites referred to in this publication and does not guarantee that any content on such websites is, or will remain, accurate or appropriate.

Library of Congress Cataloging-in-Publication Data
Brownell, Philip (Clinical psychologist), author.
Spiritual competency in psychotherapy / Philip Brownell.
   p. ; cm.
 Includes bibliographical references and index.
 ISBN 978-0-8261-9933-1—ISBN 0-8261-9933-X—ISBN 978-0-8261-9934-8 (e-book ISBN)
 I. Title.
 [DNLM: 1. Spirituality.   2. Psychotherapy.   3. Religion and Psychology.   WM 427]
 RC489.B48
 616.89′166—dc23

2014007766

Printed in the United States of America by Gasch Printing.

Peter said, "Lord, we left our own homes to follow You."

Jesus answered, "There is no one who has left a house,
a wife, brothers, parents, or children

For the sake of the kingdom of God

Who will not receive many times as much
at this time and in the age to come—

Eternal life."

To my kingdom family

And especially those working with broken people in difficult situations:

With humankind what we attempt is impossible

But with God all things are possible.

Contents

Foreword

The reader of this book is put somewhere between a blik and a bumble bee. For those not familiar with the word "blik," it was coined by R. M. Hare at Oxford in 1950, and is an unverifiable and unfalsifiable interpretation of a person's experience.

For other readers who believe that, because of aerodynamic design, a bumble bee can't fly—that's a well-circulated myth. Even though the bee is a tanker-truck that transports nectar and its left and right wings flap independently, it does fly. What the bee lacks in design, it makes up with brute force.

So, we are left between a blik and a myth. I have pitched my mental tent here and speak from just outside the entrance flap. Speaking of flap, this is why I find this book so timely and useful. It's because of the flap about God, the Bible, and most things spiritual.

The popularity of strident atheists in today's culture has either introduced, or strengthened, the resolve of many people who chose to dismiss a spiritual dimension. For those who have the responsibility of helping a person through the mental maze, a map may be needed. This book provides the map.

In the first part, a reader encounters "the" or "a" spirit. One definition offered is "something imparted or bestowed upon a person, built into them by God." Welcome to the world of blik and myth. We can't see the object, only the manifestation of possible existence.

After bouncing off of the blik, we impact the myth. Religion, for some, is to believe in myths. Yet, religion and spirituality are "parallel continuums, twirling around each other like the latticework in a strand of DNA. . . ." This can be overlooked, minimized, or misunderstood. But to do so may twirl incompetence around psychotherapy. Hopefully a reader is open-minded enough to consider the distinct probability of encountering this combination in fellow human beings.

Even for those who truly believe a bumble bee can't fly, there comes a moment when a myth calls for further examination. Dr. Brownell offers this with professional respect and clarity.

For almost a half-century I have often observed the presence of something ageless within the human body. When talking with an elderly woman, she looked at me and said, "When you see me, you see an old woman. But inside is a 16-year-old girl." And for a brief instant she was, and I was privileged to meet the youngster. Blik.

As a fellow writer I have also experienced the possibility of a spiritual dimension. This happened through a relationship with Jesus Christ. Yes, I believe in God, in the human manifestation and written revelation of Him. But stop here. That doesn't make me anti-intellectual or a victim of delusions, as the more ferocious scoffers portray. My fields of interest range from philosophy to theology, with musings among science and logic. Even being able to pronounce some of the words encountered in these topics should result in some credit.

There are many references to the Christian faith, along with other religions, but Dr. Brownell claims that "just as this book is not a psychology of religion, nor a philosophy of religion, it is not a Christian theology of psychotherapy." Then what is it?

It's a journey taken by a seasoned psychotherapist who examines all the dimensions of the "unified whole." He takes his bag of therapy tools, checks the mental map, then heads toward the town of Spiritual Authenticity and rents a room. At least that's the way I see it.

I also see the vulnerability and competency of the traveler. He feels, cares, and factors in the spiritual aspect of a human being, if needed. If I were a client, it would be reassuring to see this book located somewhere in a therapist's office.

It is apparent that a person's mental health depends on their connection with reality, or lack of. Although truth is under suspicion in a relativistic culture, I continue to seek and believe that it exists. Perhaps it's akin to what is called "critical realism." There are topics such as therapeutic relationship, complex situational dynamics, the interpretation of experience, and the move to behavior enactment that also require further education on my part, beyond this initial exposure.

In the meantime, Dr. Brownell offers the reader a three-legged stool with a comfortable "extra-therapeutic factors" cushion upon which to sit, observe, and think. One leg is solidly stabilized by philosophy, another by psychotherapy, and the remaining one by theology. Position it somewhere between the blik and the bumble bee.

May "the" or "a" spirit be with you.

Patricia Roberts-Adams
Portland, Oregon/Reno, Nevada

Preface

This book has been roaming around in my mind for at least 15 years. In my imagination it has taken several forms, and it has been addressed to several different kinds of readers. It has also evolved within this present iteration.

There is always some "finding out" when it comes to writing, and that is because of the nature of writing. After I started writing for myself, instead of writing for professors, I realized why professors assign writing. People learn from it. I know that I learn from it, and that is partly why I write. It is the process of reaching out into the world to get information and relate it to what I'm thinking about, and it is related to the process of reaching out into the world to think in the first place. I don't just collect facts; I grapple with ideas and correlate the facts with the ideas that grip me. I often interact with my colleagues and run constructions by them to see what they will do with them. In that regard I prize my relationships with Peter Philippson, Dan Bloom, Seán Gaffney, and others on the discussion lists of the New York Institute for Gestalt Therapy and the listserv known as Gstalt-L. Thus, writing becomes an extension of myself, a growth experience that seems a bit beyond what I ever thought it might be.

Andy Clark (2011) relays an anecdote, attributed to Richard Feynman, in which a historian refers to Feynman's notes as the record of his thinking, the work having been done in his head, and Feynman responds by saying, "No, it's not a *record*, not really. It's *working*. You have to work on paper and this is the paper. Okay?" (p. xxv).

I can relate. I have lived long enough that I have worked on paper, on a typewriter, and now on a computer. I have learned to think through my fingers on the keyboard. My cognitive process—my mind, if you will—extends through my fingertips, onto the keypad, and into the computer program, and my thoughts often flow out into the world so that my self extends beyond the bounds of my physical body. I cannot do the same thing just talking to people; dictation doesn't work for me. I must write it. Also, if I am working on an organizational board in which I must talk, for example, to participate in a phone conference, I am close to useless, and it is frustrating, because following the conference, I will typically sit down on my computer and write a long and detailed email laying out everything I could not say—literally could not find the words to say, not just could not find a place to say them in the flow of the discussion. People often wonder why I did not share all that "stuff" when I had a chance, and the answer is that I was not my normal self. My normal self is a writing self, and a keyboard-writing self.

Why do I bring this up? It's because people need to be themselves when they work as psychotherapists, and one cannot fake such things as competence. If the extension of one's mind does not naturally flow out into the world down spiritual corridors, if one has not developed a spiritual way of being in this world, then spiritual competence is going to be a struggle, and dealing in spiritual matters in psychotherapy will seem like a bad fit until one has mastered it over time.

That might seem like I am building up to claim only spiritual people can do spiritual work in psychotherapy. That would be untenable. After all, I had to learn how to type on the typewriter, going from paper and pen, and I had to experience countless days of writing dialogues with my colleagues on professional e-mail lists before I came to realize that I had become a certain kind of person—the kind who thinks best through his fingers on a keyboard. Just so, people who are not immediately sensitive to the hues of light shining through stained glass, the smell of incense burning on metal in cold, stone cathedrals, or the heat of sacrifice on the altar can learn to see beyond such extensions of the self and work out their own spiritual competencies. I hope this book will at least point the reader in a direction that facilitates such growth.

This, however, is not a book that covers all bases. That has been part of its pruning over time. This is not a book that explores all the major issues with specificity in reference to a majority of spiritual traditions and worldviews. That has been part of the focusing of the project in the reduction of time. Given that I don't have time (perhaps there never was enough time) to research all the nuances of the major spiritual and religious systems so as to provide an exhaustive reference, I am falling back on what I know best, and I am letting it serve as both specific example and metaphorical illustration. The reader from a different spiritual tradition will, hopefully, be able to apply the principles outlined in the examples and points that I make. Furthermore, I am not even providing an exhaustive treatment of my own spiritual tradition in psychotherapy. Rather, I'm going to explore this from my perspective and roam around in it. I will go here and there, miss some things and hit others. I admit this approach from the beginning. This book will not be all things to all people.

I am a Christian, but having said that, I am not what some might think of as a Christian. I am an ordained clergyman, and I once served on the multiple staff of a large church in the Sacramento Valley of California. In my Bible I carried a picture of what I looked like in college, and it showed a young man in a navy peacoat, with shoulder-length hair and a beard. The secretary at that church told me, "I don't think a pastor should have *ever* looked like *that!*" I never burned my rock and roll. I drank wine, and I went to movies. On the other hand, in college I also drove an old, green panel truck with the words in yellow across the side that said, "Jesus Saves!" I sat in the hallways with my Bible open and got into conversations with people about spiritual matters, and to this day I hold to a literal, historical, grammatical hermeneutic in exegesis.

I am conservative in my theology, but I defy the stereotypes. As one of my colleagues once said, "I am too Christian for the psychologists, and too psychological for the Christians." I am not like the preachers who feel their calling and task from God is to point out where everyone is wrong. I think we're all wrong to some degree, and so it's a pointless effort. My education in clinical psychology, my training and growth in gestalt therapy, and my experience in clinical practice have led me to appreciate the complexity integral to human life, and that includes the spiritual dimension of living. I've existed as a man trying to live according to Christian spirituality for almost 45 years, and for part of that time I was a professional Christian. I speak through my fingers into your world about some things that I know. I don't know everything. Life is more than what it seemed in seminary. I have learned that there are spiritual experiences people have that are different from my own, and I believe that spiritual competence in psychotherapy requires that the psychotherapist know something before beginning but be able to learn something from each client as the process unfolds.

What I have intended in the writing of this book is to explore spirituality in the practice of psychotherapy in order to contribute to the competence of clinicians.

Philip Brownell
From above Mizzentop on Harbor Road
Warwick, Bermuda

REFERENCE

Clark, A. (2011). *Supersizing the mind: Embodiment, action, and cognitive extension*. New York, NY: Oxford University Press.

Acknowledgments

I would like to acknowledge the contributions that many have made to my life, because out of my life came this book.

To my parents, Warren and Barbara—what a wonderful and crazy incubation you two provided. That includes my brothers (Mark, Tim, and Jeff) and my sister (Cathy).

To my children, Matthew, Zachary, and Anastasia—trying to parent (protect, nurture, discipline, enrich, provide, guide, encourage, and inspire) you is a lifelong graduate course in adjustment and humility. In spite of me and to the credit of others in accord with the providence of God, you three are incredibly wonderful people.

To my wife, Linda—some have said that you are a female version of me or that I'm a male version of you. They are all wrong. You are someone God prepared beforehand, before we were even born, to come into my life (and me into yours) at a precise moment to bless us in accord with His love for us, because He is a giver of good.

To Lee Toms, Pat Roberts-Adams, and Paul Clayton—Lee Toms was my pastor, and I served with him on a multiple staff church. I listened to his preaching, I watched his work ethic in the ministry, and I discussed various aspects of the Christian life and ministry with him. Pat Roberts-Adams was a spiritual mentor for years and tracked me through some pretty difficult times. She is a fellow writer, but beyond that she is an avid reader and learner. I don't think I could ever catch up. Paul Clayton is the first person I can say truly responded to the gospel through my presence in his life; I never got bored thinking about that. He is a child in the Lord, and he's still running with endurance the race that is set before him.

To my friends and colleagues in the world of gestalt therapy, many of them agnostic at best: Dan Bloom, Peter Philippson, Seán Gaffney, Brian O'Neill, Sylvia Crocker, Sally Denham-Vaughn, Carol Swanson, Ruella Frank, Pablo Herrera Salinas, and Jan Roubal, among others. You have helped fashion my thinking through countless discussion group exchanges, conference planning events, and research-oriented discussions.

To the people at Springer Publishing Company, especially Nancy S. Hale for her patience and help in getting the book completely done.

Introduction: Spiritual Competence in Clinical Practice

The philosophy which is so important in each of us is not a technical matter; it is our more or less dumb sense of what life honestly and deeply means. It is only partly got from books; it is our individual way of just seeing and feeling the total push and pressure of the cosmos.

—William James, 1907/2003, p. 1

The same can be said of competency. Competency is not obtained completely from books, and when it comes down to it, one demonstrates his or her competence as an individual way of seeing and feeling in the pressure of one's corner of the cosmos. If a person has a stroke, that person wants a doctor who knows something about strokes, has an appropriate attitude toward the patient, and can apply information to specific facets of an otherwise novel situation and actually *do something* to ameliorate the patient's condition. In this sense, competence is pragmatic and can be observed and evaluated.

Competence is also ethical. Professional ethics comprise systems of thought, cultural values, and professional experience grounded in the rigors of philosophical discipline (Hanson, Kerkhoff, & Bush, 2005). Something is considered to be right or wrong—helpful, compassionate, and caring or destructive, callous, and cruel—and the arbiter in any given case is often nothing more than a person's conscience.

The man with a conscience fights a lonely battle against the overwhelming forces of inescapable situations which demand decisions. But he is torn apart by the extent of the conflicts in which he has to make his choice with no other aid or counsel than that which his own innermost conscience can furnish.

(Bonhoeffer, 1949/1995, p. 68)

The American Psychological Association (APA) has provided aspirational principles and guidelines to help people exercise ethical decisions of conscience. Table I.1 shows examples of the numerous other organizations that also provide such ethical codes (since I am a psychologist, I will refer to the APA's ethics code in subsequent issues of ethics, but the reader might do well to cross-reference in the code that applies most appropriately to his or her organization or profession).

Regardless of all these codes of ethics, it still requires individual judgment to keep from doing harm, to maintain respect for others, and to practice in areas in which one has knowledge and ability.

In order to evaluate spiritual competence in psychotherapy, a person must comprehend the nature and demands of psychotherapy as well as the nature of spirituality and the requirements for competently addressing the needs of spiritual people encountered during psychotherapy. It is not necessary, nor is it even possible, to know everything about all the diverse religious and spiritual streams flowing among

TABLE I.1
EXAMPLES OF ETHICS CODES

Organization	Online Reference
American Psychological Association	http://www.apa.org/ethics/code/principles.pdf
American Association of Pastoral Counselors	http://www.aapc.org/policies/code-of-ethics.aspx
American Counseling Association	http://www.counseling.org/Resources/aca-code-of-ethics.pdf
American Association for Marriage and Family Therapy	http://www.aamft.org/imis15/content/legal_ethics/code_of_ethics.aspx
National Association of Social Workers	http://www.socialworkers.org/pubs/code/default.asp
European Association for Gestalt Therapy	http://www.eagt.org/code_of_ethics.htm

the communities of faith in this world. What is necessary is that one begin to see spiritual and religious life as an important consideration, right up there alongside cognition, affect, and development. It is also necessary to know some facts about various religious and spiritual people, their worldviews, values, and practices, and to develop an attitude of curious fascination with regard to the ways in which people inhabit spirit. In one way it is a different world (Yancey, 2003) with its own culture, but in another it is a whole set of worlds, each with its own culture.

THE NATURE OF PSYCHOTHERAPY

Some consider psychotherapy to be an application of science, but others claim it to be a form of art. Although the science of psychotherapy demands evidence-based practice, the artistry of psychotherapy requires an aesthetic sensitivity (Francesetti, 2012). The therapist-as-artist subjectively discerns its form and contributes to its emergence in relationship with the client, who, conducting a corresponding piece of artistry, appreciates the process and contributes to its progress. As such, Gerald Corey (2013), in his survey of psychotherapeutic approaches, stated that psychotherapy "is a process of engagement between two people, both of whom are bound to change through the therapeutic venture. At its best, this is a collaborative process that involves both the therapist and the client in co-constructing solutions to concerns" (p. 7).

Corsini and Wedding (2007), in the eighth edition of their book surveying a number of approaches to psychotherapy, claimed that any form of psychotherapy is a learning process that concerns the way people think, feel, and act. As such, psychotherapy is intended to make people think differently (cognition), to make them feel differently (affection), and to make them act differently (behavior).

Many people believe the concept of psychotherapy originated with Sigmund Freud in 1900 (Bankart, 1996), with his work titled *The Interpretation of Dreams* (since republished in numerous editions and translations). Others trace the origins of psychotherapy five years earlier to the collaboration between Josef Breuer and Freud, and the publication of their book *Studies in Hysteria*; Breuer's patient, Anna O., is said to have called the hypnosis she experienced as "the talking cure"

(Winick, 1997). Because of these associations, psychotherapy, "the talking cure," has been attributed largely to Sigmund Freud. With the advent of such a talking cure, the psychotherapist became the doctor of the *interior* (Cushman, 1992), and psychotherapy's focus became what takes place when two people sit down to speak with one another about one person's subjective experience. It is any form of treatment using verbal or non-verbal communication between a therapist and a patient/client/consumer that is understood to be a professional relationship.

(Brownell, 2010a, p. 4)

Thus, psychotherapy entails a unique pairing. That is, the process and the experience are not identical and transferable between one therapist and another, or even with the same therapist between one client and another. While manuals can delineate procedures leading to uniformity of practice, no two therapists using such manuals will conduct themselves in exactly the same way, every time, for each and every client.

There is a way in which one person draws another out, turns another on, turns another off, or sends another into retreat. It is not that such a person intends to do something like this to the other; it is a by-product of the way they each exist, interact with one another, and the specific settings in which they find themselves with the specific extra-therapeutic factors that affect each one of them. For psychotherapy to work, there must be "chemistry" between the therapist and the client—they must "click" with one another. They must establish contact and build a relationship (Norcross, 2011).

People tell their therapists things they would never tell anyone else, and that is the way it is supposed to be. The therapist is the trusted confidant, but not just that; the therapist is trusted for his or her ethical stance (being trustworthy as a person with altruistic values) and for his or her competence as a professional (as a psychotherapist).

The word "psychotherapy" is a compound formed from two Greek words, *psychē* and *therapeuō*. *Psychē* means "soul." There are two Greek words associated with curing or healing, and one of them is found in the compound—*therapeuō*, meaning "heal" or "cure." On that basis alone, the compound refers to a process that heals the soul, with "soul" being a more general term that in many places is best translated as "person." There is another word indicating mind (*nous*), so it is best to retain the more general sense of person for *psychē* and allow the association of mindfulness with psychology to emerge at will. The other Greek word that is worth considering is *iaomai*. While *therapeuō* originally meant to serve a superior, and to cure that person of various ills, *iaomai* was the more direct word for healing, and its result was a person who became *hugiēs*, or healthy or whole. *Iaomai* includes healings and cures from physical and psychological ills. Thus, the implication in the compound "psychotherapy" (and associated words) is that the therapist serves the client for the purpose of healing that person and rendering him or her healthy, sensible, and of sound mind (Brown, 1976).

With these things in view, consider Jesus as psychotherapist. For some that would be an oxymoron, because they consider psychotherapy and religion to be opposite to one another, with no place available in religious thinking or practice for psychology—the study of the soul. Obviously, I am not one of those people. Consequently, I often see scripture through the eyes of a psychotherapist, through the eyes of someone who has listened to the way people really are, the secrets they keep from others, and as someone who has witnessed the anguish they experience in trying to live among other people as well as the exhilaration and excitement they experience on the occasion of an intimacy.

Jesus sat down with a woman he met at a well outside a dusty town in Palestine. He asked her for some water, and then he told her that she was living with a man outside of marriage and had been married several times before. She was astounded, and she ran away to the townspeople saying, "Come see a man who told me all about myself"[1] (literally, "Come see a man who told me everything that I did").

Now, the point here is not that Jesus, as psychotherapist, exercised omniscience and knew facts about his "client" that she had not revealed. The interesting thing to me is the effect of being with Jesus.

She did not recoil in shame, as if feeling judged by a legalistic and oppressive religious figure whose interest was her sexual sin. She described Him as a man who told her *everything that she did*. Actually, He did not tell her everything that she had ever done; He went to the heart of an important but single aspect of her life. It only seemed so big as to feel like everything she had ever done. Her experience was also not simply at the level of the facts of her life, as a category description of how many times she had been married. Her experience was that Jesus had gone to the kind of person she was, and with just a few facts stated openly between them, she got in touch with who she believed herself to be—as a person.

Jesus had touched her soul in such a dramatic fashion that she wondered aloud whether He might be the Messiah. She inquired with him about a nagging question she had had—where was the correct place to worship God? It was in this dialogue that Jesus provided one of His most salient teachings: God is Spirit. It's not a matter of where to worship God but how to worship God (in spirit and in truth), bringing together two important features of spirituality (process and relationship).

The privilege of being a psychotherapist is that psychotherapists are involved in touching people in the way that Jesus touched the woman at the well. Psychotherapists touch people's souls, and there is healing in that. Research on psychotherapy has shown that significant healing comes directly from the quality of the psychotherapeutic relationship. This is contact between two people *as people*. This is not one person playing a professional role in order to do something helpful to the other one. On the other hand, no psychotherapist is omniscient; so there are skills involved in promoting the self-revelation of the client and competencies required to advance the presence of the therapist. With increasing awareness, people learn (both therapist and client) more about what they do and how they do it, and there is a beauty to this process—a good form to it that can be promoted, perceived, and appreciated. In fact, a skilled psychotherapist will do just that, bringing together the science of psychotherapy with its artistry.

THE ISSUE OF COMPETENCE

Competence involves not just what a person knows, but also what a person can do and what happens when that person does what he or she can do. "Competence in professional psychology refers to developmentally appropriate levels of knowledge, skills, and attitudes and their integration in various foundational domains of functioning" (Johnson, Barnett, Elman, Forrest, & Kaslow, 2012, p. 558).[2] Rodolfa et al. (2005) asserted that competent professionals are "qualified, capable, and able to understand and do certain things in an appropriate and effective manner" (p. 348). They claimed that competence is a matter of "what a person brings to a job or role (knowledge), what the person does in the job or role (performance), and what is achieved by the person in a job or role (outcomes)" (p. 349). They proposed a set of functional competencies that are each related to a concomitant set of foundational competencies. The functional domains of competence are

(a) assessment (diagnosis and case conceptualization); (b) intervention (understanding and applying evidence-based treatments); (c) consultation (guidance, expert assistance); (d) research (contributions to the professional knowledge base); (e) supervision or teaching (training and evaluation of professionals); and (f) management (administration). Each of these is impacted by relating it to a set of orthogonal foundational competencies, and the foundational competencies are (a) self-reflective practice; (b) scientific knowledge; (c) relationships; (d) ethical and legal standards; (e) individual and cultural diversity; and (f) interdisciplinary systems.

Considering that competence is something in which a psychotherapist continually grows, competence can also be understood as developmental. Competence is always a work in progress. However, it is helpful to see phases of this development in which a psychotherapist undergoes graduate or doctoral education, internship, postgraduate supervision and residency, possibly further specialization residency or fellowship, and then continuing development. The combination of functional and foundational competencies and developmental stages of growth have been referred to as the "cube" model (Rodolfa et al., 2005) for professional competency in psychology, and this combination provides a good heuristic of the issues involved when considering competency in psychotherapy.

In regard to spiritual competency, then, knowledge, performance, and outcome can be assessed in the matrix in Figure I.1.

Thus, for example, a person could evaluate to what degree he or she might be spiritually competent by considering to what degree he or she is self-reflective and knowledgeable about religious issues, careful in regard to relationships, ethical and sensitive to diversity among communities of faith, and able to utilize interdisciplinary systems (in the case of psychotherapy, perhaps the disciplines of philosophy and theology or religious studies) in the areas of assessment, psychotherapy, consulting, research, and management.

If, as is the case, researcher bias has been shown to be a factor, shouldn't people consider the possibility that psychotherapist bias might be in play as well? The issue of spiritual competency is a relevant one precisely because it has not been developed and considered; it is a blind spot in the training of many psychotherapists. In the darkness of that blind spot, the bias of the psychotherapist lurks unexamined, and spiritual competency in psychotherapy is the developmental process of bringing all these features of the matrix into the light, dispelling darkness over time.

FIGURE I.1
COMPETENCY MATRIX

	Self-reflective Practice	Scientific Knowledge	Relationships	Ethical and Legal Standards	Individual and Cultural Diversity	Interdisciplinary Systems
Assessing						
Intervening						
Consulting						
Researching						
Supervising						
Managing						

The three most commonly used methods of assessing competence are subjective assessment by supervising clinicians, multiple-choice examinations to evaluate factual knowledge, and abstract problem solving (Epstein & Hundert, 2002). These methods are used to determine what a person knows and what a person can do. As stated, what a person knows and what a person can do are not static categories. As the cube model illustrates, these things evolve and develop over time, and so the means of assessment should accommodate such growth.

The assessment and development of spiritual competency requires an organized approach to the development of such competency. Those tasked with the obligation to attend to adequate preparation of clinicians need to attend to their own educational competencies so that their students and trainees emerge from their studies knowledgeable and capable in regard to the role of spirituality and religion in life.

SPIRITUALITY AS A CULTURAL ISSUE

Spiritual competence in psychotherapy is best understood as belonging to that part of the foundational competencies involving individual and cultural differences,[3] also known as multiculturalism (APA, 2003; Saunders, Miller, & Bright, 2010; Sue, Bingham, Porche-Burke, & Vasquez, 1999). One's culture includes spiritual and religious elements; one's field is a complex situation in which spiritual and religious influences are present. Just as a psychotherapist living in Western Europe would not think of working with a client from Asia without gaining some appreciation of Asian culture, psychotherapists need to consider the spiritual and religious cultures of the people with whom they work. They need to evaluate their competence to work with clients who hold significant religious or spiritual worldviews. They need to consider how religion and spirituality have or have not been a factor in the lives of their clients, especially when clients represent marked difference in ethnic, cultural, and national categories. For instance, one would obviously engage a translator if forced to work with a client from another country who speaks a different language, but would one think to engage a consultant to understand the client's different religious or spiritual "language?"

The issues of spirituality, religion, and secularism are in stark contrast as multicultural considerations when it comes to working with migrant populations. A given therapist, having lived and worked in a context of secularism, might find it difficult to understand a client coming from a different country, one in which religion is a major force (Limberg, 2013). For that matter, a therapist working in a country where religion is a major factor would need to understand the relative secular perspectives of a client coming from somewhere that does not value religion and spirituality. This is true of the differences across various cultural elements and communities even within the same country. Furthermore, when religious and spiritual constructs and practices bleed into public policy, depending on the jurisdiction in which one practices, one needs to become competent with regard to the effects of such policies on both the therapist and the client (Singh & Cowden, 2011).

Seen in another way, all these kinds of cultural influences are part of the extra-therapeutic factors that both therapist and client bring into the meeting and that affect the development of their relationship. They are at play in the very beginning stages of their contacting, and they account for a majority of the outcomes in psychotherapy (Brownell, 2010a). Thus, the multicultural issues of spirituality and religion are crucial considerations.

Unfortunately, spiritual and religious beliefs have been marginalized in psychology; that might be because spirituality and religious worldviews, commitments, and practices are not often considered relevant to psychological process and thus not provided as a standard element of graduate training in psychotherapy. That could be a holdover from the bias of Freud, who considered religion to be pathological. It could be a reflection of the sociopolitical context in which any given training program exists, including an unspoken expectation that religion not be introduced into the "public square." There could be many reasons why this deficit has existed, but exist it has.

According to a study conducted by Crook-Lyon et al. (2012), 250 psychologists from Division 12 of the APA (Clinical Psychology), 296 from APA Division 36 (Psychology of Religion), and 250 from APA Division 45 (Society for the Psychological Study of Ethnic Minority Issues) were surveyed, and 76% agreed that religious and spiritual issues were inadequately covered in training. In the same study, 77% agreed that spiritual and religious issues are multicultural issues, and 67% did not view spirituality and religion as distinct from multiculturalism. Clearly, more work needs to be done.

COMPETENCE, ETHICS, AND CULTURAL SENSITIVITY

Gonsiorek, Richards, Pargament, and McMinn (2009) asserted something that almost seems like common sense—that religion is important both to people who retain their religious affiliations and those who turn away from theirs. It is inevitable, they observed, "that such deeply held aspects of the human experience will regularly express themselves in clients' presentations for psychological services" (p. 386). Therefore, they concluded, competent service provision should be expected, and that would indicate "a sufficiently broad and detailed combination of course work, supervised experience, continuing education, professional reading, consultation, and other standard training vehicles that together are satisfactory to licensing boards and ethics committees" (p. 386).[4]

According to the APA's ethics code, psychologists should practice only in areas of such competence: "Psychologists provide services, teach and conduct research with populations and in areas only within the boundaries of their competence, based on their education, training, supervised experience, consultation, study or professional experience" (2.01a; APA, 2010, p. 1063). Using that as a model, those engaged in the provision of psychotherapy should do so only within the boundaries of *their* competence, which, as has already been established, is a function of what they know, what they can do, and what takes place when they do it.

If they lack competence, then they should get appropriate training: "Psychologists planning to provide services, teach or conduct research involving populations, areas, techniques or technologies new to them undertake relevant education, training, supervised experience, consultation or study" (2.01c; APA, 2010, p. 1064).

Unfortunately, there is a gap with regard to the competence of most providers when it comes to clients' spiritual and religious identities and practices. Note that not only have spiritual and religious issues been poorly covered in training programs, even though most people believe they are part of a multicultural perspective, but they have also been shown to be missing in terms of provision of service. If competence involves knowing something about what one is doing and then having the outcomes prove the ability to apply knowledge to critical areas of life, then such competence is lacking in many cases.

Rosenfeld (2011) observed that many therapists deal with religious issues in psychotherapy without sufficient training. Citing a dated study, he pointed out that three-fourths of social workers had almost no content on religion or spirituality during their graduate education (Canda & Furman, 1999), and he reported a similar condition for psychiatrists and clinical psychologists. This observation was supported by later research[5] cited by Crook-Lyon et al. (2012), noting that "most psychologists have limited awareness and understanding of issues surrounding clients' religion and spirituality. . . . Few graduate training programs address religious or spiritual issues" (p. 1).

This incompetence, unfortunately, shows up in practice when the understanding of religious clients leads to poor treatment planning and service provision. Kevern, Walsh, and McSherry (2013) conducted a study to evaluate the efficacy with which care plans captured and made use of data on the spiritual and religious concerns of mental health users in a UK Health and Social Care Trust. A questionnaire was given to 71 service users and the findings compared with the information that made it into files held on their behalf at three key points in the care planning process. The importance that service users accorded to spiritual and religious matters was not reflected in the electronic records, some of the information was wrong or wrongly nuanced when compared with the clients' self-descriptions, and service users themselves were misinformed about the kind of information that *was* being stored about them. The study concluded that spiritual and religious concerns were not being considered in the construction of care plans. It is likely that in spite of training focused on spiritual concerns being important in mental health, the individual service provider's local competence is a crucial factor in adequate treatment planning.

With this in view, it is clear that people who do not have training in working with spiritual and religious issues ethically ought not practice with clients presenting with those issues or for whom such issues are integral elements of the field/significant extra-therapeutic factors. In fact, even with training it is likely that service providers will need to take stock of their own beliefs, worldviews, and biases with regard to spirituality and religion, and if a service provider is aware that he or she is inherently antireligious, it is probably best to develop a good referral resource for use with clients who need something the antireligious service provider may not be able to provide.

With spiritual and religious beliefs and practices being integral to clients' ethnic and cultural identities, Principle E of the APA's ethics code is also relevant. Principle E states that psychologists respect the dignity and worth of people, including the rights they have to privacy, confidentiality, and self-determination. It asserts that psychologists should be aware and respect cultural, individual, and role differences like those "based on age, gender, gender identity, race, ethnicity, culture, national origin, religion, sexual orientation . . ." and related categories, taking these kinds of things into consideration when working with members of such groups. It also says that psychologists attempt to eliminate biases from their work and do not knowingly participate in or condone activities based on prejudice (APA, 2010, p. 4).

Following the APA benchmark, then, psychotherapists ethically ought to attend to the blank spots in their training and the biases in their own worldviews. Psychotherapists who believe that religion is the cause of suffering, religious people are weak-minded, and that there is no reason to make religious or spiritual concerns integral to the process of psychotherapy would be unethical and incompetent to work with clients who strongly believe in God or those who adhere diligently to a spiritual discipline.

This would likely fly in the face of experienced psychotherapists who believe that they can remain "objective" or whose approach is basically phenomenological and thus tracks the experience of the client (so if the client is religious, there is no problem because the therapist simply takes his or her lead from the client). The problem with that is that it reflects a one-person psychology that does not deal adequately with the presence and subtle influence of the therapist, making for a two-person psychology (*at least* a two-person psychology, if not for a more collective view allowing for the influence of society and culture on both therapist and client). Rather, therapists need to realize that religion and spirituality as issues and matters of concern are likely to be "in the room" one way or the other, and in order to be competent they need to account for them, to become knowledgeable, to challenge their own religious/antireligious commitments, and to develop the ability to respond effectively.

THE PURPOSE OF THIS BOOK

The purpose of this book is to contribute to spiritual competency in the practice of psychotherapy. I have been thinking of this book for several years. The issues covered evolved through conversations with colleagues, presentations at professional conferences, training workshops, and previous writing projects. I wanted to write something that transcends a gathering of facts. At the same time, I cannot escape the realization that this can only be from the perspective of one person's gathering of facts and implicit, relative meanings.

Nevertheless, I wanted to write something that touches the soul, and I admit that is a grand ambition.

Recently, I attended a church service in a large city, and this service was supposed to be devoted to worship. The church had brought in worship leaders from a church in a prominent southern city, and supposedly they were to be given the entire New Year's Eve worship service—to usher in the new year on the right note. The worship leaders began to work the situation. They sang upbeat numbers, all well choreographed and staged. There was a live band. There was a backup choir. It was a big production, but it wasn't going anywhere and just seemed to be what professional musicians can do. The worship leaders sensed this. They were telling emotional stories about their autistic child. They were inviting the congregation to "get into it." But it was going nowhere. The worship leaders toned down the volume until it was a hush, and one of the leaders sidled over to the keyboardist, stepped in beside him, and then took over. He deviated from the plan. He roamed the keys and the notes seemed to be searching for a theme, and then a classic hymn from the reformation emerged in the notes of the piano. I had been sitting, rather bored with the whole thing, but when I heard that hymn, a wave of passion swept over me, and I stood up. Others all over the church did the same. Then, the worship leader modulated to *Agnus Dei*, a well-known aspect of the mass set to contemporary music by Michael W. Smith, and people began to sing it spontaneously. Some began to moan. The place was flush with the sense of God, and I closed my eyes and dropped my head in worship. Then, it all stopped. The pastor of the church had sent one of his staff up to make announcements and to lead the congregation in a canned prayer. The whole tone of the situation dropped out in a disappointing crash.

I wanted to write a book on spiritual competence that would encourage and stimulate an experience of the Spirit and not just make announcements or lead the reader in canned and predictable statements about professional responsibilities. The approach I have taken is analogous to what Perls, Hefferline, and Goodman (1951/1972) called a gestalt analysis. In a gestalt analysis, one does not point directly at some figure and explain it or at some fact as a form of proof. One observes all the various elements of the situation in which the figure appears, and one describes the "things" as they are given, in the context in which they are given, however one encounters them. A picture emerges. A story unfolds. An experience comes about.

People commonly say that one person cannot really know what something is like until he or she walks in the shoes of the person engaged in that something. Supposedly, you can't know what having a baby is like unless you have given birth. You cannot know what sex is like until you lose your virginity. You cannot know what psychotherapy is like unless you've experienced it. That argument, obviously, has its limitations. We can know something about a condition without having to experience it. I have worked with numerous people suffering from a postpartum depression, and I understand what the dynamic is like even though I, myself, have never been pregnant and given birth. I used to work in the delivery room of a Naval hospital, and I've been in the delivery room for the births of all three of my children. No, I was not the one having labor pains, panting, and sucking on chips of ice, but I could hear and see, and I was in the room and part of the experience from my corner of it. I know something about it because I immersed myself in the elements of the situation. I know something of the experience of postpartum depression because I have immersed myself in the elements of my clients' experiences and learned from them.

So, the purpose of this book is to give enough of a gestalt analysis, to look at the issue of spirituality and how it manifests at various times and in various persons, to immerse the reader in it so that a picture emerges and an experience comes about. It would not be good enough that one might read this book, gather some facts, and then simply know something about the subject; rather, I hope that people might engage with spirituality enough to "get it," to comprehend themselves as spiritual beings, and to understand their spiritual and religious clients, respecting the place of spirituality in psychotherapy. That builds knowledge, supports growth in ability, and hopefully leads to a more effective, ethical, and competent practice.

THE STRUCTURE OF THE BOOK

The first part of this book examines spirituality itself. It might seem obvious what that is, but there are actually many takes on the subject. Part I lays the ground and allows the reader to find his or her own starting point. It contextualizes spirituality in various religious understandings and provides a workable definition. It also includes a discussion of the common polarity between spirituality and religion and an exploration of the approaches to the study of religion—that is, from the perspectives of philosophy, psychology, and theology. While there are various typologies one might encounter with regard to the study of spirituality, one can simplify them into two elements: spirituality as process and spirituality as relationship. There is an obvious overlap in that there is a process to relationship and every process will include certain relationships, but this approach first explains the two-fold typology and then, in the rest of the book, explores how spirituality as process and relationship can be understood in practice. The last chapter of Part I explores the personal and existential nature of spirituality.

Part II consists of four chapters, each taking one aspect of an evolving convergence in psychotherapy. Each chapter explores spirituality in psychotherapy directly. The first chapter of Part II describes how spirituality as process and relationship is present and relevant to the therapeutic relationship. The second describes the overall complex situation. The third describes the holistic but subjective experience of people involved in psychotherapy (including the cognitive elements of mindfulness and the interpretation of experience), and the last chapter describes spiritual work in the context of the experimental nature of experiential learning.

Part III includes several chapters that take a different approach. In this section, I tell stories more than build arguments. I also relate, as in most of the book, from that spiritual tradition I know the best and in which I am most competent—Christianity.[6] My hope is that the reader whose spiritual and religious tradition differs might be able to "translate" these stories and metaphors into his or her own context, and I hope that those without any grounding in such a tradition will at least gain an appreciation for the complexity and richness inherent to our clients' situations. Instead of starting with the processes of psychotherapy, these chapters present common problems or situations that a psychotherapist might encounter in clients presenting with relevant spiritual issues. In the least, Part III provides a broad appreciation for the kinds of dynamics any given therapist might reasonably encounter in religious and spiritual clients.

I started off this introduction claiming that competency is an individual way of seeing and feeling in the pressure of one's corner of the cosmos. Although we are all accountable for our competencies, that is still true. It's up to the reader to make the most of this book, but here are a few suggestions on how to read it:

- You may want to skip Part I—an exploration of the concept of "spirit" and how that relates to religion—and go to Parts II and III.
- You might want to explore more for yourself one of the four consilient elements of psychotherapy in Part II (dialogue/relationship, field/situation, interpretation of embodied and subjective experience, and existential/behavioral experimentation) for its spiritually relational and process-oriented features with regard to a religious tradition more akin to your own background and culture.
- You may want to take one of the issues covered in Part III and see whether there are any corollaries in other religions.
- You might want to attempt writing treatment plans for some of the issues in Part III.
- You might want to use this book as a resource for a personal meditation and to reflect on the way you experience spiritual process and spiritual relationship.

One other thing needs to be said. I may show evidence of it along the way. This is not a book that tells people all about spirituality in psychotherapy. It is from my own perspective, and there are other books in the genre of the psychology of religion, for instance, that are much more exhaustive and scholarly than this one. While I attempt to relate to spiritual things outside my own religious and spiritual tradition and experience, I speak most freely and with the most competence from a stance within my own ground. Further, while I attempt to relate things to what others have written, and so provide various references, this is not, as I have said, an exhaustive literature review. The things I am sharing should be investigated more by the reader and tracked down for their counterparts in other religions and in the literatures of theology, psychology, and philosophy. What I do hope to do here is to open a door into spiritual and religious experience and the processes associated with that in psychotherapy. In that regard, my hope is that you will not just know about some things, but that you will also actually experience some things, and that your ability to work with spirituality in psychotherapy would increase.

NOTES

1. δεῦτε ἴδετε ἄνθρωπον ὃς εἶπέ μοι πάντα ὅσα ἐποίησα (*The Greek New Testament*, 1983, United Bible Societies, pp. 334–335)
2. Johnson et al., quote Epstein and Hundert (2002) to further define competence as "the habitual and judicious use of communication, knowledge, technical skills, clinical reasoning, emotions, values, and reflection in daily practice for the benefit of the individual and the community served" (p. 226).
3. This does not mean that spiritual competency is not relevant to the other functional and foundational competencies.
4. This book is intended to be a resource in the development of such competence.
5. See Walker, Gorsuch, and Tan (2004); Young, Wiggins-Frame, and Cashwell (2007); Brawer, Handal, Fabricatore, Roberts, and Wajda-Johnston (2002); and Russell and Yarhouse (2006) cited in the reference section.
6. I am Christian but perhaps less rigidly sectarian than most.

PART I

What Is Spirituality?

There are many ways of understanding spirituality. If one is hoping to build spiritual competence in psychotherapy, it helps to know what spirituality actually is. Is it simply another word for religion? Is religion essentially different from spirituality, or do spirituality and religion form a polarity? This is a subject that others have investigated, and I will take a position here, as they have done.

This section is important, as it lays a ground and presents a heuristic that will be utilized later in the book to examine other issues. I believe that two essential aspects of religion/spirituality are process and relationship. In a phenomenology of religion and spirituality, one will find these two considerations at the core of what is taking place. In considering spiritual issues in the lives of clients, the psychotherapist will be considering what kind of processes are going on in the client's spiritual lives and to what the client is relating in that process. Some religious and spiritual traditions have a larger emphasis in one or the other of these categories, and each person establishes his or her own integration of them, forging a personal spirituality.

CHAPTER 1

Spirit

The sky watches us and listens to us. It talks to us, and it hopes we are ready to talk back.

—Ten-year-old Hopi girl, Robert Coles, 1990, p. 25.

What is this thing called "spirit?" If people consider spirituality in psychotherapy, certainly the basic consideration is spirit itself. Is spirit the same thing as soul, or for that matter as mind? Aristotle (2006) spoke of the soul as related etymologically to respiration, and, as will be seen, spirit is related to breath. Furthermore, both are aspects of the immaterial part of a person, as is "mind" or "self," so there is overlap in these concepts.

The "soul," or *psyche*, is the term used in the Septuagint, the Greek translation of the Hebrew Old Testament, for *nephesh* in Tanach, the Masoretic text of the Hebrew Bible,[1] but the Latin word for "soul" is *anima*, from the Greek *anemos* (or air, breath). The term *nephesh* is most often translated as "soul," but what it points to is the holistic entity having breath and life, and so could also be understood as a reference to the person, as it is translated on occasion. The person is an embodied being having the capacities of life (it is animated), intellect (it has *nous*, or mind), and relationship. Wink, Adler, and Dillon (2012) pointed to William James' belief that the objective person has three classes: the material *me*, the social *me*, and the spiritual *me*. The spiritual person, in that way of looking at things, includes one's internal state of consciousness, moral concerns, and religious aspirations. The person is substantially one, a unity, but exhibits a property dualism in the relationship between body and mind (Johnson, 1990, 2008). As the body is engaged in the world, the mind emerges from that lower level of organization and supervenes on the body, providing agency (thus, a reductive physicalism is rejected, the mind is not the brain, but a non-reductive physicalism is accepted, the brain in the world gives rise to the emergent mind, the self, the subjective sense of being a person). Yet, this is a logical consideration and a philosophical rationale for valuing neuropsychology as relevant to the psychotherapeutic process. By the time anyone encounters a fellow human being, this emergence and supervenience is fully integrated and operational in the situated person. Thus, a soul is an embodied entity in which the soul is the life of the body. According to Aristotle (trans. 2006), the soul keeps the body together: "the soul seems rather to hold the body together; at all events, when the soul has departed, the body disperses in air and rots away" (p. 23). He regarded the attributes of the soul to include knowledge, perception, opinion, desire, wish, and appetite.

Thomas Aquinas was a medieval Aristotelian scholar of significance who upheld a holistic view of persons. In describing his anthropology, DeRobertis (2011) asserted that for St. Thomas it would be nonsense to refer to worldly existence of a body without a soul or a soul without a body. It is only possible to reflect and abstract the concepts of "body" or "soul" because people have already encountered both of them in their original states as holistic human beings:

> It is the human existent that one encounters in the real-life world of day-to-day experience, never a body, never a soul. Thus, in common vernacular, to have encountered "a body" is to have found a corpse. To have encountered "a soul" or "a spirit" is to have seen a ghost.
>
> (p. 152)

The work of Edith Stein[2] (2002, 1931/2009) brought together a Thomistic view of persons with the phenomenology of Edmund Husserl. She also read Martin Heidegger's *Being and Time* and was influenced by his use of the concept of Dasein. Being is situated among others in a world already going on and is part of the overall, complex situation. It makes little sense pragmatically to consider soul apart from the rest of a situated being, to consider mind apart from soul, to consider self apart from mind, or to consider spirit apart from soul. These are not substantive in themselves; they are potentialities in the holistic being of the person.

This chapter explores the potentiality of spirit. It starts with some definitions and then moves to explore how spirit is described by various spiritual and religious traditions. In all, it is helpful to maintain awareness that we are not considering something that is isolated from the action of the mind, the self, or the soul. At the same time, we are also not just using different words for the identical thing.

VARIOUS DEFINITIONS

If you look up the word "spirit" in the American Psychological Association's PsycInfo database, you will see various ways in which the word is used. For instance, sometimes the word spirit is used as a technical construct. Turel and Connelly (2012) referred to "team spirit," by which they meant an individual trait capturing a person's psychological attachment to a particular group. At other times, the word spirit can indicate a quality of character or attitude in which a person or group acts to get things done or relates to others. Witesman and Wise (2012) referred to a reformer's spirit in describing the traits necessary to lead in organizational change. Diaz and Schneider (2012) refer to spirit as the will and purpose of a society. "Spirit" can refer to the typical characteristics for a person or a group of some kind, and when magnified, a person can become identified with a set of such characteristics. Thus, one can refer to a spirit of fair play and good sportsmanship, but one can also describe someone as a leading spirit in the pursuit of good sportsmanship.

Another sense of the word "spirit" points to the belief in spiritual beings. Consoli, Tzaquitzal, and González (2013) provided a case study in which the Mayan cosmological constructions (cosmovision) included a sense of spiritual beings influencing spiritual capacities in human beings, the spiritual and the mundane of ordinary life being fully integrated. This sense of spiritual beings at work in the lives of people was also referenced in contemporary indigenous Central American cultures, where whole societies are described as influenced by "mass spiritual possession" (Wedel, 2012) and also in Thai culture, where migrant workers call upon shrines to deal with spirits of wildness and chaos (Johnson, 2012).

As mentioned, sometimes "spirit" indicates a human capacity. Tougas (2013) associated awareness with spirit, and thus akin to mind, soul, consciousness, psyche, imagination, and even self. This notion of spirit as self is also intrinsic to Eastern spiritual understanding (Keshavan, 2012).

In traditional Chinese medicine, the human being is a microcosm of the whole of existence and in balance between nothingness (the spiritual realm) and beingness (the material realm; Field, 2009; Shi & Zhang, 2012) that is reminiscent of the split in western cultures between the ontological and the epistemological, between the metaphysical and the material.

The English word "spirit" comes from the Latin *spiritus*, referring to the breath. In New Testament Greek, the word *pneuma* also meant breath, but it could also mean spirit. In Hebrew, the term *ruach* referred to the breath or spirit, and in Arabic, the word *ruh* did the same. In all these cases the idea associated with the word spirit is of breath or wind, and by extension, in a poetic fashion, that part of a human being that moves, cannot itself be seen, but can move things that can be seen.

Spirit refers to the inner, immaterial aspects of personhood. It is a way of describing one's anthropology. For instance, Kark Rahner (Shults & Sandage, 2006) argued that human beings are spiritual beings, because their life in the world is a striving for the Absolute and is an openness to the future. Since the divine Spirit is present everywhere without regard to the limits of time, then human spirit is that capacity for meaningful contact with the divine Spirit. It is a relational capacity at the heart of this kind of anthropology.

SPIRIT OR SPIRITUALITY IN ABRAHAMIC MONOTHEISM

A commonality exists among three of the great religions in the world. They share terminology, and they share a perspective in history. The three great faiths called Judaism, Christianity, and Islam were born of an event that each remembers as a moment in history, when the One True God appeared to an Iron Age sheikh named Abram and bound him in a covenant forever. Abram is the later Abraham, the father of all believers and the linchpin of the faith, indeed the theology from which the three communities of God's worshipers emerged. For some this was the beginning of the history of monotheism (Peters, 2004).

It could be said with reasonable accuracy that the Hebrew scriptures, what is known as "The Old Testament," comprise the ground, or background, for the foreground distinctives that set Christianity and Islam off, making them separate religions. Therefore, I will use the Old Testament to present a beginning place for understanding the concept of "spirit" in Abrahamic monotheism.

Spirit in the Old Testament

When one conducts an inductive study of the concept of "spirit" in the Old Testament, several meanings emerge from the various contexts in which the word appears. Table 1.1 compares the lexical definitions of two words commonly translated as "spirit" and provides references for each. Following Table 1.1, quotes from representative scriptures display how these words are used in context and provide a better understanding of the range of meaning involved.

The lexical definition and the references where these concepts are found are useful, but reading the contexts themselves is more informative. The reader is recommended to take some time and to read the contexts around many of these various instances where the word "spirit" occurs to grasp the range of meaning in the word. I will provide a few examples here and comment on them.

In Genesis, the Pharaoh of Egypt had dreams. "Then Pharaoh awoke, and behold, it was a dream. Now in the morning his spirit was troubled, so he sent and called for all the magicians of Egypt, and all its wise men" (Genesis 41:7b–8a). When they could not interpret the dream for him, he eventually found Joseph, and Joseph interpreted the dream, causing Pharaoh to then say, "Can we find a man like this, in whom is a divine spirit? . . . Since God has informed you of all this, there is no one so discerning and wise as you are" (Genesis 41:38–39). There is a contrast here between spirit as a disposition or attitude, a characteristic of the person, and spirit as either an imparted capacity or an influential entity imbued with divine power.

In Genesis 45:27, Jacob learned that his son Joseph was still alive, and his spirit revived. His constitution strengthened. His fortitude increased. His inner person refreshed, and he became determined to see his son Joseph once more before he died. In contrast, according to Exodus 6:9, when Moses spoke to the Jews in Egypt and told them that God was going to set them free, they did not believe him because their spirits had been broken by bondage, and they were despondent. In another case, Caleb was characterized as having a different spirit compared with those who tested God in the wilderness in that he followed God fully (Numbers 14:24).

In Exodus 28:3 God is said to have endowed people with a spirit of wisdom so that they might create garments for the newly appointed priesthood. In a similar way, but with different phrasing, God asserted that He had called by name Bezalel and "filled him with the Holy

TABLE 1.1
DEFINING SPIRIT IN THE OLD TESTAMENT

Hebrew Word for Spirit	Lexical Definition	Scripture References
Ruah	The word comes from a root that in various Semitic languages of the time meant breathe, blow (Syrian); breath, spirit, wind; soul, spirit (Arabic). It took forms in Hebrew meaning (1) breath, wind, or spirit—that is, of hard breathing through the nostrils or of sign and symbol of life; (2) wind; (3) spirit—that is, as breathing quickly in animation or agitation so as to indicate temper or disposition; (4) spirit of the living, breathing being dwelling in the bashar (flesh or body, often in parallel to nephesh or soul) of men and animals; (5) spirit as the seat of emotion; (6) seat or organ of mental acts; (7) referring to the will; (8) moral character; (9) Spirit of God (Brown, Driver, & Briggs, 1907/1978). "The idea behind ruah is the extraordinary fact that something as intangible as air should move; at the same time it is not so much the movement *per se* which excites attention, but rather the energy manifested by such movement. The basic meaning of ruah, therefore, is more or less that of 'blowing'" (Kamlah, 1971)	Genesis 1:2; 6:3; 41:8; 41:38; 45:27; Exodus 6:9; 28:3; 31:3; 35:21; 35:31; Numbers 5:14; 5:30; 11:17; 11:25, 26; 11:29; 14:24; 24:2; 27:18; Deuteronomy 2:30; 34:9; Judges 3:10; 6:34; 9:23; 11:29; 13:25; 14:6; 14:19; 15:14; 15:19; 1 Samuel 1:15; 10:6; 10:10; 11:6; 16:13–16; 16:23; 18:10; 19:9; 19:20; 19:23; 30:12; 2 Samuel 23:2; 1 Kings 10:5; 18:12; 21:5; 22: 21–24; 2 Kings 2:9; 2:15, 16; 1 Chronicles 5:26; 12:18; 28:12; 2 Chronicles 9:4; 15:1; 18:20–23; 20:14; 21:16; 24:20; 36:22; Ezra 1:1; 1:5; Nehemiah 9:20; 9:30; Job 4:15; 6:4; 7:11; 10:12; 15:13; 20:3; 21:4; 26:4; 26:13; 27:3; 32:8; 32:18; 33:4; 34:14; Psalms 31:5; 32:2; 34:18; 51:10–12, 17; 76:12; 77:3; 77:6; 78:8; 104:30; 106:33; 139:7; 142:3; 143:4; 143:7; 143:10; Proverbs 1:23; 11:13; 14:29; 5:4; 5:13; 16:18, 19; 16:32; 17:22; 17:27; 18:14; 20:27, 28; 29:23; Ecclesiastes 1:14; 1:17; 2:11; 2:17; 2:26; 3:21; 4:4; 4:6; 4:16; 6:9; 7:8; 7:9; 8:8; 10:4; 11:5; 12:7; Isaiah 4:4; 11:2; 19:3; 1914; 26:9; 28:6; 29:10; 29:24; 30:1; 31:3; 32:15; 34:16; 38:16; 40:7; 40:13; 42:1, 5; 44:3; 48:16; 54:6; 57:15; 57:15,16; 59:19; 59:21; 61:1, 3; 63:10; 63:14; 65:14; 66:2; Jeremiah 51:11; Ezekiel 1:12; 1:20, 21; 2:2; 3:12; 3:14; 3:24; 8:3; 10:17; 11:1; 11:5; 11:19; 11:24; 13:3; 18:31; 21:7; 36:26, 27; 37:1; 37:14; 39:29; 43:5; Daniel 2:1; 2:3; 4:8, 9; 4:18; 5:11, 12; 5:14; 6:3; 7:15; Hosea 4:12; 5:4; Joel 2:28, 29; Micah 2:7; 2:11; 3:8; Haggai 1:14; 2:5; Zechariah 4:6; 6:8; 7:12; 12:1; 12:10; 13:2; Malachi 2:15, 16

(continued)

TABLE 1.1
DEFINING SPIRIT IN THE OLD TESTAMENT (*continued*)

Hebrew Word for Spirit	Lexical Definition	Scripture References
Ob	The word comes from a root meaning a water carrier that makes a hollow sound; from that it took forms meaning (1) a wineskin, (2) a necromancer or wizard that carries or channels a spirit, (3) a ghost, (4) necromancy—the act of conjuring up a spirit (Brown, Driver, & Briggs, 1907/1978).	Leviticus 19:31; 20:27; 1 Samuel 28:7, 8; 1 Chronicles 10:13; 2 Chronicles 33:6; Job 32:19; Isaiah 29:4

Spirit in wisdom, in understanding, in knowledge, and in all kinds of craftsmanship to make artistic designs for work in gold, in silver, and in bronze, and in the cutting of stones for settings, and in the carving of wood, that he may work in all kinds of craftsmanship" (Exodus 31:1–11). Here spirit is seen as a skilled capacity for creative and artistic expression. It is a targeted and specific capacity or characteristic of the person rather than a global disposition, and as such, it is also something imparted or bestowed upon a person, built into them by God.

In Numbers 5:14, 30, spirit is equal to an emotion: "if a spirit of jealousy comes over him and he is jealous of his wife. . . ." In 1 Samuel:9–15, Hannah is "oppressed in spirit," meaning that she was desolate, disconsolate over being barren, and weeping from her sadness.

Sometimes, the sense of the word spirit is of a spiritual being, as when God sent an evil spirit to terrorize Saul (1 Samuel 16:14–23), or when David played music for Saul, Saul felt refreshed, and the spirit departed from him.

Sometimes spirit is used in reference to God's Spirit, as in Numbers 11, when the burden of leading the people was great, but Moses did it with the help of God's Spirit. However, God suggested that Moses share that burden, and he told Moses to gather 70 elders of Israel and that God would "come down and speak with you there, and I will take of the Spirit who is upon you, and will put Him upon them; and they shall bear the burden of the people with you, so that you not bear it all alone." So, they did that, and when God's Spirit came upon the 70 elders, they prophesied. In the same way, God commanded Moses to commission Joshua, "a man in whom is the Spirit," to take authority among the people of Israel. Joshua was described as being "filled with the spirit of wisdom" (Deuteronomy 34:9), with the result that the people listened to him. Similarly, the judges of Israel were people upon whom "the Spirit of the Lord" came in order to accomplish some kind of work. In the story of Gideon, Gideon first met the Angel of the Lord face to face, and God told him to tear down the altar to Baal, but the power to effect that work came when the Holy Spirit came upon him (Judges 6:11–40ff) and the two interacted. In 1 Samuel 10:6, 9, the Holy Spirit came upon Saul and changed him, turning him into "a different man."

Spirit, then, is a human capacity of emotion and thought that animates the physical body and provides a conduit of communication and power between human beings and God.

Spirit in the New Testament

Spirit is variously defined. As in Table 1.1, referring to usage in the Old Testament, Table 1.2 provides lexical definitions and scriptural references (not an exhaustive list, but a representative one), where the reader can check the context of usage in the New Testament. Following Table 1.2, however, there are also examples of the way various contexts read so as to sense how the term "spirit" is being used.

Although the reader can investigate these contexts for him or herself, I will provide a few examples and comment on them. The purpose here is not to elucidate a theology of spirit (a modest attempt at that will be provided in the next chapter), but to illustrate various ways in which "spirit" is observed in the New Testament. Again, this is so one might comprehend what it is—spirit—that we are dealing with.

In Matthew 3:16–4:1, the Bible reads, "After being baptized, Jesus came up immediately from the water; and behold, the heavens were opened, and he saw the Spirit of God descending as a dove and lighting on Him, and behold, a voice out of the heavens said, 'This is My beloved Son, in whom I am well-pleased.' Then Jesus was led up by the Spirit into the wilderness to be tempted by the devil."

In this section, spirit is personified and given the power of agency, the ability to act. Specifically, it is God's spirit, the spirit who descended

TABLE 1.2
DEFINING SPIRIT IN THE NEW TESTAMENT

Greek Word for Spirit	Lexical Definitions	Scripture References
Pneuma	(1) Blowing, breathing, as in air in motion; (2) breath as the life-spirit, soul—that which gives life to the body; (3) as part of the human personality (as opposed to *sarx*, or flesh); as source and seat of insight, feeling, and will; (4) spirit as an independent spiritual being (as opposed to a being that can be perceived by physical senses); (5) the Spirit—as that which differentiates God from everything that is not God and characterizes God's presence, character, and influence (Bauer, Arndt, & Gingrich, 1957). The Greek root *pneu-* denotes a dynamic movement of air. Its derivatives indicated to blow (air, into a musical instrument), to breathe (so as to be alive); to emit a fragrance; to radiate heat, anger, courage, etc. One form of the word indicated the process of blowing, breathing, panting, of inspiration (from a deity). The suffix *-ma* indicated the result of the action; thus, in this case "wind" or "breath." Because of the association of breath and life, pneuma approached the meaning of psyche, or soul. In the New Testament, it is the power human beings experience that relate them to the spiritual realm, "the realm of reality which lies beyond ordinary observation and human control" (Brown, 1978, p. 693).	Matthew 3:16; 4:1; 5:3; 10:20; 12:18, 28, 43; 14:26; 22:43; 26:41; Mark 1:23, 26; 2:8; 3:30; 5:2; 6:49; 8:12; 9:20, 25, 26; 14:38; Luke 1: 17, 47, 80; 2:27, 40; 4:14, 18, 33; 8:55; 9:39, 42, 55; 10:21; 11:13, 24; 13:11; 24:46, 37, 39; John 3:5, 6, 8; 4:23, 24; 6:63; 7:39; 11:33; 13:21; 14:17; 15:26; 16:13; Acts 2:4, 17, 18; 5:9; 6:10; 7:59; 8:29, 39; 10:19; 11:12, 28; 16:7, 16, 18; 17:16; 18:5, 25; 19:15, 16, 21; 20:22; 21:4; 23:8, 9; Romans 1:4, 9; 2:29; 7:6; 8:2, 4, 5, 9–11, 13–16, 23, 26, 27; 11:8, 12:11; 15:19, 30; 1 Corinthians 2:4, 10–12, 14; 3:16; 4:21; 5:3–5; 6:11, 17, 20; 7:34, 40; 12:3, 4, 7–9, 11, 13; 14:2, 14–16; 15:45; 16:18; 2 Corinthians 1:22; 2:13; 3:3, 6, 8, 17, 18; 4:13; 5:5; 7:1, 13; 11:4; 12:18; Galatians 3:2, 3, 5, 14; 4:6, 29; 5:5, 16–18, 22, 25; 6:1, 8, 18; Ephesians 1:13, 17; 2:2, 18, 22; 3:5, 16; 4:3, 4, 23, 30; 5:9, 18; 6:17, 18; Philippians 1:19, 27; 2:1; 3:3; Colossians 1:8; 2:5; 1 Thessalonians 4:8; 5:19, 23; 2 Thessalonians 2:2, 8, 13; 1 Timothy 3:16; 4:1, 12; 2 Timothy 1:7; 4:22; Hebrews 4:12; 9:14; 10:29; James 2:26; 4:5; 1 Peter 1:2, 11, 22; 3:4, 18; 4:6, 14; 1 John 3:24; 4:1–3, 6, 13; 5:6, 8; Jude 1:19; Revelations 1:10; 2:7, 11, 17, 29; 3:6, 13, 22; 4:2; 11:11; 14:13; 17:3; 18:2; 19:10; 21:10; 22:17 (Strong, Kohlenberger, & Swanson, 2001)

out of heaven, who directs Jesus into the wilderness for a purpose. This same sense of a personal spirit of God, a Holy Spirit, is strongly evident in the epistles of Romans, 1 Corinthians, Galatians, Ephesians, 1 John, and Revelation. In Acts, it is possible to lie to the Holy Spirit, pointing to an interpersonal capacity in relationship between human beings and the Holy Spirit.

In Matthew 5:3, the Bible reads, "Blessed are the poor in spirit, for theirs is the kingdom of heaven." This harkens back to Psalm 51:16–17, where it says, "For You do not delight in sacrifice, otherwise I would give it; You are not pleased with burnt offering. The sacrifices of God are a broken spirit; a broken and contrite heart, O God, You will not despise." Being poor in spirit positions "spirit" as pertaining to the character, the condition of the inner person. It addresses attitude, in which attitude refers to a settled way of thinking or feeling. In the case of Psalm 51, "spirit" is in parallel to "heart," and heart is the seat of conviction. So the sense here is that spirit refers to the inner disposition of the person—what a person thinks, feels, values, hopes, wants, and so forth.

Dallas Willard described this condition as it was referenced in Matthew 5 as being spiritual zeros, "the spiritually bankrupt, deprived and deficient, the spiritual beggars, those without a wisp of religion" (Willard, 1998, p. 100). In this regard, then, what is in view is the realm of the spirit, that which is spiritual, which would then be an attribute of the kingdom of God. God's kingdom (and then the things of God) is spiritual—of the spirit—and about which a person might know something or have direct, experiential knowledge.

In Matthew 12:43–45 the Bible reads,

> Now when the unclean spirit goes out of a man, it passes through water-less places seeking rest, and does not find it. Then it says, "I will return to my house from which I came," and when it comes, it finds it unoccupied, swept, and put in order. Then it goes and takes along with it seven other spirits more wicked than itself, and they go in and live there; and the last state of that man becomes worse than the first. That is the way it will also be with this evil generation.

In this case, spirit is conceived of as an entity, but an immaterial entity, and more specifically as that kind which is "unclean." It belongs to a spiritual realm opposed to God. So, here it is more than a ghost, which could be seen as benign. This is a disruptive and malevolent, immaterial being that has the capacity to inhabit human beings with torment.

In John 3:5–8 the Bible reads,

> Jesus answered, "Truly, truly, I say to you, unless one is born of water and the Spirit he cannot enter into the kingdom of God. That which is born of the flesh is flesh, and that which is born of the Spirit is spirit. Do not be amazed that I said to you, 'You must be born again.' The wind blows where it wishes and you hear the sound of it, but do not know where it comes from and where it is going; so is everyone who is born of the Spirit.

In this case spirit is again the Holy Spirit, the Spirit which is from God, has the capacity of giving life, and is a person with agency. Beyond that, though, spirit in this context is decidedly opposite from whatever is flesh. Jesus claimed that in order to enter God's kingdom a person had to be born twice—once by natural means (water), and once by spiritual means (the Spirit). These are two kinds of birth. One is the coming to life in the world of a physical body, and the other is a coming to life to God in the world with a capacity for relationship. Thus, human beings have at least two capacities: spiritual and physical.

This distinction between what is physically discerned through the senses and what is metaphysically discerned through the spiritual capacities of an individual was the same one Jesus had in mind when He said,

> Woman, believe Me, an hour is coming when neither in this mountain nor in Jerusalem will you worship the Father. You worship what you do not know; we worship what we know, for salvation is from the Jews. But an hour is coming, and now is, when the true worshippers will worship the Father in spirit and truth; for such people the Father seeks to be His worshippers. God is spirit, and those who worship Him must worship in spirit and truth.
>
> (John 4:21–24)

Spirit in the New Testament, then, is a capacity of the inner person, a disposition akin to its use in the Old Testament addressing matters of heart, thought, affect, and will, but it is also strongly a capacity for relationship with God (i.e., through worship). Spirit is also personified in the Holy Spirit, who is depicted as having agency and potency. If God *is* spirit, then at some level the question "What is God?" is impacted by the question "What is spirit?"

Edith Stein (1931/2009) stated that a "thing's substance is what it is and its substance is different from its being; God is 'Who is' and this—according to Augustine—is the best way to say what He is" (p. 7).

God told Moses (when Moses asked who he should say sent him), "Say 'I am' has sent you." Who is God? I am that I am (the tetragrammaton). Who is God? Being. What is God's substance? Being, but being that addresses other (i.e., Moses)—spirit.

Spirit in persons is the quality of being that in human persons is created in the image of the divine Person, after the God Who is being. Spirit is the shared capacity of existence, the conduit by which one being engages in contacting another being.

Spirit in the Koran

Spirit in the Koran can refer to a heavenly force attendant on the visitation of angels, the immaterial aspect of human beings, a spiritual being, and the Holy Spirit (Shellabear, 1932; Table 1.3). The Holy Spirit in Islam is Gabriel, the foremost angel (Salih Al-Munajjid, 2013), who came to the aid of Jesus at the bidding of Allah and is God's chief messenger. An Islamic person can engage in spiritual retreats, spiritual resolves, and spiritual works (Keller, 2002). The concept of spirit in Islam closely parallels that of spirit in Hebrew (Macdonald, 1932).

In 2:87 the Koran reads,

> We indeed gave Moses the book and We sent messengers after him one after another; and We gave Jesus, son of Mary, clear arguments and strengthened him with the Holy Spirit. Is it then whenever there came to you a messenger with what your souls desired not, you were arrogant? And some you gave the lie to and others you would slay.

Here is a case in which both words associated with the concept of spirit reside in the same context. In one case, the Holy Spirit is in view (ruh), and in the other case it is the soul, the self, the inner inclinations of a person (nafs) leading them to accept one person and reject in various ways another. In addition, the Holy Spirit is seen to be an agent of strengthening. "According to the Holy Qur'an, the Holy Spirit is the angel which brought revelation: 'The Holy Spirit has revealed it

TABLE 1.3
DEFINING SPIRIT IN THE KORAN

Arabic Word for Spirit	Lexical Meanings	Koran References
Ruh	"Spirit, breath (of life). Used in the Quran twenty-one times, referring to the divine spirit in the sense of communication of life force. Often interpreted as an immaterial, immortal element of a living being, as well as the true self, or soul, apart from the body. Also a designation for Jesus and the angel Gabriel. Often used interchangeably with nafs (self), although Sufis distinguish between ruh as the higher principle of soul and nafs as the 'lower' or 'animal' self." Oxford Islamic Studies Online, Oxford University Press spirit; (rah al-quds) the Holy Spirit (Kassis, p. 1040)	2:87, 253; 4:171; 5:110; 15:29; 16:2, 102; 17:85; 19:17; 21:91; 26:193; 32:9; 38:72; 40:15; 42:52; 58:22; 66:12; 70:4; 78:38; 97:4
Nafs	"Self or soul. Used in the Quran as a general designation for the self or true self; interpreted as the spiritual reality of all living creatures. In philosophy, the specifically human nafs is often described as the potential to actualize the fullness of self-awareness, often equated with the intellect (aql). In Sufism, often described as the 'lower self,' associated with physical rather than spiritual impulses, by contrast to ruh, understood as the 'soul' or 'higher self.' Often understood primarily in a negative sense. In the more theoretical Sufi writings, also used in the neutral, philosophical meanings." Oxford Islamic Studies Online, Oxford University Press NAFS n.f.—soul, self, life, person; heart [Ar, Ali, Bl]; mind [Pk]; (used as a reflexive when followed by a pronominal suffix) -self, -selves, own, own behalf; each other, one another (as in 2:54). Several phrases employ nafs such as (min tilqj' nafri) of my own accord; (rdwada 'an nafsihi) to solicit; (shaqq al-nafs) great distress or trouble (for oneself); (tba nafsan) to be pleased to do something (Kassis, p. 824).	2:9, 44, 48, 54, 57, 72, 84, 85, 87, 90, 102, 109, 110, 123, 130, 155, 187, 207, 223, 228, 231, 233, 234, 235, 240, 265, 84, 86; 3:25, 28, 30, 61, 69, 93, 117, 135, 145, 154, 161, 164, 168, 178, 185, 186; 4:1, 29, 49, 63–66; 4:79, 84, 95, 97, 107, 110, 111, 113, 128, 135; 5:25, 30, 32, 45, 52, 70, 80, 105, 116; 6:12, 20, 24, 26, 54, 70, 93, 98, 104, 123, 130, 151, 152, 158, 164; 7:9, 23, 37, 42, 53, 160, 172, 177, 188, 189, 192, 197, 205; 8:53, 72; 9:17, 20, 35, 36, 41, 42, 44, 55, 70, 81, 85, 88, 111, 118, 120, 128; 10:15, 23, 30, 44, 49, 54, 100, 108; 11:21, 31, 101, 105; 12:18, 23, 26, 30, 32, 51, 53 (and on to 245 instances of this word)

(i.e., The Qur'an) from the Lord' (16:102). The Holy Spirit is mentioned by two other names, Gabriel (vs. 97) and the Faithful Spirit (26:193)" (Muhammad Ali, 2002, p. 43, footnote 87a).

In 4:110, 111 the Koran reads, "And whoever does a wrong or wrongs himself but then seeks forgiveness of Allah will find Allah Forgiving and Merciful. And whoever commits a sin only earns it against himself. And Allah is ever Knowing and Wise."

Here the sense of soul, the inner person, is in view and also the self, used in a reflexive construction ("him-self"). When the term "soul" is used, it is of the immaterial aspect of a person rather than standing for the person him or herself. In 4:110, it is in the sense of a conscience. In the reflexive use, however, it does seem to stand for the person, "self" not meaning the inner subjective experience but rather the person. One sins against himself, his own person, as opposed to against someone else.

SPIRIT IN EASTERN THOUGHT

When moving to an Eastern mindset, one finds less interest in the person of a divine being and more interest in the way of life among transient and finite beings and of the energy that animates them. Taoism is one form of Eastern thought, but Hinduism and Buddhism are also examples. There are others, of course, but I will stay with these three as being representative.

Spirit in some forms of Eastern thought is the force for motion and change that is associated with all things, all things being related in one whole of existence (Capra, 1976). There is a nonduality in this; spirit is matter and matter is spirit. *Ching* (essence), *chi* (vitality), and *shen* (spirit) are the three substances of energy in the Taoist worldview. These three are believed to be involved at every level of being, from microscopic organisms to the furthest stretches of the universe (Kim, Yang, & Hwang, 2006). Further, there is a relationship among them such that *ching* (or *jing*) gives rise to the energy field of a person, which is known as *chi* (or *qi*), and that affects the quality of one's spirit, or disposition toward life (*shen*).

> The Master's power is like this.
> He lets all things come and go
> effortlessly, without desire.

He never expects results;
thus he is never disappointed.
He is never disappointed;
thus his spirit never grows old. . . .

When taxes are too high,
people go hungry.
When the government is too intrusive,
people lose their spirit.

(Lao-tzu, 1995, vss 55, 75)

One of the preeminent scriptures of Hindu religious thought is the Bhagavad Gita. Spirit as it is seen in this document is a force in all of life, some *thing* that transcends individuals but provides them with life.

In the following example, note both the antecedent of "spirit" as a "thing" (not a person or an actual being), and note how this spirit is related to people:

> The Spirit, which pervades all that we see, is imperishable. Nothing can destroy the Spirit. The material bodies which this Eternal, Indestructible, Immeasurable Spirit inhabits are all finite. Therefore fight, O Valiant Man! He who thinks that the Spirit kills, and he who thinks of It as killed, are both ignorant. The Spirit kills not, nor is It killed. It was not born; It will never die, nor once having been, can It cease to be. Unborn, Eternal, Ever-enduring, yet Most Ancient, the Spirit dies not when the body is dead. He who knows the Spirit as Indestructible, Immortal, Unborn, Always-the-Same, how should he kill or cause to be killed? As a man discards his threadbare robes and puts on new, so the Spirit throws off Its worn-out bodies and takes fresh ones.
>
> (Bhagavad Gita, chap. 2)

Spirit in this context is the life force that inhabits and animates physical bodies, but that is a decidedly Hindu way of seeing such a thing, and it is a force that transcends individual, embodied persons.

In Buddhism, spirit is more akin to mind. Mark Reck, a practicing Buddhist and gestalt psychotherapist, put it this way:

> I think the closest thing to "spirit" that Buddhism references would be encompassed in their concept of "mind." For Buddhists, "mind"

(especially as articulated by various Tibetan commentators) connotes both the general mentation of everyday life (the "concrete" form; Tibetan, yid) and what renowned Buddhist scholar Herbert Guenther describes as cognitively-sensitive "vibrant spirituality" or "projective intentionality" (the "actualized" form; Tibetan, thugs). So maybe "spirit" in many (Western) traditions may be akin to the "actualized" form of mind (thugs) in Buddhist traditions?

(Personal communication, November 3, 2013)

In accord with this understanding, one form of Buddhist meditation (Vipasanna) uses the focused awareness of the mind to attend to various aspects of one's existence over time. It is a discipline and a process, a way of life. The Pali term for insight meditation is *vipassana bhavana*, which means "the cultivation of the mind toward the aim of seeing in the special way that leads to insight and understanding" (Gunaratana, 2002, p. 33).

SPIRIT IN THE NEW AGE

New age spirituality is an eclectic mix of spiritual constructs and beliefs about spirit. Spirit in the new age is linked to physics, ecology, and metaphysical systems, and in the hands of some authors it becomes an entirely alternative cosmology, based, for instance, on the sinking of Atlantis and the destruction of a Martian civilization (Melchizedek, 1998). It builds on established religious constructs, but redefines or recontextualizes them. For instance, God is "resymbolized as Primal Energy, the Creative Surge, the Immanent Mother, the Womb of Being, the Universal Cosmic Consciousness, the Pool of Unlimited Power, the Slumbering Deep Within and the Spring of life" (Bloesche, 2007, p. 117). Biblical figures such as breath, wind, and living water can be seen as concrete, with spiritual anima or energy connected to their material presence. An example is Tolle's (2005) call to a new spirituality, one that has apocalyptic overtones in the forecast emergence of, literally, a new age:

Since time immemorial, flowers, crystals, precious stones, and birds have held special significance for the human spirit. Like all life-forms, they are, of course, temporary manifestations of the underlying one

Life–one Consciousness. . . . So, when you are alert and contemplate a flower, crystal, or bird without naming it mentally, it becomes a window for you into the formless. There is an inner opening, however slight, into the realm of spirit.

(p. 5)

Tolle goes on to assert that Jesus and Buddha, in their use of such references (to flowers, etc.), were preparing the ground for a "profound shift in planetary consciousness that is destined to take place in the human species" (p. 5).

New age thought is thick with the promise of esoteric knowledge; this is one manifestation of its gnostic origins. This knowledge (gnosis) is often cast as a timeless thing, known by a few throughout history, but only obtained through a personal journey of enlightenment (Lesser, 1999). This secret knowledge, and the promise of enlightenment, has been the lure of gnosticism for centuries.

The gnostic vision sees a spark of heavenly light imprisoned in a natural body. The body is an obstacle to God's redeeming work, not a vehicle (as with Christian mystics). According to the Gnostics, the saving gnosis awakens seekers after truth to their essential value and to their eternal origin.

(Bloesche, 2007, pp. 72–73)

Thus, some new age followers embrace the body (according to a mystic emphasis), and others attempt to escape the body (according to a gnostic emphasis). Zukov (1989) suggested that evolution rightly understood is the transformation of a being operating according to the five bodily senses to a being operating by higher, and internal values such as magnanimity and altruism—internal values of the soul or mind. He expresses a Cartesian perspective that separates that which is material about a human being from that which is immaterial, and that dualism is more than a property dualism—it is substantive. Brennan (1987), on the other hand, sees a unity in all things and uses the illustration of a candle and its flame. She says that there is the wax and the wick, there is the flame, and there is the light, but that they are all one, and the light and the flame are inseparable. Her system of healing is based on the system of energy fields, or chakras, and is a holistic, embodied perspective.

SYNTHESIS

Spirit is the immaterial aspect of a whole person, which is the capacity to contemplate, be fascinated by, engage with, tremble before, and yet yearn to be with that which significantly transcends the self and is responsible for all that exists while still being present and available for relationship. All this includes what people think, how people feel, and what people value and intend. Spirit is the medium for contact with God.

In nontheistic religious systems, spirit or spirituality is a capacity to appreciate beauty or mystery. It is spunk, grit, or fortitude, and so still a capacity of the self, but simply an attraction for that which is mysterious, puzzling, or enigmatic and at the same time somewhat beyond the mundane.

NOTES

1. Also known as Tanakh. The term is an acronym formed from the initial Hebrew letters of the Masoretic Text's three traditional subdivisions: The Torah or first five books, called the Pentateuch, the Nevi'im, or prophets, and the Ketuvim, or writings. Thus: TaNaKh.
2. As seen in her *Potency and Act* (2009) and *Finite and Eternal Being* (2002). See the reference section for the full citation.

CHAPTER 2

Spirituality and Religion

Be very careful that grace and politeness do not merge into a banality of behavior, where we're just nice, sort of "death by cupcake."

—Bono, June 28, 2013, interview
at Focus on the Family

My younger brother is an interesting man. He grew his hair long when we were all young, and he kept it that way. He grew a huge walrus mustache, and he kept it that way. His hair is now gray and that mustache is pure white. He worked as a carpenter outside in the hot sun of the central valley of California, so his skin is now etched in thick wrinkles that make him look tough, masculine, and distinctive. He looks like he stepped out of a Sam Peckinpah western or some homage to carefree bikers. His religion is syncretic, having formed through a conversion to Christ, followed by tutelage in fundamentalist groups considered cultic by some, but growingly over the years his thinking and affection has been attenuated by his interest in, and involvement with, Native American peoples. If you talk theology with my brother, you'll get a mix when he reaches into his bag. However, if you spend any time with him, you'll see him watch the earth and sky in order to read the signs his Father Spirit provides. He is one of the most sensitive men spiritually that I have ever known.

So, there is the rub between religion and spirituality that brings many people to divide them into a polarity, with a structured religious institution at one end and a spontaneous and creative flowing in contacting between the whole person and something of greater meaning and/or organizing influence at the other.

What follows in this chapter is an investigation of this polarity people create between religion and spirituality, as well as a look at spirituality and religion from a psychological stance, a philosophical stance, and a theological stance.

What one finds is that it is impossible to separate religion from spirituality and keep them pure, as if they do not commonly cross-pollinate each other. Only in the abstract world of thought can they be isolated. Out in the world where people walk around and watch the earth and sky for signs, religion and spirituality cross paths with one another on a regular basis.

Following this chapter, I will use the terms religion and spirituality interchangeably, because the conclusion I have come to is that a person can practice his or her religion with either a poverty of spirit or with a rich sense of spirituality. Thus, religion and spirituality are related and not opposite things.

POLARITY OR FALSE DICHOTOMY?

Alister McGrath (1999) defined spirituality in the context of religion. He said, "Spirituality concerns the quest for a fulfilled and authentic religious life, involving the bringing together of the ideas distinctive of that religion and the whole experience of living on the basis of and within the scope of that religion" (p. 2). That is a good integration of the two constructs and a way of seeing the complexity involved with each. Post, Wade, and Cornish (2013) found a considerable overlap between the terms, following the definitions of Hill et al. (2001): (a) spirituality is feelings, thoughts, experiences, and behaviors arising from a quest for the sacred, and in which "sacred" refers to ultimate reality or truth as perceived by the person or a divine being or object; (b) religion is quite similar, being the feelings, thoughts, experiences, and behaviors arising from a quest of the sacred, but within this search for the sacred there are also nonsacred pursuits such as belonging, meaning, or wellness. Religion also takes place within a community, and the community supports the search. Hage (2006) asserted that although the terms spirituality and religion are not entirely interchangeable, they have overlapping meanings and are most often used together in the literature. Spirituality is often described as the broader of the two terms. The word "spirituality" is derived from the Latin *spiritus*, meaning breath or life force. Spirituality generally refers to meaning and purpose in one's life, a search for wholeness, and a relationship with a transcendent being. One's spirituality may be expressed through religion or religious involvement, which generally refers to participation in an organized system of beliefs, rituals, and cumulative traditions (p. 303).

The words "spirit" and "religion" were most in vogue in print during the period between 1800 and 1860, and then they steadily declined to a low around 1990. They have been steadily increasing since then. Also, the words do not show a drastic difference in utilization between them (for instance, with spirituality being more pronounced than religion). The most variance, however, was between 1840 and 1920 (Google Ngram Chart, 2013). The word "spirituality" is virtually nowhere to be seen until quite recently.

In order to consider in what ways religion and spirituality are related to each other, it is necessary to work out an understanding of each idea. The concept of spirit has been examined in Chapter 1, so bear with me a moment while I explore the concept of religion. Then we will see how they are related to one another.

The word "religion" is a construct, a social reality invented by people in response to what happened in the 16th and 17th centuries (Schilbrack, 2012). During that period, Copernicus published his revision of cosmology, *On the Revolutions of the Heavenly Spheres*, in which he explained that the sun did not revolve around the earth but that the earth circled the sun; hence, our world was not the center of all things (Repcheck, 2007). Galileo supported his views, but in 1633 was ordered by the Congregation of the Holy Office of the Inquisition of the Catholic Church not to teach them. Thus, the church suppressed scientific inquiry, and the threat of inquisition threatened discovery. The wars between governments and peoples loyal to Catholic or Protestant churches (1524 to 1648) were also part of the ground of that period. Thus, religion became a construct useful in identifying people, or groups of people, in conflict based on their spiritual practices, institutional allegiances, and theological commitments.

The word "religion" appears neither in the Hindu, Buddhist, or Hebrew scriptures, nor in the early Egyptian, Japanese, or Native American languages (Smith, 1962). You cannot find a religion lying around in the American Southwest and then pick it up and measure it. You may be able to find a group of people with a worldview, a spiritual belief system that influences how they live, who are practicing rituals they believe link this worldly life to something beyond, but you will not find a "religion."

That is a word, a construct, created by people. Regardless, what that word "religion" refers to has existed in all times and societies, even though it was not identified as such. Traditionally, the term "religion" has referred to everything people do in order to relate to that which is divine or transcendent, what people would say is greater and beyond them but the source of everything that is with them. More currently, people who study religion have admitted that religion is about a way of life—habits, practices, purposes, passions, commitments, beliefs and ways of thinking, and distinctive ways of living together in community. Thus, religion also refers to one's embodied daily life and so can be conceived of as immanent. Whereas one religion might emphasize one of these over the other, for instance the transcendence in Islam or the immanence in Eastern religious thought, Christianity stresses both: "the transcendent God is also the God who can be found within and around us, discernable in both a dramatic religious experience and in the simple, quiet love of a child for his or her parent" (Nelson, 2009, p. 4). Religion, then, is multidimensional and complex.

Incidentally, as soon as the construct of religion was created, the opposite of religion became a possibility. Thus, the corollary to that which is religious is that which is secular. Secularity is the most logical polarity pit against religion, not spirituality.

But what about polarities?

A polarity is a reduction of an otherwise complex field into opposing extremes. Examples of polarities are right or wrong, black or white, yes or no, good or bad. People resort to polarities in order to manage the difficulties inherent to complexity. When they do, they also usually identify with one end of the polarity and reject the other. A person given to splitting, for instance, might idealize another person, seeing the other as superlative and "for" the self, but if something tarnishes the image of the idealized one, suddenly a shift can occur in which the idealized becomes the demonized and then the person sees the other as "against."

Religion and spirituality are not each at one end of a single continuum; they are not a real polarity. Rather, they are parallel continuums, twirling around each other like the latticework in a strand of DNA, connected by the "amino acids" they each supply and that link them. While the polarity to that which is religious is that which is secular, the polarity to that which is spiritual is that which is mundane.

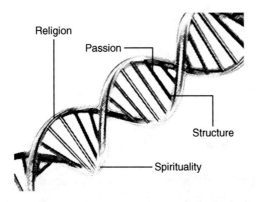

FIGURE 2.1   Structure and passion: Religion and spirituality.

The illustration below (Figure 2.1) shows religion and spirituality in parallel. As an example of how they are connected, one link is constituted of structure, contributed from religion, while also constituted of passion, contributed from the spirituality side. Numerous other examples could be fleshed out, but the reader perhaps gets the point.

It is a false dichotomy to pit religion against spirituality. A false dichotomy emerges when someone claims that his or her conclusion is one of only two options, when, in fact, there are other possibilities. For example, "You can either have meaningful spirituality or you can have dead religion; you don't want dead religion; so you'd better develop a meaningful spirituality (i.e., apart from religion)." In terms of logic, a false dichotomy is sometimes called a false dilemma, and the reasoning goes like this: either x or y is true (when x and y could both be false); y is false; therefore, x is true. Applying that to this current topic, either religion or spirituality is meaningful; spirituality is meaningful; therefore, religion is nonsense.

PSYCHOLOGICAL STANCE

The psychology of religion is a huge subject. It includes anything a person might think of in the field of psychology pointed toward an intersection with religion and spirituality. It is impossible in a book this size to bring up all the various aspects of this huge area of concern.[1] Suffice it to say, however, that some things stick out for me, and the people writing in this genre include those focused on both religion and spirituality.

In exploring the relationship between religion and spirituality, Hill et al. (2001) made the following observations about both religion and spirituality and their relationship to psychological frames of reference:

- In a person's life, religion and spirituality both develop across the life span.
- Religion and spirituality are both social–psychological phenomena; they are expressed in people groups and influenced by reference groups.
- Religion and spirituality are related to cognitive phenomena such as forms of commitment, and they involve complexity of thought.
- Religion and spirituality are related to affect and emotion (and I add—especially the self-conscious emotions of shame, guilt, and pride, but also of joy, confidence, and hope).
- Religion and spirituality are relevant to the study of personality.
- Religion and spirituality have been recognized as having importance to mental health status, that is, religion and spirituality are just as likely to be predictors of positive as they are of negative mental health.
- Religion and spirituality are negatively correlated with drug and alcohol abuse.
- Religion and spirituality are increasingly seen to have positive social functions.

Some people do find distinctions between these constructs, as depicted in Table 2.1.

TABLE 2.1
RELIGION AND SPIRITUALITY CONTRASTED

Characteristic of Theistic Religion	Characteristic of Spirituality
Supernatural/transcendent power by which people are motivated or to which people are committed.	God-oriented, where thought and action are premised on theologies, broadly or narrowly conceived.
A feeling present in the person who conceives such a power.	World-oriented, stressing one's relationship to ecology and nature.
The ritual acts carried out in respect of that power.	Humanistic, stressing human achievement and potential.

Based on Hill et al. (2001).

Psychologically speaking, according to Hill et al. (2001), one could say that religion is the attraction people find to something beyond and more meaningful than themselves, the feeling that attraction generates, and the acts carried out that correspond to both. Spirituality is an orientation toward a transcendent other (God) based on theological systems, a meaningful and reverent orientation toward the world and its natural processes, and/or a stress on human potential activation. There is both overlap and contrast between these two ways of looking at things.

Psychotherapists work with people, and there has been a poor carry-over from the academic study of psychology to the context of clinical work. So here are a few areas in the psychology of religion and spirituality that support the contention that the split between religion and spirituality is a false dichotomy and that might also be useful in one's practice.

Moriarty and Davis (2012) and Moriarty and Hoffman (2007) are pursuing a research project focused on God images. These are primordial schemas, mental representations, that "underlie individuals' personal, emotional, embodied experiences in relationship with a divine attachment figure, such as God, Jesus, or Allah" (Moriarty & Davis, 2012, p. 154). By contrast, God concepts are abstract, conceptual, and/or doctrinal understandings that serve as ground for individuals' beliefs about such a transcendent figure. God images are most closely correlated with a person's self-image such that psychotherapy to help a person's sense of self often facilitates a more positive God image. Moriarty and his associates have found that an anemic God image affects the quality of a person's spiritual experience. Conversely, a person's sense of attachment to God will affect that person's sense of self and wellness in the world. It appears that these things are all interrelated. A strong sense of self relates to a stronger sense of God, and that relates to a quality spiritual experience, which relates to increased wellness.

Related to this are the observations of O'Grady and Bartz (2012) dealing with spiritually transcendent experiences. Such an experience can radically affect a person's sense of self, self-esteem, and appreciation for God. Such a transcendent experience is a subjective experience of the sacred. A spiritually transcendent experience is a "spiritual modification of consciousness that extends beyond the ordinary vicissitudes of everyday life" (p. 161). This is not something that can be programmed by a psychotherapist, but it is something an ill-formed psychotherapist can overlook, minimize, or misunderstand. This kind of experience leads to what some would call an experiential knowledge of God; it is the difference between knowing things about God and knowing God through personal contact with divinity (Packer, 1973; Schaeffer, 1971). Speaking of the conversational nature of relationship with divinity that comprises such contact with God over time, Dallas Willard wrote,

> In the still small voice of God we are given a message that bears the stamp of his personality quite clearly and in a way we will learn to recognize. But in the contrast to other cases, the medium through which the message comes is diminished almost to the vanishing point, taking the form of thoughts that are our thoughts, though these thoughts are not from us. In this way, as we shall see, the human spirit becomes the "candle of the Lord."
>
> (p. 87)

Also related is the issue of religious and spiritual coping. Religious coping is a searching for significance in times of stress that is distinguished from regular coping in that it is related to that which is sacred and includes beliefs, rituals, experiences, and institutions associated with supernatural forces (Krumrei & Rosmarin, 2012). Coping strategies include reframing the situation in order to contemplate it as part of God's plan, prayer, seeking a deeper connection with others or a spiritual source, or a spiritual awakening. Pointing to a synthesis of over 100 studies and related sources, Krumrei and Rosmarin (2012) claimed that religious coping predicts positive outcomes in mental health and that it accounts for variance in well-being beyond that attributable to other important nonreligious coping methods. Consequently, "religious coping is important to people's adjustment to stressors," and the religious nature of religious coping methods are "not redundant with secular methods of coping, but account for unique variance. . . ." Therefore, religious coping is not a proxy for coping in general. Rather, "it seems that religion adds a distinctive dimension to the coping process" (p. 247).

PHILOSOPHICAL STANCE

Martin Buber is often credited with influencing psychology and other social sciences with his relational philosophy. He affected client-centered and gestalt therapies with his sense of an intersubjective relationship (I and Thou) versus a subject–object relationship. He was a Hassidic scholar who formulated his thinking in the crucible of his relationship with God.

As we contemplate two philosophical positions relevant to the epistemological and ontological considerations in psychotherapy (social constructionism and critical realism), it is helpful to keep in mind one of Buber's (1952/1988) observations:

> Philosophy errs in thinking of religion as founded in a noetical act, even if an inadequate one, and in therefore regarding the essence of religion as the knowledge of an object which is indifferent to being known. As a result, philosophy understands faith as an affirmation of truth lying somewhere between clear knowledge and confused opinion. Religion, on the other hand, insofar as it speaks of knowledge at all, does not understand it as a noetic act of a thinking subject to a neutral object of thought, but rather as mutual contact, as the genuinely reciprocal meeting in the fullness of life between one active existence and another. Similarly, it understands faith as the entrance into this reciprocity, as binding oneself in relationship with an undemonstrable and unprovable, yet even so, in relationship, knowable Being, from whom all meaning comes.
>
> (p. 32–33)

When it comes to the issue of religion and spirituality, or simply spiritual competence in psychotherapy, are we talking about something that is essentially concerning a Being that is indifferent to being known? Does that even matter if all we are considering is what people make for themselves in their social groups? What are the actual factors at play in the lives of the therapist and client?

Social Constructionist

Social constructionism advocates taking a critical stance toward what we usually take for granted, to challenge the idea that what we know is based on unbiased and objective observations (Burr, 2003). It stands against the idea that what we perceive exists as we perceive it and that the natural world can be plumbed by the efforts of positivistic science.[2] For instance, that which is classical music and that which is pop music are terms that do not describe the actual music; these are categories made up by people living together in societies and cultures, and they have meaning, but aside from that they are merely created—constructed—by people to classify music according to a socially developed rubric.

The way we understand the world, including the categories we use to make sense of it, are historically and culturally specific, and this pertains to religion and spirituality just as much as to music. "It is through the daily interactions between people in the course of social life that our versions of knowledge become fabricated. Therefore social interaction of all kinds, and particularly language, is of great interest to social constructionists" (Burr, 2003, p. 4). Thus, religious language is in many cases the foundation for spiritual experience. People who convert to Christianity, for instance, begin attending a church; they read Christian literature and perhaps even study theology. They learn terms like justification and sanctification that have meaning within the religious community. These terms are found in scripture and have been arranged in credal statements over centuries, and those constructs are often catalysts for contemporary spiritual experience when they are recited during worship services or meditated upon during spiritual retreat. The relatively recent shift in the sense of the words "spirituality" and "religion"—in which religion is frequently seen as the root of evil and suffering (i.e., through religious persecutions and warfare), and spirituality is seen as pertaining to ultimate concern, existential meaning, and authentic quest—is a function of the way people have been speaking about them with one another in the media, in classrooms, and in communities.

In terms of psychology, social constructionism has four main tenets: anti-essentialism, the questioning of reality, the historical and cultural specifics of knowledge, and language as a precondition for thought. Accordingly, the world is a product of social processes in which there is no predetermined nature to anything in it (such as personality), and there is no direct perception of reality—the real world. All forms of knowledge are laid down in sediments over the course of history and diversely in various cultures, and since our ways of understanding the world come from other people, we are born into a world where the conceptual frameworks and categories utilized already exist and are acquired by people as they develop the use of language (Burr, 2003). Reality is socially constructed; for all practical purposes, there is no reality outside of what people create (Berger & Luckmann, 1967/2011). Since no one's view can be said to be more true than another's, truth claims about the world cannot be made, and all truth claims become undermined. If there is a reality, it cannot be known, because it is inaccessible, and the only thing we have is our representations of various things that are expressed socially in language. This is a skeptical position in which every account must be doubted and no one account is better than another.

Religion in a social constructionist perspective is a language system for the communication and dissemination of values in society (Burr, 2003). This way of looking at the issue of religion and spirituality is a response to the question, "What function does religion serve?" Often, this is the question a psychotherapist might ask as well. What is the client doing with this religious stuff? What does religion do for the client? Therapists whose clinical perspectives are strongly constructionist in nature (i.e., many forms of cognitive behavioral therapy [CBT], narrative therapy, and existential–phenomenological approaches) often find themselves engaged in a deconstruction of the client's stories and internal dialogues without any consideration of the possibility that when those clients relate meaningful religious epiphanies they are talking about a different kind of experience—something that in a sense happens to them or comes over them and not something they create for themselves. Furthermore, clinicians who do this give themselves away as discounting the ontological possibilities in spiritual experience.

Shiah, Chang, Tam, Chuang, and Yeh (2013) conducted a study in China to compare several religious groups to see to what degree they embodied an internal spirituality or an external instrumentality (socially pragmatic value of religious practice). Religious involvement was found to be greatest among Christians, followed by Buddhists and Taoists. An instrumental purpose for religious activities was found to be highest among Taoists, followed in order by Buddhists, and Christians. The results supported the conclusion that Christianity offers the least support for an extrinsic religious orientation and the most support for an intrinsic religious orientation, but the point most relevant at the moment is that there is a distinction between an internal religious orientation that does not seem to be as socially constructed and a more pragmatic and extrinsic religious orientation that does.

Critical Realist

One person says that there is no God and that even talk about God is meaningless because no one can verify truth claims. He or she goes on to say that talk about God is simply a language game that does not accord, for instance, with the language game scientists use and so God talk is nonsense. Religion and spirituality are simply socially constructed to serve human needs in social conditions.

Another person claims that God exists and that the discussion of God is as rational a topic as the discussion of atheism. He or she goes on to say that talking about God is an aspect of discourse on experience and can be explored phenomenologically, even though God Himself cannot be perceived by the usual senses. Religion and spirituality are natural responses in a world created by God and in which God's presence can be experienced.

Archer, Collier, and Porpora (2004) said that ontological realism concerning God in the intransitive dimension is consistent with epistemic or experiential relativism in the transitive dimension. What does that mean? It means that the existence of God does not logically contradict the fact that some people experience God and others do not. For those who do not, their knowledge base has no personal antecedent for the abstract construct and term known as "God." For those who do have an experiential knowledge of God, the term "God" is filled with personal relevance and meaning.

The critical realist position on religion and spirituality calls for a level playing field. Instead of the privilege starting with atheism and the believer having to overcome its a priori assertions, the critical realist asks that the ontologically based spiritual understanding of religious experience be treated as legitimate, though not beyond question, and just as valuable as the secular explanations of such religious experiences.

This is a legitimate phenomenological issue regardless of who might ask it. Even within the scope of the religious community, one believer in Christ will discount the experience of another on the basis of a priori theological or credal commitments, and it is not different when it comes to the atheistic sociologist discounting the spiritual rationale for a religious experience and giving the sociological or psychological explanation as if that were the actual truth. Both discounting fellow believer and discounting nonbeliever fail to bracket (as best anyone can) their cherished beliefs in order to examine the experience itself on its own terms.

When I was pastoring a small, rural church along the North Tillamook coast in the state of Oregon, a woman dropped in to talk about the loss of her mother. She said, "My mother came to me." What she meant was that her mother had died. The day after her death, in the night, the woman woke up suddenly. At the end of her bed stood her mother. This was her experience, and it was reassuring to her to have contact with her mother, as if to confirm that her mother continued on in a life after death. Now, the atheist might, even before the story was all the way out of the woman's mouth, start explaining it in secular, superstitious alternatives. Even I, as the woman's pastor, smiled outwardly, but was backing up inwardly. I concluded that I did not understand what she was telling me, because I was conflicted—caught between what I had come to believe dogmatically about the spirit of a person going to be with Jesus at death and about there being a chasm between the dead and the living (and so on and so forth). I believed in the veracity of the woman's experience, but I doubted the possibility that what she claimed actually happened in the way she thought it did.

The critical realist holds that there is a real world that exists outside one's thinking about it. We do not have an absolute knowledge of that world, and we cannot investigate it with a naïve realism that sees an exact correlation between what we perceive and what is there (that is the worn approach of positivism), but we can attain to an investigative knowledge in which we are constantly learning more and revising what we have come to know.

According to Hass (2008), as we live and move in this world, we have a synergistic relationship with the world and cocreate our perception and understanding of it. Does that mean our knowledge is socially constructed? Could be; perhaps somewhat. But not absolutely. Why? Because we do not simply represent the world in our contacting (which would be a relic of dualism and the Cartesian theater in one's mind). We actually "touch" a real world that exists apart from our representing, and we have real contact of a real world. We just do not have an exhaustive understanding of that real world, and so all our faculties of discovery and interpretation are put to use trying to understand, and that is what makes it a coconstructed perceptual and interpretational process.

It is the same thing—a kind of handshake between the subjective and the objective—in regard to what we cannot perceive with the senses but can perceive in other ways. For example, after Jesus fed the 5,000 and there were 12 baskets of bread left over, He and the disciples set out across the Sea of Galilee, and the disciples began discussing how they only had one loaf of bread among them. Jesus could see what was going on, and he chided them to be careful not to fall into the unbelief characterized by the Pharisees. Then He said, "Why do you discuss the fact that you have no bread? Do you not yet see or understand? Do you have a hardened heart? Having eyes, do you not see? And having ears, do you not hear?" (Mark 8:17–18).

He was not referring to physical sound and sight. He was talking about a spiritual understanding, what some might even call an enlightenment or revelation, and that is a kind of experience that the critical realist would say is worthy of consideration, just as much as the atheist who says he or she indeed does not "hear" and does not "see" when it comes to such religious and spiritual events. Implicit in a level playing field is the dialogue between believer and non-believer—between the one who has the spiritual experience in the practice of a religion and the one who has no given religion.

However, more basic to that is the dialogue between that which is partially known and the person who would like to find out more. As N. T. Wright (1992) put it:

> I propose a form of critical realism. This is a way of describing the process of 'knowing' that acknowledges the reality of the thing known, as something other than the knower (hence 'realism'), while fully acknowledging that the only access we have to this reality lies along the spiralling path of appropriate dialogue or conversation between the knower and the thing known (hence 'critical').
>
> (p. 35)

The critical realist, then, understands that in the practice of one's religion it is entirely possible for a person to have spiritually meaningful appreciation of an ontic religious experience. It is possible to have a dialogue between what is not understood and what is. The structure of a religion does not necessarily smother the spontaneity and significance of a spiritual epiphany. There may be more to learn about the way religion and spirituality are related and what they contribute to one another. In fact, the critical realist would admit that that relationship is, in itself, a fruitful opportunity for research.

THEOLOGICAL STANCE

Theology is essentially a theistic field of study; it is a focus on the being, nature, and actions of God, including God's actions in the lives of human beings, but it doesn't have to be a narrow perspective (if such a perspective could actually be called "narrow"). If one expands the idea of "God" to include that which is simply transcendent, then a "theology" could include a basically atheistic worldview, but a worldview that finds reverence in natural structures and processes, especially those that are substantively *other* in essence and that could be considered an *über-natural theology*.[3]

Since anthropology is one part of a systematic theology, anything relevant to the human condition would be relevant theologically. For example, Paul Tillich believed that theology should be manifest in a dialogue with science, culture, and art. His overriding project was to relate Christianity to secular culture. In *Theology of Culture*, Paul Tillich (1959) offered several essays in support of this thesis. In the one titled *Basic Considerations*, he said,

> You cannot reject religion with ultimate seriousness, because ultimate seriousness, or the state of being ultimately concerned, is itself religion. Religion is the substance, the ground, and the depth of man's spiritual life. This is the religious aspect of the human spirit.
>
> (p. 8)

When understood, theology is what a person learns about God in the course of his or her relationship with God. It is the byproduct of such a relationship and cannot be neatly organized into either a theoretical or a practical discipline (Horton, 2011). A systematic study of God, however, yields a more broadly structured body of knowledge about God, based on the determined purpose of knowing God more completely, but one that is embodied in the processes of grasping, dissecting, comprehending, and possessing one's object of study. This can result in the experiential knowledge of God, but it does not have to, as people can make a secular profession out of many things, including the study of the Bible, religious history, and systematic theology. Where theology reflects the theologian's own sense of contact with the divine (or the transcendent), theology takes on religious importance and spiritual significance.

Returning to the metaphor of DNA, the strands of religion and spirituality are connected as before, but in this theological consideration, they are connected by at least two considerations that seem figural and important: relationship and process. The illustration below (Figure 2.2) shows that in both spirituality and religion, there will be a relational aspect and there will be process.

In process theology, God is part of creation. God is changing and constantly emerging and is "of" creation rather than standing apart from what He has created. Consequently, the knowledge of God is always progressing, and is "in process." This is not just the increasing accumulation of facts about God that a person might gather over time. This concerns the available fund of knowledge—what could be known. So, this kind of evolution of the being and character of God finds a home in New Age spirituality that tends to be about becoming, evolving, and having the spark of divinity within. Process theology is most associated with the thinking of Alfred North Whitehead and Charles Hartshorne. For "both Whitehead and Hartshorne, it is an essential attribute of God to be fully involved in and affected by temporal processes" (Viney, 2008). This involvement in creation, whether or not God is subject to change, makes God immanent. It makes God immanent in essence. Thus, the issue of transcendence (rather assumed in the study of a supreme being) is collapsed into immanence. God is not just with us; God is like us in that God is evolving.

In all forms of religion and spirituality, there are these two important considerations of process and relationship even though some religions and spiritual practices seem more closely associated with process or relationships. For instance, the Tao is all about the "way,"

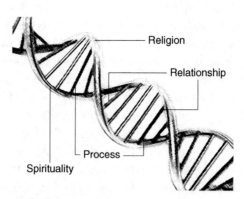

FIGURE 2.2   Process and relationship: Religion and spirituality.

not just meaning the path, but the process by which one traverses the path, and Buddhism concerns itself with the disciplines of mind to deal with suffering. The monotheistic religions of Judaism, Christianity, and Islam, on the other hand, are predominantly about the relationship people have with God. People can concern themselves with their relationship to others and the environment in Eastern religion, and they can concern themselves with the ways to work out their salvation in the monotheistic religions. These two considerations will be dealt with in more detail in subsequent chapters.

A COHERENTIST WEB OF BELIEF

I want to use a concept here to illustrate how religion and spirituality really cannot be separated for a warranted practice of either. In a web of belief, there are several touch points, and the more touch points one has, the more they all cohere in a formidable unit that justifies one's worldview. In such a web of belief, the touch points are connected by a logic of some kind; it is what binds them and holds them together. The touch points more central in the web are more important and resistant to change, but everything in the web of belief is open to moderation if a preponderance of some kind becomes persuasive. Some may recognize this in W. V. Quine's (1978) epistemological construction of a web of belief.

To illustrate with regard to certain elements in the field of psychotherapy, coherentist warrant is the web of clinical factors and theoretical tenets created through the consilience that unites them (consilience is the logic between the touch points). William Whewell asserted that coherence is a type of consilience, because coherence extends any given hypothesis through a grouping of terms, constructs, practices, and so forth that constitute a new class of phenomena without having to adjust the hypothesis to make them fit. That is, they just do fit; they go together, pointing to a commonality.

For instance, in CBT's imaginal desensitization, the client does not insert him or herself into the actual problem scenario; he or she simply imagines being in it, and then the desensitizing takes place in that imaginal space. Gestalt therapists create the same imaginal space, but they approach the process as an experiment, not knowing exactly what might result, and helping the client to pay attention and monitor him- or herself in the process. It is virtually the same thing. The cognitive behavioral therapist and the gestalt therapist share a consilience of practice, and that forms part of a coherent web—people coming at the same phenomenon from two different perspectives. They are linked through the shared logic of the procedure between them (which is not an exact similarity but a sufficient similarity[4]).

So, with regard to the fields of religion and spirituality, are there any consilient touch points that might constitute part of a coherent web of belief such that one might assume that religion and spirituality are consilient terms? Remember that religion is a construct useful in identifying groups of people on the basis of their spiritual practices, institutional allegiances, and theological commitments. The practices in question are the rituals by which people embody and enact their spiritual beliefs.

Wade Davis (2008), in a Ted Talk given in Monterey, provided one example after another of the spiritual rituals enacted by various people groups extending from Polynesia to Tibet to the Native Peoples of South America. In one example, for instance, he referred to a Tibetan nun who had lived in solitude for years. Instead of the stress of isolation, on her face was the tranquility of peace. In his book *The Spirit of the Disciplines*, Dallas Willard (1988) identified the spiritual practice of solitude as being one that Jesus practiced. Indeed, the retreat is something common to spiritual practice among many people, and it is something we consistently find that people repeat both within religious institutions and outside of them.

In fact, ritual (or discipline) is a basic structure in religion within which people can understand and experience a deeper spirituality. Foster (1978) lists several such disciplines such as meditation, prayer, fasting, solitude, simplicity, service, confession, and worship. Willard's list of such disciplines includes solitude, silence, fasting, frugality, chastity, secrecy, sacrifice, study, worship, celebration, service, prayer, fellowship, confession, and submission.

Christian prayer is consilient with contemplation. Gunaratana (2002) pointed to the similarities among several religions by saying that prayer is the direct address of a deity and contemplation is an extended period of conscious thought about an issue, religious construct, or passage from scripture. They both require concentration. Hindu yogic meditation also requires concentration, perhaps through focusing on a single object. In Buddhist meditation, concentration is also required, but with the addition of awareness.

Gerald Cory (2000) pointed to several ways in which there is a consilience among traditions for religious practice, including that of mysticism.

> A Christian mystic has a mystical incorporation with the Christ and is filled with the Holy Ghost; a Hindu or Yogi becomes one with the Brahman, or world soul; the Buddhist achieves oneness with the unitary consciousness or The Void; The Taoist grasps the unity of the Tao; the nature mystic achieves a total incorporation with nature. . . .
>
> (Cory, 2000, p. 109)

Naturally, there are some differences as well. If, for example, we associate the word "church" with religion, then spirituality could be something a person attends to in the solitude of his or her own soul, and as such is an individual thing. Religion, on the other hand, is a group concern. One may practice his or her spirituality alone, but one cannot practice one's religion (i.e., participate in church) without that being a communal and relational thing.

If one stands back and considers that in a psychological stance, a philosophical stance, and a theological stance, one encounters a common overlap between religion and spirituality, then a coherent web, a consilience, emerges. In theology, one finds both religion and spirituality being used interchangeably. The philosophical understanding of each shows a commonality between them, and in psychology also the two are used interchangeably. Reading the signs of life in order to find significance is both religious and spiritual.

NOTES

1. Let me just recommend that the reader start an independent study of the subject with two books: (a) *Psychology, Religion, and Spirituality*, by James Nelson, and (b) *The Psychology of Religion and Spirituality for Clinicians: Using Research in Your Practice*, by Jamie Aten, Kari O'Grady, and Everett Worthington, Jr. Nelson is comprehensive and explores areas not usually found in texts on the psychology of religion; he brings in continental philosophy as well as relying on psychological research. The second book makes some nice applications of the psychology of religion to clinical practice.

2. Although the poverty of positivism has been demonstrated, and we are in a post-positivist world, remnants of positivism can be found in various approaches to psychology.
3. Above or beyond nature as pointing toward God, this would be nature as transcendent in itself.
4. The cognitive behavioral therapist is attempting to bring about a preconceived change, reach a known goal, but the gestalt therapist is using the same technique as an experiment in order to answer the question, "What might happen for X if he or she does this?" The logic goes to the process and the potential in the imaginal space in question; what they do not share is the logic of the outcome.

CHAPTER 3

Spirituality as Process

Victory, defeat—the words were meaningless.
Life lies behind these symbols and life is ever bringing new
symbols into being.

—Antoine de Saint-Exupery, 1942, p. 127

A process is something that is going on, something happening, something moving. It is a wave. Koiné Greek had a way of capturing process; it was in the verb structure. That language was not so much interested in time but nature, that is, not so much interested in when something happened, but how it took place or how it was in the process of taking place. Yes, of course they needed to account for time, but that was not the major consideration.

"The basic genius of the Greek verb is not its ability to indicate *when* the action of the verb occurs (time), but *what type of action* it describes, or what we call 'aspect'" (Mounce, 2003, p. 126). There is a continuous aspect in which the action of the verb is an ongoing process. This would be like saying, "I am walking," or even "I walk" (with the understanding that it means a continuous action of taking one step after another, after another, and so on). There was also an undefined aspect to the verb, meaning that the action was thought of as a simple event, without commenting about whether it was or was not a process. "I slept." "She cried." "We ate." Thus, when Jesus spoke to his disciples and characterized the kind of life His followers were to lead, He said, "If anyone wishes to come after me, let him deny himself and take up his cross and follow me" (Mark 8:34). In that sentence, the words "deny" and "take up" are in the undefined aspect, not saying much

59

about the nature of those actions except that they were to occur, but the word "follow" is in the continuous aspect, meaning that the disciples of Christ were to live a life characterized by the continuous process of following.

Now we turn to consider spirituality as process.

WHAT IS A PROCESS?

We live in a small, one-bedroom apartment, below a large house owned by a lovely Swiss couple, on a hill overlooking the Great Sound in Bermuda. Outside our front door is a concrete patio. On the hill straight across the patio is a jungle of trees, shrubs, and vines. There are flower beds on either side of the patio, and the grassy yard, which is expansive, falls away from the moon gate next to us down the hill toward a condominium complex called Mizzentop. From there, the Great Sound stretches out on the other side of Harbor Road toward the city of Hamilton.

Every year, when the season begins to change from winter to spring, the ants emerge from the jungle and the grassy yard, or from under the concrete of the patio through a few cracks in the cement, and they stream up and down the outside of the house, or across the patio, and they hunt for food.

We also have cats, two indoor cats and two outdoor cats. All cats are hunters, but they are hunters of opportunity. The indoor cats hunt food in their dishes, paper grocery bags left on the floor, bugs, and shadows. The outdoor cats hunt lizards and rats.

One day, Cheetah, a skinny and older outdoor cat with an asthmatic condition, caught a lizard. He killed it and left it on the patio. So did I. But I watched for the ants, because I was curious what might happen.

Ants are social insects that live in colonies that are sometimes described as superorganisms because of the way the ants organize into a unity, all members working together with various roles, all of which support the colony. When you see them, they are constantly in motion.

At first there were just a couple of ants. They were scouting the area. They wandered here and there. It looked to be a random reconnoitering. Then, they found the dead lizard. Pretty soon there were more ants, but it still looked to be a random finding. However, in short order, the ants began to appear in a stream. It looked as if most of them were coming from a place across the patio and underground toward the lizard carcass, but there also began to be some ants headed back toward the place from which they came. Eventually, the ants covered the dead lizard, and I watched them take its body apart, one small bit at a time. Eventually, there was nothing left of the lizard but its delicate skeleton. Then, the ants filtered out and were gone, except for still a few wandering ants in random patterns of searching.

I have learned that ants communicate by scent. So in the process of finding the dead lizard, communicating back to the other ants, and then slowly consuming its body, the ants must have given off a particular scent. Whatever the actual mechanisms, the method in their activity seemed organized, purposeful, and efficient.

It was a process, and a process is a series of actions or steps taken to achieve a specific end. In the example of the ants, even the apparent random wanderings of the scouts were a purposeful part of the colony's process, because the colony is always "in process."

People are said to be in process when they are a "work in progress."

Siddhārtha Gautama, the Buddha, went through a process of enlightenment (Batchelor, 2010). At first he was the son, the prince in a kingdom that his father ruled. He was a member of a warrior family. His father's role was as benefactor and overlord, tilling land, collecting taxes, attending to the public works for the common good, and taking care of diplomacy with neighboring states. His mother died a week after his birth. Siddhārtha was a thoughtful, contemplative young man who perceived the common lot of humanity in terms of sickness, old age, and death. He empathized with the suffering of those he saw. At first, he sought after the same things others did and in the same way that others did, but he reached a turning point in which fulfilling duties to his caste seemed empty, and he began to wonder if that was all there was to life. He began to desire to find a way to dissolve greed, hatred, and delusion. While still a youth, he shaved off his hair and beard, put on the yellow robe, and went out from his safe home into homelessness; he joined the life of wandering mendicants. He sat at the feet of various teachers who advocated such things as "nothingness" or the "sphere of neither perception nor nonperception." These did not satisfy, but he learned meditation techniques that later proved valuable. At one point, he practiced ascetic disciplines that he hoped would provide an open door to what he had sought, but they too did not satisfy; so, he decided to give up the way of asceticism, which left him alone to pursue his own, unique way. "These are two characteristics of the spirit of the Buddha: on the one hand, he was able to question, to try different things; and on the other hand, he was able to go his own way, to depend upon himself . . ." (Batchelor, 2010, p. 21). These are the processes of life that led him to search. When he attained enlightenment at the foot of the Bodhi tree, it was based on the processes of the cultivation of virtue, concentration, and understanding. Consequently, what he taught for the remainder of his life was morality, meditation, and wisdom.

In Christianity, the word "salvation" can be understood as either justification or sanctification. If it is justification, it is a dot, a point on the page, and it occurs as the culmination of one kind of process (that process leading to salvation). As such, it comes to completion, happens once, and it's done. However, sanctification is like a line on the page that just keeps going on and on. It is a process that is captured in St. Paul's words: "So then, my beloved . . . work out your salvation with fear and trembling; for it is God who is at work in you, both to will and to work for *His* good pleasure" (Philippians 2:12,13). The aspect is continuous both in terms of the command to keep working out and the observation that God is continuously at work in the lives of such people both to will and to work for His pleasure. In terms of spirituality, what it points to is a synergistic relationship between God and human beings in which on the human side we are "working out" (applying the disciplines conducive to spiritual growth) what on the God side is continuously being worked within (God in the process of developing salvation within us). The details of this process constitute the what and the how of one's spirituality.

THE WHAT AND THE HOW OF SPIRITUAL PROCESS

On the night of my graduation from high school, my mother was too drunk to attend. Things had been getting out of hand leading up to that day. I had run away from home and slept over at a friend's house for several days. He and I had joined the Navy on a delay program so that by the time we graduated we were already set to go to boot camp 120 days later. I wanted to escape the home I grew up in, because it had become too crazy.

As I put on my robe for graduation at the high school and found my way to the chair for the ceremony, back home my mother called a couple of friends from our local church. She asked for help, because she had reached the bottom of her barrel. They came to the house. They told her about Jesus, something she had actually known about already, but this time she took on the whole story as meant for her, and she prayed with them to accept Jesus as her savior. She enrolled herself in rehab. Both she and my father started going to Alcoholics Anonymous (AA) meetings. She started attending church and joined a Bible study. By the time I was on active duty and would come home on leave, she was solid in what she believed, and we would argue about religion, because I thought it was a joke.

Three and a half years later, I was sitting in my room in the same house I had left to join the Navy, and I was asking Jesus to be *my* savior. There was a process getting me to that point, but my salvation, in the sense of my sanctification, had just begun. It's been almost 44 years since then, and along the way I've been part of churches, participated in home Bible studies, prayed my way through crises, read many pieces of Christian literature, and been influenced by several incredible people. These are the kinds of things involved in Christian spirituality from a process perspective. They constitute the "what" and the "how"—what people do and how they do it.

Every religion comes with a process, that is, each recommends disciplines, practices, or exercises by which people might grow spiritually. For instance, if you are Buddhist, then you meditate, write haiku, paint, do calligraphy, or contemplate a koan (Richmond, 1999). The process of spiritual growth, however, is not simply the practice of disciplines. It is the maturing of one's perspective over time through the consistent application of one's faith to the challenges of life. There is no way to capture that in a few words. It's the difference between being told that San Francisco is a city by the bay on the one hand and walking at Fisherman's Wharf, smelling the crabs boiling in their metal pots and seeing steam rise into the chilly air, hearing the gulls call to one another as they circle overhead, and then settling down to eat at one of the restaurants there, tasting the sourdough bread with a slab of butter.

There are many practices that people in various religions observe to facilitate this maturation over time. Table 3.1 presents some of them.

This table does not represent an exhaustive list, but it will suffice to show both the breadth and the overlap across various religious traditions in which spirituality is expressed. Further, these practices are not items people check off on a to-do list, once done then forgotten. These are things people do repeatedly, and so there is a process to

TABLE 3.1
SPIRITUAL PRACTICES

Religion	Practice
Christianity (both Catholic and Protestant)	Corporate and/or private prayer, fasting, acts of mercy, Eucharist/Communion, chanting, celibacy, meditation/contemplation, celebration/worship, confession, servanthood, solitude, study, self-control, fellowship, etc.
Judaism	Contemplation, diligent study of the Torah, reciting daily prayers (such as the Shema and Amidah), adhering to dietary laws, observing Shabat, fasting, doing deeds of love/kindness
Islam	Ritual prayer, fasting, Dhikr (recitation of the names of God), Muraqaba (self-care through meditation), Sarna (losing oneself in worship music and in whirling dance)
Buddhism	Development of the heart/mind and of kindness, meditation (zazen), writing poetry (such as haiku), painting, calligraphy, or attending Zen gardens
Hinduism	Silent or audible repetition of a mantra (a sound, syllable, or group of words considered capable of producing transformation), yoga (breathing techniques and postures), mudras (gestures)
New Age	Memorization and silent repetition of passages from the scriptures of various religions, ceremonial invocation, physical exercise, modified yoga and dietary restrictions, eclectic integration of indigenous spiritual practices from diverse cultures

them, and they are processes within processes. The table also points to part of a coherent web in that across various religions there is a ritual vocalization of mantras, scriptures, and corporate prayers; there is worship that includes music and in which there may also be dancing; there is a variety of creative expression of religious affection, something Jonathan Edwards (1746/2011) described as those affections that are spiritual and gracious, that arise from the influences and operations on the heart that are supernatural and divine.[1]

Such a characterization might be given to the Jewish contemplation of the vision of the *Merkavah* (the heavenly chariot described in the book of Ezekiel). When a person is worthy and blessed with the ability to gaze at the Heavenly Chariot and the angels accompanying in heaven, that person has to follow various exercises—observe the process appropriate to the moment. He has to fast for a number of days, place his head between his knees, and whisper so only he can hear the praises of God, all the while with face to the ground.

> As a result he will gaze in the innermost recesses of his heart and it will seem as if he saw the seven halls with his own eyes, moving from hall to hall to observe that which is therein to be found.
>
> (quoting Lewin, Otzar ha-Geonim, in Jacobs, 1986, p. 493)

In Hinduism, sacrificial offerings have been made to various deities at various times, and this has evolved into the self-renunciation of desire, the pursuit of the knowledge of truth, and practices of concentration (yoga). These Hindu principles are sought and practiced as ways of living (Derrett, 1986). In the most celebrated combination of such principles, the Bhagavad Gita (a homily from the mouth of Krishna, who appears as a universal spirit), the process is described as follows:

> He whose consciousness is without attachment, whose self conquers in all directions, who has left desire behind, he, by the renunciation, achieves the highest success, transcending all action. To those who are constantly concentrated and worship full of love I give that consciousness-attachment by which they read me.
>
> (Bhagavad Gita 18:49, 10:10)

In the 5th century in Ireland, Patrick's influence led to a tremendous response among the people such that in the century to follow, the church in Ireland had become largely monastic (O'Laoghaire, 1986). That church was governed by abbots of important monasteries. In such monasteries, prayer, study, and manual labor were cultivated in earnest, and the object of study was the Scriptures.

Monastic life epitomizes this idea of process, because monastic life is an established rhythm in the use of time—the beat between prayer and work—showing

> that all time belongs to God and our use of time finds meaning only if we do our tasks, both religious and secular, to honor and serve God. . . . God calls us to seek his face in prayer and to do his work in the world. Monastic spirituality affirms that we must do *both* activities if we hope to fulfill the purpose for which God created us.
>
> (Sittser, 2007, p. 97)

Contemporary monasteries still offer this kind of resource to the spiritual person. It is not necessary to join the monastery and to become a monk; today many people utilize the monasteries as retreats where they can provide for themselves a restorative experience, and for those who make repeated visits to the monasteries, they are useful and meaningful, specifically as part of the process of spiritual growth (Quellette, Kaplan, & Kaplan, 2005). One monastery in Conyers, Georgia, for instance, provides people with the opportunity to rest, reflect, and renew. People come to The Monastery of the Holy Spirit as a place where they can get away from the stressors of everyday life to revitalize the spirit and rejuvenate the soul. The Amaravati Buddhist monastery in Hertfordshire, England, both conducts organized retreats associated with the monastery and allows people to simply stay at the monastery on an informal basis to deepen their understanding of Buddhism and of themselves in an environment that encourages reflection. Visitors come from all over the world. Some stay for a day, a weekend, or longer, perhaps to learn meditation or to have a time of refuge from the stresses of the world.

The process of growth in spiritual maturity is lifelong, and it is comprehensive, including every aspect of life. The spiritual life is not a compartmentalized commodity. It is not something people do only on particular days or at particular times. Being a spiritual person is more a matter of who one is, even though it certainly includes what one does. The Bible describes such a person as a *pneumatikos* (an adjectival form of the word pneuma/spirit). As such, a spiritual person discerns the things of God in the midst of a world not really cognizant of God. It is a seeing by the eyes of the spirit and a hearing by the ears of the spirit. It is a comprehending that is more proprioceptive than perceptive—that is, like balance, it is something a person senses going on within. It is something Jesus referred to when he told people that they had eyes but didn't see and ears but didn't hear (they had no spiritual sensitivity, no spiritual proprioception); He was talking about a spiritual capacity that runs the course of human life in persons growing in spiritual maturity. It is the ability to hear God—to hear *from* God.

This ability to hear God is a source of sensitivity and guidance that psychotherapists need to heed. I am sure that in other religions and spiritual traditions, those practicing those faiths have some kind of corresponding inner guide. At this point, the veracity of such an inner leading is not the issue.[2] For the therapist, the issue is what is happening in the client and what is part of the client's life world. If a psychotherapist is not cognizant of such things, he or she can interpret away what is happening and/or minimize it to the point of irrelevance or, worse, pathology.

It is interesting to note that Jesus had such a proprioceptive process. It was at work in Him to guide Him in what He did. He described that process by saying that He did nothing of His own initiative, but that the words He spoke were given to Him by His father and the things He did were the works of His father. When you read the gospels, you can see over and over again how He seems to find Himself in the midst of a situation looking to God, His Father, for what comes next.

> Truly, truly, I say to you, the Son can do nothing of Himself, unless *it is* something He sees the Father doing; for whatever the Father does, these things the Son also does in like manner (John 5:19). . . . For I did not speak on My own initiative, but the Father Himself who sent Me has given Me a commandment *as to* what to say and what to speak. I know that His commandment is eternal life; therefore the things I speak, I speak just as the Father has told Me.
>
> (John 12:49, 50)

A process is something that is going on, something happening, something moving. It is a wave. Where I live above the Great Sound in Bermuda, I can see the water. The water is always changing. Some days the waves are tiny things that bump into one another to such a degree that no clear wave can be seen, just the tops of countless peaks in the chop. At other times, the Sound is calm and almost like glass; that is when the wind that generates ocean waves is calm. At other times, the waves are quite visible as swells moving across the surface, generated by wind somewhere else out in the ocean. The process of wave formation is an ongoing series of interactions between moving air and moving water. Just so, spiritual development and maturation is a constantly moving interaction between the person and what transcends the person, yet touches the person and is experienced as immanently significant.

NOTES

1. He was writing explicitly about Christianity, but within the Christian churches, broadly speaking, one will find rich forms of worship with

various kinds of creative expression, including the ecstatic experience that often results in spontaneous dancing or the quiet reverence of a swinging thurible.

2. It *is* necessary to evaluate what is going on in clients, especially those exhibiting psychotic process, and so there is a place for considering the ontic field (what the situation actually is outside of anyone's thoughts about it), but consult Chapter 7 for a more balanced treatment of this.

CHAPTER 4

Spirituality as Relationship

*Abide in Me, and I in you. As the branch cannot bear fruit of
itself unless it abides in the vine, so neither can you unless you
abide in Me. I am the vine, you are the branches; he who abides
in Me and I in him, he bears much fruit, for apart from
Me you can do nothing.*

—John 15:4–5

In the second year of my doctoral program, I began working at a
co-occurring diagnoses psychiatric hospital in southeast Portland,
Oregon. The place had three main sections, one of which was an intensive care unit where people were sent to detox, where lower-functioning
patients resided, and where people were brought on police holds if
they were suspected to be a risk to themselves or others. Because
I had to attend classes during the day, I worked the permanent evening
shift. Although my hours were scheduled around my classes, I worked
full-time. I came at about 3:00 p.m. and got off about 11:00 p.m. I func-
tioned as a mental health therapist, one of two, and I worked alongside a psychiatric registered nurse, who passed medications. For a
while, staff came and went, and there was no consistency to the people
I worked with, but after several months that solidified. At that point,
I knew with whom I'd be working each night.

Sam[1] was a young, black female. She was short, quick-witted, and
had a sarcastic bite to her that I liked. At first we did not get along, but
after having to cover each other's backs in dealing with threats on the
unit, we learned to respect one another for a no-nonsense approach to
safety and milieu management.

Holly was a middle-aged, heavier white woman who had been a nurse for some time; her experience had been gained at the state hospital, working the psych units there.

So every day I came to work. I put my coat in the staff room, and then I went out on the unit to sense the atmosphere. I said hello. I got the report from the staff that was about to go off duty, and I watched them leave. I settled in for the evening, one evening shift at a time, ran my groups, conducted my one-to-ones, charted on my patients, and at the end of each shift I passed the report to the night staff coming on duty. Then I collected my coat, walked out of the hospital, and breathed free air in whatever kind of weather was happening in southeast Portland at the time. I drove home thinking about my doctoral program and my children back at the house, and I left the hospital behind. That happened week after week for about 4 years.

Holly at first thought I was impatient, uncaring, and rigid, but one evening the police brought us a man on a hold off the streets. His long hair was matted and knotted. His clothes were dirty, and he smelled. He was incoherent, disoriented, and virtually noncommunicative. We put him in a quiet room, and a team gathered with staff from other units. When we undid his shoes and started to take his socks off, his toenails came off with them. He had been wearing the same clothing, and the clothing had been damp and foul for so long that his toenails had started turning to goo. We realized he would need to be taken to a walk-in shower and completely cleaned up, and I was the lead male. It was up to me. I put the gloves on and followed the man into the walk-in shower. Another staff person stood behind me for backup. I took the man's clothing off and found that he'd been defecating in his pants for some time. It was caked and hardened. It took me an hour and half of soaping and scrubbing and rinsing and soaping and cleaning every crevice repeatedly to get all the dirt and decay off him, and he sighed and moaned the whole time.

Holly told me later that everything changed between us that night, because she watched me tenderly take care of the man in spite of his being in one of the foulest conditions she had ever seen.

So Sam, Holly, and I became a tight team. The unit was in order when we were there. We only had to look at each other in a situation to understand what needed to be done. We had good working relationships. However, we never went home with each other, went drinking with each other after work, or communicated with each other outside of work. While at work we shared things about ourselves, but we didn't bleed on one another. We worked together.

There are many kinds of relationships, but there is a commonality among them that helps to define what a relationship is. A relationship is "contact" over time. What follows is a further exploration of this definition.

WHAT IS A RELATIONSHIP?

Norcross and Lambert (2011) defined the therapeutic relationship as "the feelings and attitudes that therapist and client have toward one another, and the manner in which these are expressed" (p. 5). A quality therapeutic relationship is critical to positive outcomes in psychotherapy (Norcross & Wampold, 2011), but what makes for quality if all a relationship amounts to is the feelings and attitudes people have toward one another and the manner in which these are expressed? It is the way in which two people meet, the nature or quality of their meeting, and what it is like for each person in that meeting.

Yontef and Bar-Yoseph (2008) have suggested the construct of "contact," in which contact is a meeting between self and other. Thus, a person can have contact with the environment as well as with a person, and a relationship can be understood as contact over time.

Two factors contribute to the quality and nature of such a relationship: impact (the intensity or significance of any given point of contact) and frequency (the actual number of points of contact).

When I was in the Navy, I used to drive up and down the Pacific coast on my days off. One of the places I developed a relationship with is Big Sur, and that is not because of how many times I have been there, but the impact of the place on me the few times that I have been there. Here are two.

The first time I went to Big Sur, I grabbed a bottle of wine and a loaf of sourdough bread, got into my Volkswagen bug, and headed down the coastal highway out of Monterey. I stopped at Pfeiffer Big Sur State Park and parked the car. I started climbing a trail up the side of one of the mountains, and when I cleared the tops of the trees and got away from the big bushes, I climbed until I felt tired and then sat down. From that vantage point, I could see down into the park, and I could see out to the horizon, where the ocean met the boundary between air and sea. It was quiet. The quiet was so intense I could hear ringing in my ears. Eventually, the ringing stopped, but the quiet was still intense. It was disturbingly peaceful. I became aware of my heart beating and my lungs filling with air. I tried to calm myself and match the tranquility of the place. That is when a large hawk flew by. It was level with my eyes and about 20 feet out from the side of the mountain. I could see it clearly, and when it went past, I could hear the air whooshing from its wings. In that moment, I felt one with the mountainside, the hawk, the air, the sight of the ocean, and with all of creation. I was not the king of the creatures as a human being; I was one of the creatures as a member of that moment.

The second time I went to Big Sur was September 13 and 14, 1969, 1 month after the widely publicized pop festival in Woodstock. The Esalen Institute hosted a celebration. It turned out to be the occasion for Neil Young joining Crosby, Stills, and Nash, and the festival also featured Joan Baez, John Sebastian, and Joni Mitchell. The bands all played in front of a pool overlooking the ocean, with a grassy hillside on the other side sloping up to the highway. The music was not that great, and the comments were filled with idealistic dribble reflective of the times. However, something happened in the midst of it all for me as I sat there in the crowd. Suddenly, three pelicans appeared stage left, gliding on the warm air rising from all those bodies sitting in the sun. They drifted slowly across in front of the pool, about 6 feet above the heads of everyone seated on the grass, and when the people saw them, they let loose with a collective sigh and then a hush fell over everyone. For one moment we were all focused on the three pelicans floating above our heads, drifting and serene. When the pelicans reached stage right, everyone let out with spontaneous applause and shouts of appreciation. I have never forgotten that moment. Three birds hushed a crowd of thousands.

To this day, I have a relationship with Big Sur. It feels like an old friend, like somebody with whom I tasted youth.

In Bermuda, traffic congestion is high around 8:00 a.m. and 5:00 p.m. because the roads were built for horses and carriages, and there are too many automobiles on the island. So, many people take a ferry to work. I drive to the parking lot where the road goes up the hill to Blu Bar and Grill, an upscale restaurant that overlooks the Great Sound at the Belmont Golf Course. I park and catch the ferry at the Belmont ferry stop on the other side of Harbor Road. It is customary to express thanks to bus drivers and ferry crew; so I have always done that. When I get on in the evening, I let them know where I'm getting off; everyone does that so the Captain can plan his route. I do that every time I ride the ferry. I ride the ferry Monday through Friday, week in and week out. One day, too many people were getting aboard for me to tell the crew member where I was getting off, and I sat down thinking that I'd let him know when it was needed. However, before I could do that, he walked past, looked at me, and whispered, "Belmont?" I nodded with the good feeling that I had been seen. That sense of being seen was an increase in the quality of contact that had been developing between us over the many times we had seen one another while I was riding the ferry.

There are all kinds of relationships. There are intimate relationships. There are business relationships. There are superficial relationships, and there are temporary relationships. There are also therapeutic relationships.

Spirit is the medium, and faith is the means by which one establishes and develops a relationship with God. It takes time, it involves impact, and it requires a quality of contact.

THE WHAT AND THE HOW OF SPIRITUAL RELATIONSHIP

Spirituality as relationship includes meetings between self and other over time and with impact, where "other" is understood to be a transcendent other or focus of ultimate concern. If the meeting with an ultimate concern is in question, then that becomes a categorial intentional object[2] in which the reality of a construct such as justice or love becomes figural and tangible as an actual other in the life of the subject. Thus, one kind of spiritual relationship is a reverie on beauty in nature, without it necessarily being about the creator of nature. The spiritual capacity in people allows us to relate to such things even if we do not believe in God.

These meetings between self and other can be understood as contact.

Contact was a movie directed by Robert Zemeckis, in which a young female scientist sought intelligent life in the universe, and it found her. Two races of people divided by great distance created a way to touch one another.

One way of understanding contact is to say that it is the physical touching between two things or people. To extend that, contact is the communication that goes on between one and another, which could be activated or operated through physical touch, like the connection for the passage of electrical current. However, it can also be an interpersonal touching as well, and so constitutes the connection that allows the passage of emotional, intellectual, or otherwise psychological "current" between a person and environmental others. Just as there can be a poor connection that inhibits the flow of electricity, there can be a poor quality of contact between people that diminishes the effect or impact of the other in a person's life. Furthermore, just as the circuit that allows the free flow of electricity can be broken, people can break contact, and in psychotherapy this is often called resistance.[3]

Some people have a poor sense of the other and consequent poor contact because they do not form clear figures of interest with regard to their own experience. That is, some people may not have a sufficient awareness of themselves, what it feels like to be in a situation, and what they want in those situations. If you ask such a person what he or she is aware of, one might say, "I don't know." If you ask what he or she wants, one might shrug his or her shoulders with a blank expression. These people are out of touch. They are not meeting themselves in the course of their lives, not paying attention, not fully experiencing what they are living through, and therefore they are not even fully living. Such a person is not grounded well enough to be able to provide the self-support necessary to enter into full contact with another. It will seem confusing or scary, and they will break contact by withdrawing into themselves, deflecting into irrelevance, projecting a self-made version of reality onto others, or just avoiding contact to begin with.

One significant way that people obstruct or avoid contact with God can be called "hardening." It is a term pointing to the stubborn stiffening of a person (Bauer, Arndt, & Gingrich, 1957). It is a disposition of the will set against, not in the sense of aggression but in the sense of determined resistance, and it is associated with unbelief. This is the person who says, "I don't care what you say, I just don't believe it." He or she digs in the heels.

Hebrews 3:7–15

Therefore, just as the Holy Spirit says, "Today if you hear His voice, do not harden your hearts as when they provoked Me, as in the day of trial in the wilderness, where your fathers tried Me by testing Me, and saw My works for forty years. Therefore I was angry with this generation, and said, 'They always go astray in their heart, and they did not know My ways'; as I swore in My wrath, 'They shall not enter My rest.'" Take care, brethren, that there not be in any one of you an evil, unbelieving heart that falls away from the living God. But encourage one another day after day, as long as it is still called "Today," so that none of you will be hardened by the deceitfulness of sin. For we have become partakers of Christ, if we hold fast the beginning of our assurance firm until the end, while it is said, "Today if you hear His voice, do not harden your hearts, as when they provoked Me."

Psalm 95:7–11

For He is our God,
And we are the people of His pasture and the sheep of His hand.
Today, if you would hear His voice,
Do not harden your hearts, as at Meribah,
As in the day of Massah in the wilderness,
"When your fathers tested Me,
They tried Me, though they had seen My work.
"For forty years I loathed that generation,
And said they are a people who err in their heart,
And they do not know My ways.
"Therefore I swore in My anger,
Truly they shall not enter into My rest."

Notice that hardening is something that happens in a current moment, in the "today" of subjective experience. Hardening is a moment-by-moment resistance to the initiatives of God, Who is described as expressing a voice, speaking (Wolterstorff, 1995), and desiring a relationship by reaching out for contact (cf. Isaiah 1:18). When a person does not resist or break such contact, then a dialogical relationship with God is possible (Buber, 1923/1958). Dallas Willard (1999) expressed this saying, "Today I continue to believe that people are meant to live in an ongoing conversation with God, speaking and being spoken to. Rightly understood, I believe that this can be abundantly verified in experience" (p. 18). Because we are born into an en-Spirited natural world (Smith, 2010) that is already going on at our arrival, we are always in the presence of God speaking. God speaks generally through that which God has created, and God speaks specifically to individuals through diverse means (i.e., in scripture, through other believers, in sermons, through religious and spiritual literature, in the midst of worship, in music, in society, and pointedly in nature, etc.).

One is, however, not stuck with a theistic understanding of spiritual relationship. Jean-Luc Marion (2002) stated, "What shows itself first gives itself . . ." (p. 5). He was talking about any phenomenon. Corresponding to Marion, Jean-Louis Chrétien (2004) asserted that one does not know the call of any given phenomenon but in one's response to it. So if one's response is a hardening against that call, against that givenness, then one just doesn't know the phenomenon at all. This was St. Paul's argument (1 Corinthians 2:13–15) when he said that a spiritual person can understand spiritual things, but a nonspiritual person cannot. There is a contacting in the appreciation of spiritual phenomena that transcends a purely physicalist system. One can stand by the ocean at sunset and watch the expanse of the sea under the crimson clouds and feel reached by that spectacle, touched by it, moved by it. The sunset is given and known in the response of the person standing on the sand. There is contact. That contact can speak to a person about the creator or not; it can simply be that the sunset in its beauty implies to the person something more that transcends his or her mundane life.

Still, for those whose spirituality is a theistic system, there is something more than the apprehension of a spectacle that, regardless of its givenness, is indifferent to being known (Buber, 1952/1988). Contact with God over time establishes a relationship. Impactful contact with God establishes peak moments that Otto (1923/1950) described being filled with *mysterium tremendum* (awe and fear) and *mysterium fascinans* (fascination and attraction). Further to that, the mysterium is not simply mystery in the sense of a secret or a puzzle. Rather, it is the detection of something that is wholly other, "that which is quite beyond the sphere of the usual, the intelligible, and the 'canny,' and is contrasted with it, filling the mind with blank wonder and astonishment" (Otto, 1923/1950, p. 26). What, for such a perspective, is a spiritual relationship? It is the feelings and attitudes that flow between a person and a transcendent other of consideration in which there is the potential for interpersonal knowledge and intimate contact.

NOTES

1. Names are changed here; although this is a true story about real people, some details are altered.
2. An intentional object constitutes the aboutness of experience, and it can be a perception of a physical object in one's world or it can be the conception of an object of thought. The "categorial" intention comes from the phenomenology of Husserl and others.
3. However, it could just as easily be seen as self-regulation and a healthy adjustment to prevailing unhealthy circumstances.

CHAPTER 5

Personal Spirituality

There is no object that we see; no action that we doe; no good that we injoy; no evil that we feele, or fear, but we may make some spirituall advantage of all: and he that makes such improvement is wise, as well as pious.

—Anne Bradstreet, 2006, p. 155

Personal spirituality might seem like a redundancy. Is not all spirituality personal? Surely so, just as all experience is personal, and yet not all experience is personally meaningful in the sense of having application or relevance for oneself. A person might be touched by the concept of types in the Bible. A type is a person or historical event that anticipates another person or event or even theological construct that appears later on. It presages it, as if someone journeyed back in time and made a monumental marker for the future. Types attest to the transcendence of God, but are they personally meaningful, do they touch? Or are they simply intellectually stimulating and speculative? Are they confusing and enigmatic?

In order for spirituality to be personal, one's religion must be existentially meaningful, characterized by personal authenticity, and it must exhibit ethical consistency.

EXISTENTIALLY MEANINGFUL

Technically, existentialism is not a philosophy (Friedman, 2000); yet, commonly it is thought of as an abiding interest in meaning and significance (Bartz, 2009; King, 2012; Park & Edmondson, 2012;

Truscott, 2010). It is not a formal school of philosophy, and so it's easier to identify what existentialist thinkers, the people themselves, are concerned with than to identify the facets of existentialism as a system. Existentialists wonder about the experience of being human, having determined that people are neither substances with fixed properties nor subjects interacting with a world of objects (Crowell, 2010). They want to know how best to live one's life. They ask questions everyone must deal with in order to take life seriously: what is death, what is the significance of existence, what is the place of God in human existence, the meaning of interpersonal relationship, the role of the knowledge of one's self-existence, etc. As such, existential concern is an individually personal interest; it is not so much a concern with others.

Every once in a while people see stories on the news about someone who apparently has it all in life, only to ask the question, "Is this all there is?" Then ensues a search for meaning, and usually the person gives up the fancy house, shiny car, and the fast-paced life for something less flashy but more significant. I routinely meet people like this in my private practice in Bermuda. They have been top flight executives making millions, but they are drifting and wondering whether there might be something they are missing.

Not one of these people I've met could be said to have a viable spiritual life. It's not that they cannot appreciate beauty, for they enjoy it as much as the next person. It's that beauty evokes a pleasurable experience that lacks an iconic quality. The icon points to something of greater value beyond it. So the man who sees a beautiful woman without appreciating her iconic value sees no further than that woman and the pleasure she brings him. A man who sees a beautiful woman and also experiences her iconic value sees beyond her to the One who made her or to life as a meaningful drama that includes her. He does not only enjoy the fact that such a beautiful creature exists, but also feels moved that there is a Being capable of creating men and women, intimate relationships, companionship, and sexual pleasure (or that life is filled with significance that transcends mere pleasure).

People who have existential content to their spirituality are able to see life as iconic. People who lack such meaning in their spiritual lives may collect beautiful works of art, and they may contribute to philanthropic endeavors. They may have been doing what they thought people were supposed to do in accumulating wealth and material things, but it hasn't been enough. It has not satisfied. More specifically, people who lack iconic capacity in their Christian lives live a kind of "formula Christianity," in which they apply principles that are supposed to result in success, greater fulfillment, status as a great Christian, and so on. These people are no different from the man who sees a beautiful woman and can only see the pleasure she might bring him. It is a this-world-only perspective that lacks much significance. One of the standard catechisms says that the purpose of humankind is to glorify God and to enjoy Him forever. It doesn't just say that our purpose is to enjoy God forever. There is something of iconic value in what we are, being created in the image of God. There is something greater than our next spiritual high, our next sense of being blessed by the worship music, and so on.

An increased interest in existential value usually also coincides with reaching the middle years in life, and so these people often think they are simply going through a "midlife crisis," meaning that they just have to find the right formula for doing midlife, and they'll achieve an easy ride through that phase as well. However, it doesn't work that way, and when that fails, they often get depressed.

An existential depression can be thought of as a spiritual condition. It is not the sole malady of the well-to-do. Anyone who suffers the dissolution of load-bearing walls in the structures of their beliefs can succumb to such a condition, and it is both an infirmity and an opportunity. The dissolving of worldviews pours a kind of growth hormone over one's horizons. This does not necessarily mean that a person who is in such a remodeling phase will throw away every spiritual belief, but it does mean that a new attitude toward spiritual discovery might feel very revolutionary—disturbing but also exciting.

PERSONALLY AUTHENTIC

When I was on the staff of a large church in the central valley of California, I subscribed to a piece of Christian literature, a periodical titled *Leadership*. It was published by *Christianity Today*, and is still so.

One day I picked up my latest issue of the journal and started leafing through it. I stopped on a page that had a cartoon on it. In the cartoon, a group of people were organized into a circle. The circle is supposed to be a structure that enhances sharing, openness, communication, transparency, etc. It is a place for authenticity, but all the people were wearing masks.

Personal spirituality is a matter of authenticity. A person is authentic when people see and hear on the outside of that person what the person knows of him- or herself on the inside. This is not to say that an authentic person will never act out of character or act in a way he or she cannot personally endorse. We sometimes give away unconsciously and nonverbally something we cannot admit or even see for ourselves. I call that leaking out sideways or knowing in the back of your head. What I know in the front of my head is all I have to go on, and that is the raw material of authenticity.

When I act in accord with what is in the front of my head and what I carry with awareness in my body, then I am being authentic and I am running on good faith. Bad faith (Brownell, 2008) is behavior out of sync with who a person believes him- or herself to be. It is hiding. It is being hypocritical and acting by putting on a mask so that one appears for public consumption with two faces—one for others and one for oneself.

Personal spirituality requires personal authenticity. To stifle who you are just to fit in or find favor with others is like feeding yourself from someone else's menu (you probably won't like it very much). Worse than that, it's like not feeding your *self* at all.

The 12 steps of alcoholics anonymous is a spiritual system. The first three steps establish that we: (a) admitted we were powerless over alcohol—that our lives had become unmanageable; (b) came to believe that a power greater than ourselves could restore us to sanity; and (c) made a decision to turn our will and our lives over to the care of God as we understood Him. This works if one actually believes there is a God (however they believe that God to be). It is problematic if one does not believe there is a God, and it is so, because in a system requiring that people be honest with themselves and others, they are asking people to mouth the first three steps even if they have to twist those words to the point of incredulity in the process. If they say they have turned their lives over to God, what are they actually believing?

I worked with a person who did not believe in God. He could not say those words and take the first three steps without being dishonest to himself, and of course the whole recovery process for him was going to be a lie, and therefore quite useless. We struggled with the words "God as we understood Him." How did he understand "God?" He didn't. He could not go near a divine, transcendent being. Eventually, going with the words "higher power" (which many in 12-step programs do), he was able to see the recovery community, his peers, as the higher power that might be able to save him. Without the struggle for authenticity, his recovery would have been weakened. Without the effort to be honest with oneself, to get "real" about what one believes and what one doesn't, personal spirituality will not be very personal.

This is where many Christian people fall down. They do wear the masks, but it's as if they don't want to pay attention to that fact. They go to church and sing the songs, but it's not a growth experience. They don't allow people to see who they really are, and they don't really even want to think about who they really are.

My wife and I once volunteered to lead a young people's group in a church that we were attending. We had them all over to our apartment just below Fort Hamilton, and we spread out the food on tables on the large porch that overlooked Bond Bay. Everyone gathered around tables, and we started to discuss what our group was going to be like. They told us, "We don't want anything heavy." They did not want anything heavy? They did not want to examine their lives and think about things that mattered. They wanted to be able to get together and have fun without having to think about who they were as people and how the person of Christ made a difference (among other things). That is intentional irrelevance—the wish to not be responsible for one's life and the hope that one will not be responsible for making that wish. It's like watching the fuse burn on a stick of dynamite but saying, "I don't want to think about that."

There are concomitant features in a life lived with such hypocrisy. One is not seen, so one is deeply isolated. One is not known, so one lacks intimacy. The defects of character are not dealt with through social interaction, and social learning is truncated because one's true self is never in question.

ETHICALLY CONSISTENT

Dietrich Bonhoeffer (1949/1955) said, "Christ does not detach a person from the world of things but from the world of sin . . ." (p. 322). He considered a retreat from the world and its institutions to be a form of idealism, but not the practical spirituality that rightfully belongs to Christ. His ethic was one in which the spiritual person is engaged in the world and concerned with its institutions, and the institutions rise to the level of their intended purpose and design through the influence of the church (which is the congregation of spiritual people).

He did not believe that secular institutions should become wings of the church, that the church should overwhelm the world and assimilate it, but that the church should exercise its influence in cooperation with the world and that the institutions of the world ought to allow it to do so.

> It is not by its overthrowing but by its reconciliation that the world is subdued. It is not by ideals and programmes or by conscience, duty, responsibility and virtue that reality can be confronted and overcome, but simply and solely by the perfect love of God. . . . This love of God does not withdraw from reality into noble souls secluded from the world.
>
> (Bonhoeffer, 1949/1955, p. 72).

After writing these words, he put his own life on the line for emphasis, and the world vented its fury against him through Nazi executioners.

After living about 70 years and visiting many countries in the world, meeting with people and assessing global conditions, the Dalai Lama (1999) came to the conclusion that people everywhere long for happiness and endure suffering; he called for a spiritual revolution:

> My call for a spiritual revolution is thus not a call for a religious revolution. Nor is it a reference to a way of life that is somehow otherworldly, still less to something magical or mysterious. Rather, it is a call for a radical reorientation away from our habitual preoccupation with self. It is a call to turn toward the wider community of beings with whom we are connected and for conduct which recognizes others' interests alongside our own.
>
> (pp. 23–24)

He advocated individual ethics to include restraint, virtue, compassion, the endurance of suffering, and discernment. He understood compassion to be empathy—the ability to enter into and share another's suffering—but also patience. He told the story of one Buddhist monk who had been imprisoned by the Chinese and put into reeducation, forced to renounce his religion, and endure great suffering. When the Dalai Lama asked the monk whether he had ever been afraid, the man replied that he had feared losing compassion for his jailers. The Dalai Lama concluded that it is the spiritual state of a person that is most significant to the ability to withstand hardship. He concluded that it is insufficient to resist evil because what is called for is to overcome evil with good, and that requires an active and aggressive ethical stance.

This is reminiscent of Paul's words in Romans 12:21: "Do not be overcome by evil, but overcome evil with good."

Islamic ethics come from an understanding of the Koran to command the good and forbid the evil.

For Hindu people, ethics is about conduct, and so spirituality is based on what people do with and toward one another in thought, word, and deed (Hindu Online, n.d.). Without a proper ethic, a person cannot develop a proper spirituality.

> The basis of Hindu ethics is this: "There is one all-pervading Atman. It is the innermost soul of all beings. This is the common, pure consciousness. If you injure your neighbour, you really injure yourself. If you injure any other creature, you really injure yourself, because the whole world is nothing but your own Self." This is Hindu ethics. This is the basic metaphysical truth that underlies all Hindu ethical codes.
>
> (HinduOnline, n.d.)

Jewish ethics would surely take into consideration the Decalogue. But there is a more comprehensive and underlying principle that is the basis for the Decalogue, and that is the love of God:

> Hear, O Israel! The Lord is our God, the Lord is one! You shall love the Lord your God with all your heart and with all your soul and with all your might. These words, which I am commanding you today, shall be on your heart. You shall teach them diligently to your sons and shall talk of them when you sit in your house and when you walk by the way and when you lie down and when you rise up. You shall bind them as a sign on your hand and they shall be as frontals on your forehead. You shall write them on the doorposts of your house and on your gates.
>
> (Deuteronomy 6:4–9)

Jesus pointed to this section of the Bible (and also Leviticus 19:18) in summing up the ethical principles of the Law and the Prophets:

> "Teacher, which is the great commandment in the Law?" And He said to him, "'You shall love the Lord your God with all your heart, and with all your soul, and with all your mind.' This is the great and foremost

commandment. The second is like it, 'You shall love your neighbor as yourself.' On these two commandments depend the whole Law and the Prophets.

(Matthew 22:36–40)

It is the love of God and the realization of the love God has for human beings that lead to behavior more in accord with God's purposes. This is a relational ethic. Ben Tertin (2013), a pastor at Imago Dei Christian Fellowship in Portland, Oregon, wrote about counseling someone when the person came saying that although he had a prescription for medical marijuana, he'd been smoking too much pot. The question was not about the legality of smoking; the codification question sends people to a set of fixed rules that often do not consider life situations. The question Tertin got around to was how profitable the pot smoking was in regard to the loving purposes God has for any person's life. That is not simply a pragmatic and utilitarian consideration on the part of God. It is a consideration of the degree to which God intends purpose and significance to specific, individual persons. That is a great gift, and it is truly a relational consideration: the transcendent God of the universe mindful of and immanent in the life of one, specific individual, who does not even amount to a cosmic speck in one way of looking at things, yet, who is so valuable as to cause Jesus to go to the cross in another.

Whether it is the existential meaning one sees in life, like that which nourished Viktor Frankl (2000) in the demoralizing experience of the Nazi death camps, or the love of God, who one is as a person— a spiritual person or a natural person—finds its expression in what one does and how one behaves toward others. These are choices. As Frankl said, "being human is not being driven but 'deciding what one is going to be,' to quote Jaspers (*entscheidendes Sein*), or to quote Heidegger: *Dasein*. I would say that being human is being responsible– existentially responsible, responsible for one's own existence" (p. 32).

And that is an expression of personal spirituality.

PART II

Spiritual Practices in Psychotherapy

An implication is an inference that can be drawn from explicit facts or conditions or the consequences that follow from them. If one thing is true, then other things must be true. In psychotherapy, some things are given, but if those things are true, then what are the spiritual implications?

What follows is a description of four ways of working in psychotherapy. These ways will be found in virtually all forms of psychotherapy to one degree or another, and so I will explore spiritual issues relevant to each in the hope of contributing to spiritual competence in psychotherapy.

To review briefly, this concern is part of a culturally competent approach to working with spiritual people. Three basic activities that therapists do when concerned for multicultural competence when working with spiritual or religious clients are: (a) engage in becoming aware of one's own assumptions about human behavior, values, biases, preconceived notions, personal limitations, etc. with regard to spiritual and religious experience; (b) attempt to understand the worldview of culturally different clients without judgment; and (c) implement relevant and sensitive intervention strategies with religious and spiritually different clients (Vieten et al., 2013).

CHAPTER 6

Spiritual Work in the Context of a Therapeutic Relationship

Through all sorts of changes the same dream, sometimes after an interval of several years, recurs to me. I name it the dream of the double cry.

—Martin Buber, 1947/2002, p. 1

There is God's call on the person, and there is the person's crying out to God; this is the double cry in Buber's dream. If God is more than the detached watchmaker of deism, if God is actually involved with the creation, then there are ways in which people have to manage that fact.

Each person has the potential to relate to God in an authentic, dialogical relationship. This is the claim of Islam through Sufism: "Each person potentially has an ability to relate to Allah in ecstatic union (fana)" (Sheldrake, 2012, p. 48). It is the claim of Judaism through the prophets and the Psalms; for example, in Isaiah 1:18 God says, "Come now, and let us reason together . . ." and in Psalm 95:7, 8 the Psalmist says, "Today if you hear His voice, do not harden your hearts. . . ." It is the claim of Christianity; in the 10th chapter of the book of Acts, Peter is shown by God that gentiles also belong to Christ. It is for Peter a process of revelation and thoughtful consideration, but it is a dialogue between himself and God and one in which he perceives a similar dialogue having transpired between the gentiles and God.

So what is involved with dialogue and with relationship? It is important in understanding therapeutic process, generally speaking, and for comprehending how spiritual issues come up in the context of therapeutic relationships, more specifically.

DIALOGUE

When I first started meeting with clients, I was fearful that I might break them. It's as if they were porcelain dolls. What if I dropped one, and it hit the concrete? I feared the client might shatter into a hundred jagged fragments. I was not talking *with* the client, I was talking *at* the client, trying to remember elements of theory, scripts from supervision about what kinds of questions to ask, and such things as that, and I was talking way too much, because in the silences my insecurity was screaming loudly in my mind's ear. My goal was to get through the hour without anybody discovering that I didn't have confidence in what I was doing. When I started working full-time on the locked unit at a psychiatric hospital, it was a God-send, because, as bad as this sounds, I realized that no matter what I did, if I completely blew it and conducted lousy therapy, if I jacked up the patient and sent him screaming down the hallway, at least the doors were locked and we could put out the fire without it burning down the entire lives of the people in question—both mine and theirs.

We all have experiences. At any given time, we each have an experience of living in this world. We experience ourselves as being in the world and of the world. We are born into a world already going on and filled with the meanings that people in groups give to it. We learn these corporate values while continuing to see what it feels like to be alive and to have a sense of individual agency. We have subjective experience.

When two people meet and interact with each other, their respective experiences intersect, and that is called an intersubjective process. People have described it in various ways using diverse words. One of these ways is to say that people interact through dialogue. So what is that?

Dialogue is a compound word. It is a transliteration of two Greek words: *dia* and *logos*. *Dia* is a preposition. Prepositions modify other words and phrases by indicating direction or position, they "aid in the expression of substantive relations" (Dana & Mantey, 1927/1955).

The words "on" and "into" are prepositions, and the meaning is different if one uses one or the other. "I put the book on the box" does not mean the same thing as "I put the book into the box." Just so, in Greek language, the same preposition could have differing meanings depending on the case in which it was used. When prepositions are used in compound words, it is for emphasis or intensity. The preposition *dia* in its root meant "two" and arose from the word "duo." In composition, it meant "two," "between," or "through." Standing alone in the genitive case, it meant "through," as in John 3:17 ("that the world might be saved through Him . . ."). With the accusative case, it meant "because of," as in Matthew 6:25 ("because of this I say to you . . ."), or "for the sake of," as in Mark 2:27 ("the Sabbath was made for the sake of man . . ."). Remotely, it could mean "by" or "through" in the sense of agency, or "by means of." These are all the considerations when compounding *dia* with *logos*.

Logos is a noun. In classic Greek, the root *leg-* meant collect, pick up, recount, speak, word, discourse, language, and account. The word *logos* took on more specific meaning in Heraclitus, where it could mean discourse in the sense of didactic discourse, or teaching. In this time period, *logos* came to point to the "subjective sphere of the activity of thinking and the thought itself" (Fries, 1978, p. 1082). In the exchanges between schools of philosophy at the time, *logos* also "took on the meaning of the individual method of argument with the most varied problems in a totally disinterested manner, the only important thing being able to defend one's own proposition" (Fries, 1978, p. 1082). Socrates, on the other hand, viewed *logos* in the sense of the common foundation of human community in dialogue (*dialegesthai*, or conversation). For Socrates, it was the process of reflection through dialogue that discovers the *logos* of things.

In Hellenistic Greek, *logos* had two main meanings in the general literature, and another more religiously technical sense as well (Bauer, Arndt, & Gingrich, 1957). On the one hand, *logos* could refer to speaking or discourse. On the other, it could refer to computation or reckoning. In the first sense, *logos* could refer to the word spoken, that is the content of the speaking, but the form of expression could also take many options (speaking, writing, pastoral counseling, teaching, etc.). It could be a statement of definite content such as an assertion or declaration. It could refer to a subject under consideration, and it could refer to the revelation of God. In the second sense, *logos* could refer to accounts being settled or the reckoning that goes into that; it could refer to the motive or reason for something. Finally, *logos* as a more technical term can refer to the independent, personified "Word" (of God) as in John 1:1—in that sense, Jesus is God the Father's expression or argument to humankind.

Most simply, it is probably wise to understand dialogue as an emphatic reference to speaking, namely two speaking, or in Socrates' idiom, conversation. It is the philosophers of intersubjectivity that have added to this concept, making it richer for psychotherapy. For instance, Burkitt (2013) claimed that although each person sees from a unique perspective, his or her vision and understanding of himself "can never be established from within: It relies on dialogue with others to give form to the external vision we have of our own selves and, through it, of the world in which we are located" (p. 8).

In the language of Martin Buber (1923/1958), one can approach another for conversation that is I-It or I-Thou in nature. The first objectifies the other and makes that person into a thing to be handled, dealt with, maneuvered, managed, treated, healed, or otherwise affected in order to satisfy the agenda of the person doing that—subject to object. The second allows the personhood of the second person to emerge and be known, to have influence, and to affect the personhood of the first—subject to subject, or intersubject.

Those following the thinking of Emmanuel Levinas (1999) and Critchley and Bernasconi (2002) would say that we owe the client, as a matter of ethics as first philosophy, to honor the client's transcendence (his or her alterity), refusing to thematize the client in our work. That is a thoroughly interpersonal approach (Bloom, 2013). That can only be attempted when the duties of the therapeutic relationship do not actually require that some kind of business be accomplished, because sometimes, in order to provide responsible, practical service, we need to accomplish some tasks and reach some goals. When it comes to the dialogue, though, when it comes to establishing contact over time and building a relationship, it will not be the tasks that loom large, but the quality of the contact.

In the therapeutic relationship, this dialogue is a mutual interaction. In fact, dialogue can be thought of as consisting of commonality, mutuality, and reciprocity—sharing interpersonal space in the process of discourse, being mutually available to the other, and proceeding with the tacit belief that one's interest and efforts toward dialogue will be reciprocated (Graumann, 1995). On the side of the therapist, it consists of being present (Geller & Greenberg, 2012) as an authentic person and then making a purposeful space for the other, including the other as much as possible so as to attain an understanding of what the current moment is like for that other person. As such, inclusion is an honoring of the client's phenomenological experience without the therapist losing his or her phenomenological experience; the gestalt therapist "does not impose [his or her] beliefs upon the client's experience of the situation . . ." (Mann, 2010, p. 179). On the side of the client, it consists of risking exposure to also be present and adopting an attitude of wonder or discovery with regard to the person of the therapist as another real person. In terms of therapy, then, it is not a matter of the therapist's skill or the client's motivations alone. "It is difficult to imagine how either the therapist or the client could contribute in them-selves, removed from the context of the interactional qualities in which the meaning of therapy is created and shared" (Moltu, Binder, & Stige, 2012, p. 86). It is about presence and inclusion.

Therapeutic presence, though, more specifically focused on the therapist, can be defined as having one's whole self in the meeting with the client by being in the moment on multiple levels (physically, cognitively, and spiritually). It requires being in contact with one's own integrated self while simultaneously being open and receptive to what is touching, immersed in it, with also a larger sense of awareness and perception. This grounded and immersed awareness emerges as being with and for the client, in the service of the therapeutic encounter. Presence involves openness to the client's internal world, including bodily and verbal discourse, and awareness of the therapist's own embodied experience in order to access his or her knowledge, wisdom, and skill. "Being fully present then allows for an attuned responsiveness that is based on kinesthetic and emotional sensing of the other's affect and experience as well as one's own intuition and skill and the relationship between them" (Geller & Greenberg, 2012, p. 7).

This kind of presence cannot be accomplished by the therapist tak-ing on a role—playing a role and exuding a persona—such as that of "expert." It cannot be attained by the therapist attempting to keep professional distance, although certainly there will be a realization of who is privileged, whose story takes center stage, and for whom the two are meeting.

There is also a danger of running therapy as if it were a goal to be met, to essentially conduct sessions in the mode of I-It. If this is done, then the therapist is interested in not much more than providing in-formed consent, arriving at a diagnosis, putting together a treatment plan, getting the client to sign the treatment plan, and collecting the fee. On the side of the client, it is also common to approach the session in the mode of I-It, hoping to get some answers from the therapist—solutions or suggestions—that will resolve the problem and make the pain or dysfunction go away. Each of them might as well be a kiosk for the other. In that mode, people do things *to* each other. Either way, it is a one-person psychology (viewing the client as a self-contained set of symptoms that need to be reduced or viewing the therapist as a detached repository of services that need to be acquired). Each of them might as well be standing at a vending machine trying to get candy bars to drop on cue.

In psychotherapy, I-It is usually perfunctory, being routine, mechanical, and carried out with a minimum of reflection. If I am conducting an intake session, then I am putting demographic data into the computer. The I-Thou process is much more interesting and can be challenging. This is where two people are actually meeting. This kind of meeting occurs in sparks. It takes seconds and moments instead of hours. It may repeat during the course of a therapeutic hour, but it is not sustained throughout it. That would be too intense.

If people feel safe and supported in the therapeutic encounter, they usually can risk lingering with the therapist in order to be known. Often they are then overcome with emotion, especially if the therapist "sees" them in their difficulty. In this respect, nonverbal discourse is quite powerful. Often, when I am with a client who is having a tough time and is sharing elements of his or her broken life, sorrow, and loss, I will tear up with him or her. This is not a gimmick or an "intervention." This is dialogue stimulated by contact. It is nonverbal discourse, but discourse just as much as if I were speaking the words "You touched me with your sadness." In fact, showing that the client did in fact touch me is probably *more* powerful.

There is what we say, and there is how we say it. They comprise the gestalt of discourse. They go together as foreground (what we say) to background (how we say it), but we read the background first and establish that as context. In our development, from infancy we learn to self-regulate our emotions in nonverbal processing and interpretation of contextual events. When we have gained the cognitive functions of language, we put the verbal together with the nonverbal, and we make a meaning out of that, but the more powerful element in that equation is the background of the nonverbal discourse. The kinesthetic, nonverbal discourse is contextual ground for understanding the meaning of what a person says, because body and mind are actually parts of one whole to begin with; we interpret holistically as a reflection of the embodied whole we happen to be ontologically (Johnson, 2007). That is the embodied hermeneutic of interpersonal life.

IMPLICATIONS

I ride an old ferry to work and back each day. One day it was raining when I stepped on board. People were hurrying to get inside the cabin and find a seat. I found one and sat down, started pulling my iPad out to read, and looked up from my backpack. Across from me, about 4 feet away, a young woman was getting situated, and she looked up from what she was doing at the same moment. Our eyes met. We each stopped moving. We held the gaze. It felt like more than the few seconds it actually was. Nothing was said, but it was a meeting.

Most people glance off one another visually. They don't really want to be seen. They don't want to encourage others or have to deal with other people noticing them or intruding. We did not glance off one another. We stopped. We met. I felt seen. It was contact.

Most people in my experience don't come to therapy expecting to be seen. I don't think they think of it that way. I think most people come hoping to find relief or some kind of solution, and many come because they have some kind of vague idea that therapy is the thing to do if you feel emotionally overwhelmed. But they don't expect to be seen, and they certainly don't expect to have to *see*.

What are the spiritual implications of meeting, of connecting, of experiencing contact, and building a relationship in psychotherapy? Scholarship in the field has established that spirituality is a legitimate concern in cultural issues that include religion and spirituality (Gockel, 2011; Meyerstein, 2006; O'Grady & Bartz, 2012) and that paying attention to spiritual dynamics in the therapeutic relationship can help the process of therapy (Comas-Diaz, 2006; Falb & Pargament, 2012).

Process

Just as dialogue is a two-way street, such that a person can have an influence in the life of the other and must also be open to being influenced by the other, this issue of spirituality in the therapeutic relationship has a double consideration. The process of therapy and the relationship itself will affect the spiritual and religious lives of both the client and the therapist. The spiritual condition of the client and that of the therapist will affect the process of therapy. Keeling, Dolbin-MacNab, Ford, and Perkins (2010) listed several issues that contribute to the complexity of spiritually related issues involved in the therapeutic process for both clients and therapists, and these are relevant to the dialogical relationship: (a) the amount of similarity and difference (perceived and actual) between clients' and therapists' spiritual beliefs and practices, (b) the amount of spiritual disclosure, (c) the quality and character of the therapeutic relationship, and (d) geographic and cultural influences.

It is hard to separate the basic approach or method of a therapeutic orientation from the contacting between therapist and client. Is the spiritual experience of the client interpreted, corrected, reframed, or observed and described phenomenologically? Is it accepted as real or actual or simply as a delusion, hallucination, faulty thinking, or irrational belief? Is it just a relative truth, like a fantasy or a projection? Is it true at all?

Is there a blind spot or a compartment into which the therapist assigns spiritual and religious experiences and issues? Does the therapist even bring such things up? Are there questions about the role of religion and spirituality on the intake form? Is it part of the picture from the beginning or something that may or may not be grafted in later on? Is there an ability to be dialogical about sexual preference but not about religious or spiritual identity? A therapist needs to be willing and able to go where such questions lead with the issue of spirituality, and going there, the therapist needs to be authentic in the process (Shafranske & Cummings, 2013). The therapist may not identify spiritually the way the client does, but the therapist, in order to conduct a spiritually competent and culturally sensitive practice, needs to practice inclusion with regard to the spiritual and religious experience of the client.

When considering spirituality as process in therapy, the current interest in mindfulness allows people to enter into an Eastern spiritual or philosophical way of looking at life. Both the Tao, or way of contacting and relationship, and the focused awareness of Buddhist mindfulness in many approaches to therapy are not just compatible with therapeutic process, but also represent a large part of the therapeutic method and attitude of the therapist. In gestalt therapy, for instance, the therapist is not as interested in why someone does what he or she does as much as how that person does what he or she does. Because Taoism lends itself to virtually any system in which one uses it, the way or the how of therapeutic process can go hand in hand with the focused awareness of what one is doing.

As already mentioned, mindfulness is a growing component of many therapeutic processes. On closer look, mindfulness comes from a Buddhist spiritual worldview, and as such can be defined as "the awareness that emerges through paying attention on purpose, in the present moment, and non-judgmentally to things as they are" (Williams, Teasdale, Segal, & Kabat-Zinn, 2007, p. 47). I once shared with a client suffering from stress, "You might be interested in learning some mindfulness exercises; they are principles taken from Buddhism. . . ." That was as far as I got. The woman rolled her eyes, sucked air into her lungs, and exhaled, "Oh no! Not that! I am a Christian." She started to gather herself up to leave, and even though I tried to tell her that the mindfulness principles were not themselves the religion of Buddhism, she was having none of that. She left and went back to share with her colleagues that I was not a Christian so that when later one of them was referred to me, she did not want to come. When that person finally did come, however, I had to show her my diploma from seminary and assure her that I was Christian, and I took pains to respond to her concerns referring to Biblical scriptural passages that pertained. All this is relevant to the mutuality, the shared ground, the commonality that is foundational to the building up of relationship through contact. The first woman broke contact because she did not sense any basis for mutuality, commonality, and reciprocity, but the second woman, feeling satisfied that I at least had some kind of common ground, some shared spiritual identity, remained, and we built a good relationship from that point on. Had the first woman been able to remain *in process* long enough, I could have gone to noticing that at the mere mention of Buddhism she wanted to leave, and I could have paid attention with her to her experience and what meanings she was making up about what I had said, who I was, what I intended to do, how antithetical all that was to her spiritual identity, and perhaps how safe she was with me. We could have dialogued about it, and I could have shared with her my surprise and dismay that I had somehow communicated that I was Buddhist, because although I admire several Buddhist colleagues for their devotion and spiritual practice, and while I think there is value in being serious about one's spiritual process, I also am a Christian.

Does this mean that only Christians can work with Christians, Jews with the Jewish, Buddhists with Buddhists, etc.? Some might say so, but not necessarily. If the mutuality is around shared respect and interest in one another's spirituality, then many clients can enter the circle of contact with a therapist who does not share their exact spiritual and religious identity. What is crucial is for therapists to know their own spiritual ground and to be able to meet the client in an authentic fashion. Having said that, therapists need to know that some, perhaps many clients, will not feel comfortable with an unspiritual therapist, someone who at a very fundamental level believes that spirituality and religion is foolishness. Also, a therapist whose spiritual ground is in the Eastern process-oriented religions will likely approach that mutuality with a different mindset (and even bias) than a therapist whose spiritual background is in the religions that advocate a personal relationship with God. These are the kinds of things that need to be addressed in a supportive and interested fashion, because they will be there in the reality of the therapeutic contacting whether addressed or not, and if not addressed head-on, obviously they will likely become acted upon in less intentional ways.

Relationship

The obvious spiritual practice associated with both relationship and spirituality is prayer. Prayer can be conceived of as talking with God. It will become apparent in this section that one cannot truly compartmentalize the process from the relationship in spirituality, and an example of this is on this subject of prayer.

There are many ways to pray. One can pray in a congregation with others, such as in corporate prayer in church; one can pray spontaneously and extemporaneously; or one can write out one's prayers and read them. One can pray in solitude. One can pray in one's mind while in solitude or one can pray out loud while in solitude. If a person believes in the evil personified in an ontological being called Satan, then praying out loud is something that being could hear, but if praying in one's mind, not so. It brings up an interesting consideration. Between whom is the dialogue in prayer?

Also of consideration is the quality of contact while speaking to God. For many people, a well-thought-out and written prayer is more meaningful than a spontaneous one. For others, a written prayer read or recited seems like a speech made at God rather than a conversation held with God. For that matter, in church services, sometimes one begins to wonder whether the prayer is actually addressed to God or to the congregation.

While some of what I will cover here also belongs in the next chapter (on the complex situation), an understanding of the dialogical elements between the person of the therapist and God and the person of the client and God needs some development.

In the movie *Fiddler on the Roof*, leading into the song titled *If I Were a Rich Man*, Tevye talks with God. He says, "You made many, many poor people. I realize, of course, it's no shame to be poor. But it's no great honor either. So what would be so terrible if I had a small fortune?" Throughout the movie he continues like that, having conversations with God about everyday life and the unfolding circumstances in the situations in the lives of the people in his family and his village. As one watches this, sometimes it appears that he is not actually talking with another being but conducting empty-chair dialogues as in gestalt therapy. He's not so much talking to someone else as he is talking to different parts of himself, and in the process he's not directing his enigmas and challenges to a being he believes is greater than himself as he is sorting out what he himself is in the process of doing. This is at the crux of what prayer is, and it's an important consideration if a therapist is going to enter into the crucible of prayer with his or her client in the course of therapy.

The letter of James[1] says that the readers have not, because they ask not, and that when they ask, they don't receive if they ask with the wrong motives (i.e., out of pure selfishness). Jesus confronts his disciples who had been attempting to cast out a demon, and He tells them it requires prayer.[2] Before Jesus raises Lazarus from the dead, He talks with His Father. In the upper room, in connection with the last supper, Jesus talks with His Father. These references to prayer are not talking about conducting empty-chair dialogues. Prayer is not a gimmick to process a person's own "stuff." It is at once a connection with the divine Being and a tool to move that Being into action so that things change in the lives of real people. It's a way of moving the universe. So people talk with God to both connect with God, to be known by God, and also to attempt to make things happen for themselves and others. Prayer is not just a noetical act. Prayer is an intersubjective process between a human being and a divine Being. Prayer is also not just a speech delivered to God but a dialogical process in which one is engaged with God. The relational and dialogical nature of this process is captured in the picture of the relationship between Jesus and His Father in the first few sentences of the gospel of John.

It says, "In the beginning was the Word, and the Word was with God, and the Word was God."[3] Theology aside, the words "the Word was with God" in Greek are "ὁ λόγος ἦν πρὸς τὸν θεόν." The word "πρὸς" is a preposition, indicating the basic orientation of being or the direction of awareness, and in the accusative case (which is the case in this passage) it can mean several things: to or toward, beside, against, with, and at. Do you see that the basic idea is one of contact? It is one of touching to be oriented toward, at hand, standing with or beside, or even to be resting against (Dana & Mantey, 1927/1955). The sense is that Jesus and His Father are face-to-face. This is what Martin Buber

(1923/1958, 1952/1988) sensed in his consideration of a dialogical relationship between a human person and the person of God.

In the course of therapy itself, the therapist might engage with the process of prayer in several ways. The therapist can pray both in session and out of session about the client, for the client, and about the process of the work with the client. In that last respect, the therapist can pray for him- or herself, in session or out of session, quietly or out loud, asking that God give insight into the client, ability to observe, ability to separate from his or her own issues, knowledge of how to help, or the courage to go into areas that produce anxiety and insecurity. Prayer can become a means of support for the therapist. The therapist can also pray with the client in session. The therapist can explore dialogically with the client the process of the client's own journey of learning with regard to the subject and the use of prayer as a resource.

Prayer is not just talking to God, however. If prayer is a conversation with God, then hearing back from God becomes important. The element of reciprocity in dialogue here looms large. "Reciprocity is the fluid, genuine interchange between two thinking, feeling beings. Reciprocity means that you do something and I respond. I do something and you respond. Our relationship grows and our lives are deeply interwoven" (Lucas, 2003, p. 77). God is not simply transcendent; God is also immanent. How a being can be simultaneously transcendent and immanent makes for a good meditation, but one way I put these things together is to realize that although God is holy, in the sense of being separate from creation and in a category of His own, God is also present with and in creation, and so active in the lives of human beings. Relationally, God does not only hear what people say to Him in prayer, God also is present with and speaks to people through inspiration, guidance, and communion.

Taking the last one first, I do not mean "communion" as in the ordinance or sacrament conducted in the church (although a case could be made for that as well). I mean communion in the sense of the sharing or exchange of intimate thoughts and feelings and the sharing in a common cognitive and/or affective experience. For instance, as the early church formed and began going about its business, it devoted itself to the teachings of the apostles and to "κοινωνία" (koinonia, or communion).[4] They not only broke from a common loaf of bread and drank from a common cup in the sacrament remembering Jesus's death, but they also had a common lot with one another in their daily living. The contacting that is possible between a person and God is often not in words or thoughts, but in the felt sense that one is with God—that God is in one's presence.

This is the experience of the numinous, as described by Rudolph Otto in the *mysterium fascinans* and the *mysterium tremendum* (being fascinated and drawn toward God, but being aware that God is wholly other, transcendent, and "too much"). It is the humbling awareness of one's creatureliness while meeting the divine Being Whose orientation is "toward." For me, this communion with God is an experience of peace and wholeness. I get the sense that things are as they should be, I am accepted, I am known. It is not that God is going to do some specific thing for me; it's that God is and will be with me (and His orientation is toward me).

The words "inspiration" and "guidance" are similar to each other in that each one involves actually hearing from God. This is not the communion of knowing one is in God's presence. This is getting a message from God.[5] Whereas inspiration is usually reserved for a message from God that applies to all people, guidance is a message from God that applies to only the person to whom it is given. There are countless books on this subject. In one, Dallas Willard (1999) suggested that among the many ways a person might hear from God were through reading of scripture, observing and contemplating nature, listening to a sermon, or talking with a fellow believer. I would add that God can make Himself known in the mundane of life as well. A person could hear from God while reading a novel, watching a secular movie, or attending a political rally. When it comes, it is often experienced as an impression that arrives complete rather than a string of words one has to reassemble and make meaning out of, like reading the words on this page.

So in therapy, there are parallel processes going on. With regard to one's relationship with God as both client and therapist meet and assemble their own therapeutic relationship, the relationship they each have to God is in parallel. The patient may be silently praying while the therapist is silently praying. They may pray together out loud at various times. I had one client who always wanted to end our sessions with the Lord's prayer, and it almost felt like we were concluding a worship service. The client and the therapist may be hearing from God, and they may feel as if God is in the midst of their meeting with one another. It is common for me to start talking with a person and then get the feeling that our meeting is no coincidence. Many times the client will actually say that as well. When I realize that providence has brought me together with a particular client, it is as if God is saying to

me, "Okay, Phil. Here's this one. I am entrusting this person to you."
It brings me to the knees of my heart and I start talking with Him
immediately.

The large point here is that each person does indeed have the potential to relate to God in an authentic, dialogical relationship. The fact
that God is both a being who is similar and dissimilar to us complicates the process, but it does not prevent it.

NOTES

1. James 4:2–3.
2. Mark 9:29.
3. John 1:1.
4. Acts 2:42–45.
5. And yes, this also falls within the range of hearing voices, and so can
   resemble psychotic process. So a psychotherapist has to go beyond the
   "voices" the client might be hearing to understand what else is going on
   (that can be used diagnostically to separate religious experience from psychotic process).

Spiritual Work in the Context of a Complex Situation

It was the Year of the Dragon, when my life's tide was said by Chinese astrologers to be at its most powerful, when change was inevitable. But all this was nonsense to me, for I was an educated person, a doctoral student in linguistics at UC Berkeley.

—Amy Tan, 2003, p. 41

There is always more going on in any given situation than we can take in and understand. That is one reason I enjoy watching movies over and over again. I watch for script and dialogue, plot, movement, staging, camera angles, lighting, cinematography, special effects, acting, character development, and editing. I can watch for nuances in the craft of one particular actor, or consistencies and style of a particular director. Yet even while I am watching movies, and focused on the screen, there is still more going on. There is the lighting in the room, the cats climbing on the furniture, the trees outside blowing in the wind, and the sound of the fans.

The process of perception entails an overflowing perceptive field. If you look at a building standing in a city, you also see the sky around it, other buildings, and you may hear the sound of the street noise or smell the smog. Your focus would be the building, but it is a percept with no line drawn around it; it is a visual percept that simultaneously comes triangulated with other senses (Hass, 2008).

The complex situation is filled with this kind of overflow of experience, and this situation has been called various things. Kurt Lewin (1940, 1943, 1951) called it the life space, Henry Murray (1938) referred to needs-and-press, Kurt Goldstein (1995) referred to the relationship between the organism and the environment, Perls, Hefferline, and Goodman (1951/1972) wrote about the organism–environment field, and Gardner Murphy (1947) wrote about the biosocial situation. Whatever one may choose to call it, this is the current context of life, and it is likely the most salient factor influencing behavior (Lewis, 1997) and outcomes in psychotherapy (Duncan & Miller, 2000). In the common factors literature, it is referred to as "extra-therapeutic factors."[1] That means everything outside of the techniques that accord with a particular clinical approach and the therapeutic relationship itself. Here I will refer to it as both the field and the situation.

THE SITUATION

Typically, people come to me for couples therapy. Often one of the persons in a relationship will tell me something like, "My wife wanted me to come, because she says I'm messed up and need to get fixed before we can get back together." In that construction of the situation, the husband is the problem, and it's all about him—as if he existed in isolation from all other elements. The two may have gotten involved with each other as an affair that ended their respective previous relationships. Their sex life may have cooled. He may distrust her and go looking through her phone to see whom she's talking with, but she might be talking with male "friends" and keeping her phone away from him. She might be staying out and not accounting for her time, and when he asks about that, she might get angry and blame him for being paranoid. On the other hand, he might be staying up late on the computer interacting with people in faraway places, and when she comes out to see what he's doing, he might rapidly shut the computer down or switch screens. She might wonder about *his* phone contacts and check them out. However, as presented to me, couples therapy often starts off with one person blaming or being blamed, which is a simplistic, one-person approach that does not take into consideration the complexity of the situation.

"Situation" is a term referring to the complex set of factors related to a biopsychosocial system that is self-adapting in nature and comprising both ontic and phenomenal features. It is both (a) the set of forces in the real world that exert influence and (b) the subjective experience of being in such a system. One way of understanding an ontic field is to see it as a totality of binding, material–physical variables. The discipline of ontology explains the ontic field as a material–physical context holding forth possibilities that social conditions "be" in particular ways and that to explain such conditions assumes some kind of relation with them. When we talk about these things, we can speak about the ontological field or the phenomenological field, but when we do, we are once removed, speaking in abstraction about something that is actually lived out one moment to the next, and something that is constantly evolving.

In terms of time, the field is now. It is all things having influence in the current moment, and can be conceived of as a sphere, or even overlapping spheres, of influence (Crocker, 1999). We can talk about the field conditions at some time in the past, but if we do that, we are reconstructing them and doing history. That is an abstraction based on memory. The ontological field, then, is a story we tell ourselves about the ontic properties that have just this moment occurred or that took place at some developmental moment in the past, and likewise, the phenomenological field is thematizing raw experience that has already been experienced. It too is an abstraction and a thinking-about rather than a living-through.

A working relationship in psychotherapy is an ontic field with phenomenal features. That is, it is not a snapshot we take and then ponder together. It is a video we are shooting, but one we may never review. Therapists do not do phenomenology at this base level when they work with clients around experience (either the current experience of what is unfolding in the relationship between them or the past experience of developmentally relevant experience). They may explore the phenomenal worlds that overlap one another in their contacting. They may notice what is going on between them, and therapists, for instance, may pay attention to arising countertransference, but that would be at a different level of the process. Some forms of therapy take apart past incidents, behaviors, cognitive patterns, or self-regulating adjustments, but when that happens, it is still phenomenal work in an ontic field but with a concomitant meta-narrative. When we meet with clients, we are engaged at an embodied, situated, and rather basic level that we can never escape. Some of the meaning is automatic (as in the influence of mirror neurons), and some of it is hermeneutic. The meaning making is a hermeneutic and phenomenological process as meta-narrative to the base phenomenal process that takes place in the ontic field of both therapist and client. To further complicate things, the hermeneutic process can give rise to emergent[2] meanings and significance that then become elements of the ontic field as well and that affect the phenomenality of both client and therapist. Thus, there are actual people in real situations, and there are perspectival experiences of the field, but these things are not separate and compartmentalized.

Although people would like to reduce complexity down to more simple chunks and organizational structures, the working alliance is a two-person field that is related through extra-therapeutic common factors to larger and overlapping fields in the lives of both therapist and client. Further, the therapist–client relationship is not simply the "bubble" that forms when the two people begin interacting with one another. It includes the physical features of the office where they meet and the social structures inherent to the organization where this office is located. Beyond that, it is related to the historical and social events of the day. It is related to the multiplicity of systems that both the client and the therapist encounter on a routine basis; employment, educational, legal, and financial institutions all have parts in the lives of the client and the therapist. So one of the considerations that any given therapist might have is just how far to go in utilizing the field strategically. Does the therapist negotiate a collaboration with the client in using an element of the field outside of the clinical hour, or simply move unilaterally to do so? In this regard, multisystemic psychotherapy, by its very nature, is an intentional and strategic use of the field to either affect change in the life of clients or experiment to see what might happen as they assimilate experience.

Situations evolve. In fact, fields themselves are emergent entities that can also generate still further emergent entities. With regard to such emergence in the social sciences, people functioning in their various roles give rise to the emergent structures of society (situations or fields) that in turn exert influence on those individuals, shaping their agency (Archer, 1982, 2007, 2010; Elder-Vass, 2007). "The highest orders of emergence are nothing more than the relations between the results of interaction" (Archer, 1982, p. 475).

As I wrote in another place concerning the nature of emergence[3]:

Emergence is the process by which properties or substances arise out of more fundamental entities but are distinct from them and irreducible to them (O'Conner & Wong, 2006). Emergence relates to gestalt therapy in that gestalt therapy maintains an emergent theory of self, and therein resides a problem. Gestalt therapists face a conundrum in attempting to integrate neurophysiological evidence with the gestalt therapy theory of self, because this boils down to the issue of how the brain (or the nervous system) is related to the mind. Gestalt therapists adhere to substance monism but property dualism. That is, they believe the immaterial self arises from the functioning of the material brain as the organism contacts the environment. Property dualism occurs when "the ontology of physics is not sufficient to constitute what is there" (Robinson, 2007, np). When a gestalt therapist encounters a client, there is more there than a simple firing of synapses, the reflecting chorus of mirror neurons, and the memory of emotionally laden experience stored in the amygdala. Nonreductive physicalism maintains that mind emerges as the brain engages; the working of the fundamental nervous system generates a complex order of properties, a mind, that is distinct from, but dependent on the working of the brain. No brain; no mind (Stoeger, 2002). Thus, the gestalt therapy experience of self belongs in discussions of the theory of mind, because it is so similar to the properties of mind as to be synonymous. Conversely, gestalt therapists enhance their understanding of a client when they assess that person's neuropsychological capacities, because self depends on the individual's neurological capacities.

(Brownell, 2010a, pp. 80–81)

More will be said about subjective experience in the next chapter, but here it is worth noting that individual experience always takes place in the context of a complex situation. While the individual's behavior is not determined by situational factors, it is influenced by them. Conversely, the individual's behavior contributes to the nature of the overall situation. So the individual is emergent of the situation, and the situation is emergent of individual agents functioning in their various roles.

There is a church along the northern Oregon coast whose pastor began to change his theology. The church was fairly conservative, and the people were set in what they believed; so when the pastor began to change, it caused a problem. It resulted in a split, actually, because the pastor had been in that church for over a decade and he was well loved. When the leaders of the church asked for his resignation, a number of church members came to him and asked him to become the pastor of a new church, one created by the exodus of people loyal to him from the old church. So a new church was born, and the people purchased land and built a building. Then, the pastor quit; he left the ministry altogether, and the new church leaders went looking for a new pastor. When they found someone they thought might be a good fit, the man visited the church to meet people, preach, and see whether there was indeed a good fit. It was in late fall along the Oregon coast, and the weather was gorgeous. The sky was clear, and the sun was shining. The big trees were all lit up in the sun. The nearby bay looked pretty. The temperature was just right, and the new man thought it looked like heaven compared with the irrigated desert of the lower Salinas Valley in California, where he had been pastoring. The new church asked him to accept their invitation to be their pastor, and he accepted. He moved his family up, and after they got there the rain began. They were staying in a home on a sand dune, and the sand got tracked all through the house. The people in the church started bickering. The treasurer took issue on several matters and resigned. The elder who had provided the most support when the new man had contemplated coming had a heart attack and died. The congregation split out against itself because some of them didn't like what the new pastor was preaching and some of the things he wanted to do for outreach to the community. The conflict escalated. The attendance diminished, and the income fell. Before too long, the pastor and his family were living just below the poverty line, and his wife had to get a job working at the market 45 minutes down the coast. She was gone most of the time when the children were out of school. What started off looking like paradise ended up looking like hell, and along the way the pastor and his wife didn't do so well either.

The current nature of a situation emerges from a previous nature of the situation. That new church came into being out of bitter conflict on the one hand and loyalty to an individual on the other. When the individual left, there was not much affection and loyalty to hold things together. When the leaders of the new church fell away, there was no organizational stability. The new pastor was new. Not only did he not understand the nature of the situation, but he also did not realize that the church could not sustain much change. When he pushed through some of his initiatives and changed the position of the pulpit, for instance, it was too much. If he had understood more of the ontic features of the situation that confronted him, perhaps he could have allowed a period of predictable routine to settle in. As it was, the people had already been through a great deal of change, and they could not, as a unit, handle more. The new church became galvanized around the new pastor and the things he was trying to accomplish, and like the church from which it emerged, the new church became embroiled in conflict. Some people ended up going back to the church from whence they had come. Eventually, the new pastor himself resigned.

To focus on the pastor and his abilities, his calling to the ministry, his insight, or even his mental state, and to do that without considering the situation, would have been to misunderstand the nature of the situation and its relevance to the pastor. For the psychotherapist, it is necessary to grasp the nature of the situation in which the client presents and to investigate its implications.

IMPLICATIONS

Chief Seattle said, "All things are connected. Whatever befalls the earth befalls the children of the earth."[4] Emanuel Swedenborg is credited with putting it in a slightly different way, saying that nothing unconnected ever occurs, for anything unconnected would instantly perish.[5] These are ways of saying that all things are parts of one, giant whole. While that may be true, we cannot make sense of it if everything belongs to everything. We need more proximate connections and smaller wholes.

Kurt Goldstein (1995) talked about the study of the brain, and he insisted that studying the reflex arc outside of the brain in which it occurs was meaningless. That would be the arc unconnected, and no arc can exist unconnected to the brain. Likewise, however, no brain can exist outside of its body, for no unconnected brain can survive without oxygen and the nutrients it receives via a pumping heart. The concept of the body and embodied enactment as a basic gestalt is supported in recent literature as well. Cosmelli and Thompson (2011) posed a leading question. They asked whether consciousness is all in the head, all in the brain, or

> is the body beyond the brain an essential part of the biological basis of consciousness? To put the question another way, does the body belong to the 'minimal realizing system' for conscious experience or is the minimal realizing system for consciousness confined to the brain?
>
> (p. 164)

Yet even this is not quite adequate, because no person can exist in isolation from others. We need other people functioning in their own ways to produce contact that is nourishing and the physical means of survival. Does this lead one back to everything is everything? Yes and no. Yes, everything is connected, and we need to keep that in mind, but if we are working with an individual in psychotherapy, what is it we are working with? Are we working with a person or a system of connections? Some would say the system of connections, but if you have that individual client sitting in front of you, he or she probably needs to know you see him or her as a real person and not just a system of connections.

The implications for the spiritual and religious issues of real people while working within complex situations require that we don't lose the person in working with the field, but in order to understand the person we need to consider the features of the situation of which that person exists.

Process

Native American spirituality is tied into the rhythms of nature, in which everything is united and in process, and each aspect of the natural field has its own way as a harmonious part of the whole. The way of the people with one another came from that, and it was patient, making room in silence for thought before speaking, respecting elders, and being courteous. Those wishing to learn and practice the "old ways" adopt this natural, process orientation to life that does not make spirituality compartmentalized. That way of life is all tied up together as one connected whole. Chief Luther Standing Bear, of the Teton Sioux, for instance, claimed that from Wakan Tanka, the Great Spirit, "there came a great unifying life force that flowed in and through all things– the flowers of the plains, blowing winds, rocks, trees, birds, animals– and was the same force that had been breathed into the first man. Thus all things were kindred, and were brought together by the same Great Mystery" (Nerburn, 1999, p. 36).

Native American spirituality is an example of process thought in that it is essentially panentheist in character. God is in nature although distinct from nature; God's character and nature are linked through supervenience. In supervenience, one reality arises out of another (e.g., the mind arises out of brain activity). Panentheists generally understand supervenience to give rise to new principles that are effective at one level but not present at the simpler level (e.g., water forms from the combination of hydrogen and oxygen under certain circumstances, but water is liquid and not gaseous). Also of relevance, emergence is the process involved in supervenience and "occurs when a new property arises out of a combination of elements . . . in part-whole emergence, the whole is more than the total of all parts" (Culp, 2013). Thus, out of the simple connection between a creator, a Father or Grand-Father Spirit, and the world, with all its parts functioning in their natural rhythms, there emerge the moral imperatives associated with an attitude of respect and reverence among human beings for natural order and process according to Native American wisdom and spirituality.

This idea is also present in the imagery of the relationship between Christ and the church. The church is described as the body of Christ, and it is one whole comprising many members all functioning according to their nature as a "hand" or an "ear" or some other part. The members are not identical to each other, and each is indispensable to the others. The members are all held together by the working that only the parts can provide under the direction of the head of the body, which is Christ.

But now comes an interesting consideration. Is the body of Christ something members experience phenomenally or ascribe to as an ontic fact? *Is* it an ontic fact? Jesus said, "where two or three have gathered together in My name, I am there in their midst."[6] So when two or three believers get together focused on Jesus, does Jesus emerge from the process of them functioning as a body?

To make this a more complex situation, consider the gifting of the members of the body. The first of Paul's letters to the believers in Corinth—in the 12th chapter, verses 4 through 6—reads,

> Now there are varieties of gifts, but the same Spirit. And there are varieties of ministries, and the same Lord. There are varieties of effects, but the same God who works all things in all *persons*. But to each one is given the manifestation of the Spirit for the common good.

Here is the picture of process in a sphere of influence called the church, which is understood, metaphorically, as the body of Christ. It is a multiplicity of variety.

If this multiplicity of creative variety were diagrammed in a mathematical equation, that equation would look something like this:

$$(Gifts^v) \times (Ministries^v) \times (Effects^v)/Christ = Body\ of\ Christ/Church$$

Which is the same as:

$$Body\ of\ Christ/Church = (Gifts^v) \times (Ministries^v) \times (Effects^v)/Christ$$

The first says that varieties of gifts multiplied in varieties of ministries (or places where those gifts can be utilized) multiplied again by varieties of effects (all under the direction of Jesus Christ) *is* the church. It equals the body of Christ. That's *what* the church is. If you find a church, you should have that stuff going on. It is a functioning whole that can be observed here and there wherever the gifted people have decided to meet in the world. The second formula says that wherever gifted people function, the church begins to emerge. The body of Christ is emergent and supervenient in the second, dependent upon the diverse gifting of the Holy Spirit put to use in various activities, with a diversity of results. Under the first, people establish buildings, put a sign out front that says the church can be found there, and then go about their business in that place; the church is not supervenient of the working of its members. Under the second, the church is in stealth mode, cannot be tied down to any one place, and forms and reforms on the fly as "two or three" gather with gifts to work together toward some effect under the authority and direction of Jesus Christ in the presence of the Holy Spirit.

To further complicate the situation, the relational matrices in the church interact with the levels of spiritual maturity in the people and their giftedness. Spiritual gifts are grace gifts operating in the realm of the spirit for spiritual purposes. They are unearned, undeserved manifestations of God's power for a purpose both inside and outside the Christian community. The fruit of the Spirit refers to character manifestations in the shaping influence of an intimate relationship with God. It points to maturity through exposure and yieldedness to the Holy Spirit. The growth of these character qualities in a person is positively correlated with the depth of one's sanctification. This fruit is described in the New Testament as a coherent collection of attributes in contrast to worldly pursuits and fleshly striving:

> Now the deeds of the flesh are evident, which are: immorality, impurity, sensuality, idolatry, sorcery, enmities, strife, jealousy, outbursts of anger,

disputes, dissensions, factions, envying, drunkenness, carousing, and things like these. . . . But the fruit of the Spirit is love, joy, peace, patience, kindness, goodness, faithfulness, gentleness, self-control . . . Now those who belong to Christ Jesus have crucified the flesh with its passions and desires. If we live by the Spirit, let us also walk by the Spirit.

(Galatians 5:19–25)

When people are drawn into relationships through their interest in one another, the spiritual response to needs, and the depth of sanctification, gifts are set loose in the community, resulting in the observation that Paul made that there are varieties of gifts, varieties of ministries and varieties of effects.

(Brownell, 2010b, p. 16).

These relational factors can be represented in the schematization in Figure 7.1.

All this may seem overly complicated, but it is important because in some places a client may belong to a church where the philosophy of ministry is that their church constitutes the body of Christ rather than the members working constitute their local church. One is top-down and the other is bottom-up. In the top-down version, people may use spiritual gift indicators to find out who has what gift and then fit those people into ministries that have been predetermined by the church leadership, but the flow of the process is not a natural outgrowth of the fruit of the Spirit in relationship with others. It's a program with benchmarks. This starts from the assumption that the church exists and must therefore be the body of Christ. However, if you start from the bottom-up,

$$\left(\frac{\left((\text{N-I})\,(\text{Alt})\,(\text{D})\right)^{\text{I+comm}}}{\left(\left(\dfrac{(\text{FoS})\,(\text{GoS})}{\text{DoS}}\right)\right)\left(\dfrac{\left((\text{N-I})\,(\text{Alt})\,(\text{D})\right)^{\text{I+div}}}{\text{DoS}}\right)} \rightarrow (\text{VoG} \times \text{VoM} \times \text{VoE})\right) \bigg/ \text{PneuF} = \text{ChComm}$$

FIGURE 7.1   Relational factors in Christian community.
Where   N-I = Nonindependence;   Alt = Alterity;   D = Dialogue;   I + comm. = Relationships between an individual and others in community; I + div. = Relationship between an individual and God; FoS = Fruit of the Spirit; GoS = Gifts of the Spirit; DoS = Depth of Sanctification; VoG = Varieties of Gifts; VoM = Varieties of Ministries; VoE = Varieties of Effects; PneuF = Pneumenal Field; and ChComm = Christian Community.

then what you do is observe the spontaneous working of the members, who will naturally follow the leading in their spiritual character and the use of their giftedness into a variety of ministries (all of which cannot be preprogrammed) and who will display a variety of effects. The second is more messy and less efficient, but it is more natural.

The Christian community is a field. Sometimes a psychotherapist must understand the nature of that field (and the health of that community) in order to understand the presenting situation of the client. The schematic in Figure 7.1 shows several factors that would likely be in play for any given individual attempting to find a home in a Christian community. What if, in attempting to relate to others, the individual encounters people with a shallow depth of sanctification? What if they encounter people whose relational skills render them poor dialogue partners? What if they lack kindness, gentleness, or other fruit of the Spirit and so are just not interested in relationship to begin with? What if people like that, however, are attempting to achieve their benchmarks in the local church program? The person coming for therapy could be internalizing and directing blame at themselves for dynamics that are more features of the field.

A Sioux elder might suggest that people in such a church sit on the ground and watch what is taking place, leave room for silence before they speak, and simply get in step with the natural flow of things. That was Paul's suggestion when he told the believers in Ephesus to walk in step with the Holy Spirit. The process of following the leading of the Spirit may set a client at odds with his or her local church or pastor. The client might come troubled because he or she is trying to sort out what is going on when they attempt to "have a ministry" only to find that they are at odds with the leadership. It may be because they are at odds with the way the leadership conceives of what is going on in the church, what the church is, and who has the authority. It may be because they are one of those people lacking in spiritual maturity, fruit of the Spirit, and so forth.

In complex situations, the problem never belongs to just one person. It is a result of the ways in which people in relationships go about doing what they are doing. In churches, as in dysfunctional families, sometimes it feels better to blame somebody than to examine the actual dysfunction. Sometimes clients come from dysfunctional church families, and when they do, the therapist needs to understand the flow of the process from a spiritual perspective. Is the client inherently defective, or is there a bad fit between the client and the process at work in the client's faith community?

Relationship

The traditional Native American believes that each living thing in nature has its own spirit "in addition to being connected to and part of the Great Spirit." That is why Native Americans pray and give thanks to such things as the sun, moon, stars, to the rain and wind, and various creatures. "We realize that we cannot survive or live without our 'relations.' We also realize that they cannot live without us; hence there is a reciprocal relationship" (Lake-Thom, 1997, p. 8).

Many Native Americans personify the earth, calling it "Mother." The Sioux, for instance, preferred contact with the earth. They sat on it. They took off their footwear to go barefoot on many occasions so as to maximize contact with the earth. They abhorred the idea of digging into it for minerals or growing grass and cutting it, as if they were slashing the chest of their mother or cutting her hair (Nerburn, 1999). Native American spirituality is at once spiritist and natural. "The world was a library and its books were the stones, leaves, grass, brooks, and the birds and animals . . . we learned to do what only the student of nature ever learns . . ." (Nerburn, 1999, p. 16). It doesn't just feel like God is in everything; for the Native American, the Great Spirit *is* in everything—in the things and in the way those things work together in a natural fashion. This is a reverence for the ontic field.

I have pointed to an ontic field and a phenomenal field, and I have mentioned the pneumenal field, but now I want to point to how the pneumenal field transcends both. That is, the pneumenal field is the ontic field with a decidedly "God-in" perspective, and it is the phenomenal field with that same perspective. One of the writers in the New Testament said, "And without faith it is impossible to please Him, for he who comes to God must believe that He is and that He is a rewarder of those who seek Him."[7] According to that person, God does exist, and He is a rewarder of those who seek Him. If God exists and is a force in the ontic field, then what kind of force would that be? He could be a rewarder indeed, but He could also be mean and nasty. It depends on what kind of a God actually exists. The experience one has of this God is another matter, but that is dependent on what one believes God to be (or even if one believes there is a God). In the Garden of Eden, before the fall, the first people had an intimate relationship with God and met Him face-to-face without any sense of shame or fear. However, after the fall, they hid from God.

One's experience of standing before God based on the assurance of salvation will often bring on confidence. When I was a young Christian and had studied enough scripture to feel assured of my standing with God, I applied for a job as a group cofacilitator with a Master's-level therapist in California who was wanting to run groups. By that time, I had been a neuropsychiatric technician in the Navy, and I had facilitated groups. I felt confident because of that, but I felt overwhelmingly confident that come what may in life, with that job, with the future, that I would be okay, because I knew, I was deeply assured, that nothing could separate me from the love of God. I owned that part of the Bible that reads, "If God be for us, who could be against us?" So I went into the interview with that confidence. It must have oozed out of my pores, because the interviewer and his friend, both atheists, jumped me for my beliefs. The interview ceased being about running groups and became about confidence in God. It turned out that the Master's-level therapist at one point had gone to seminary, but at seminary he had been taught by atheist professors and had given up his faith. He no longer believed there was a God, and meeting someone who seemed confident of a personal relationship with God was unsettling.

In the Eastern spiritual traditions, there is either no God or many gods. God could be capricious. God could be angry and demanding. God could be judgmental and difficult or impossible to please. God could be preoccupied or just unconcerned with the circumstances of human beings. As J. B. Phillips (1967) wrote, "No one is ever really at ease in facing what we call 'life' and 'death' without a religious faith. The trouble with many people today is that they have not found a God big enough for modern needs" (p. v).

Providence is the theological term that addresses God's actions in the lives of people within the ontic aspect of the pneumenal field. It is God being in charge of His creation and accomplishing His purposes in the lives of human beings (Horton, 2011). He holds all of the created order in His hands, upholds it and maintains it, and He intercedes in the lives of people according to His purposes, accomplishing everything He has intended. So the complex situation in question is a large one. For the Christian, even though this large of a field is impossible to grasp in its totality, the person of God becomes the focus. The field comes together in the person of God, and God is known through the church, through revelation in nature, and through specific revelation in Scripture.

When working psychotherapeutically, people often feel out of step with God and so out of step with the correct flow of life. They feel like they don't measure up and so are not pleasing to God. Many times I have heard someone say to me, "I believe in God, but I'm not a Christian." When I explore that some more, it becomes apparent that they believe there is a God, a creator, and they believe in Jesus as God's Son, and they believe that Jesus died for their sins, but they don't go to church. Church for them somewhere along the line became the problem for various reasons, and because they don't go to church, they believe they are out of step with God. It may be that they are out of step with God, but are they totally out of step with God? Does God commune with them at all? Do they hear from God in nature, the electronic church, in scripture or other religious literature, and do their Christian friends encourage their faith at all? There is more to the situation than simply going to church. One's relationship with other people and with God, and therefore one's touch points in the evolving complex situation, are numerous, overlapping, and convoluted. Just like God himself, there is always more to the picture than we can identify at any given moment.

This leads to what it's like to be the individual in a complex situation, what kinds of meanings are made out of experience, and what is the nature of one's phenomenal field.

NOTES

1. This would also include patient factors and therapist factors. All these things are what therapist and client bring with them into therapy.
2. See below on emergence.
3. And in reference to a specific approach to psychotherapy, namely, gestalt therapy.
4. In Wisdom of the Native Americans, by Kent Nerburn.
5. Heavenly Secrets, 2556.
6. Matthew 18:20.
7. Hebrews 11:6.

CHAPTER 8

Spiritual Work and the Interpretation of Experience

You're not gonna be happy unless you're going Mach two with your hair on fire.

—Kelly McGillis to Tom Cruise in *Top Gun*

The Bible displays a phenomenological perspective. It is written from the vantage point of lived life on earth. Thus, it says that the sun rises and sets and that the earth is set and never moves; that was the controversy in Galileo's day—how to understand the scriptures given that scientific evidence suggested that the earth actually circled the sun instead of the other way around. We conduct our lives as embodied beings. We perceive and make sense of what we perceive by means of a lived body. Judgments such as tall or short and near or far are made by people who are both tall and short and near and far. We are not only limited to what it is like to live in our own respective bodies, but also by virtue of our specific placement in a situation. These things create perspective. Other people can make judgments as to what it is like to be us, and they might interpret our expressions carefully but still be wrong. Only a person, him- or herself, can know his or her own thoughts.

Phenomenology is the *logos* of phenomena, or how things appear to a conscious subject (Spinelli, 2005). It is a matter of subjective interpretation—what it is like to be a given person in a given situation at a particular moment and the implications of being that person having that experience at that particular moment.

From the perspective of continental philosophy, this is the focus of intentional concern for a psychotherapist. It is the therapist's tracking of the "aboutness" of experience, the unfolding subjective awareness of events and the meanings given to any particular aspect of that experience by the client, which are also related to field dynamics (see Chapter 7).

Of course, this tracking is taking place in the context of a relationship between the therapist and the client, so the tracking must be conducted with binocular vision. Stereopsis creates a sense of depth in which some things seem closer while other things seem further away. That which is closer is in the foreground, and that which is further away is in the background.

When I was in a composition and design art class in college, the professor said that if you want to make things look closer, make them darker and more well-defined, and if you want to make things look further away, make them more vague and muted. The binocular/ stereoptic vision created with the working of two eyes allows us to create the perspective of some things being set against the background of others. Some things are sharp and perceived to be in the foreground. Some things are blurred and perceived to be in the background. The background gives context, and the two—what is in foreground and what is in background—are linked and give rise to figure formation.

In therapy, there is the figure formation of the client, and there is the figure formation of the therapist.

THE INTERPRETATION OF EXPERIENCE

People do not live in a cascade of thinking errors, irrational beliefs, and intrapsychic conflicts. These and other constructs created by theorists are abstractions used to describe how people live in a real world, but they are not how people actually live. Rather, people get up each day, put their clothes on, and start walking through several touch points with the world. They pick up a toothbrush. They drink coffee. They look out the window and see the sunlight on the trees. They think of the office and wish they could stay home and relax. They are experience-near.

As stated previously, people are also embodied and situated. That is, we experience the world as a body. When we reach for the toothbrush, it is near or far, high or low. Those evaluations come as a function of the body through which we see it, reach out for it, and pick it up, and those evaluations are made depending on our actual location with reference to any such thing as a toothbrush. Our consciousness of such things is the self-regulating aspect of the body interacting with its environment (Cosmelli & Thompson, 2011). Perception, enactment, emotion, dreaming, and remembering are all ways a person self-regulates, and they depend on the living body rather than just a brain encased in a skull. Referring to Antonio Damasio's (1999) work in neurology, Cosmelli and Thompson claimed that the nervous system continually maps the state of the body

> through a series of core neural structures that are crucial for both body regulation and the feeling of self. In this theory, creature consciousness with a minimal phenomenal feeling of self arises as a feature of life-regulation processes effected by the nervous system in tight coupling with the body.
>
> (p. 170)

Just as experience is not a matter of a brain by itself, making our way in life and making meaning of making our way, it is not a case of a body by itself. We are extended. Our minds, the awareness of being and doing, extend beyond our bodies and into the people and things we touch through contacting (Clark, 2011). That contacting shapes our experience and the meanings we give to it. In the movie *Avatar*, the protagonist comes to a new planet confined in a wheelchair. Through a technological advance, he is enabled to inhabit a cloned alien body, and through that body he is able to run and live as one of the race of beings indigenous to the planet. As he exists through that lived body in that strange planet, among the beings who dwell there, he experiences himself in a different way and changes as a person.

I want to revisit here something I said previously: I have experienced three iterations of writing technology that have affected the product of my writing and the process of writing. At first I wrote with a pencil on paper, which was quite time-consuming. Then, in seminary, I taught myself to write on the typewriter because I did not have time to write my papers out longhand and *then* type them up, and I began thinking through my fingers on the keyboard. I was slowed at first by the need to constantly correct with "white out" what I was producing. It was awkward and time-consuming, but it was faster than hand writing, and my thoughts were shaped slightly by working on the typewriter instead of with a pencil. When the computer arrived, the fluidity of my thinking increased because I was more readily thinking through my fingers on the keyboard. When the Internet was created, I found myself dialoguing with colleagues on professional e-mail lists every day, and the interaction was fast-paced. I lost the keen awareness of the keyboard, and instead my awareness was of the people on the list and what I wanted to say to them. Eventually, I could think better on a subject by dealing with it through my fingers on a keyboard than I could if I had to write it longhand or even speak it through a phone conversation. On the occasion that I had to use those other means of communicating, my ideas were stillborn.

People make meaning through a series of figure–ground judgments, and they do that from their embodied location in a situation, that is, with a perspective. We put what others say together with how they say it and we make a meaning out of that. We evaluate both verbal and nonverbal discourse. We also do that by placing the current moment's actions against the background of previous experience. So if the parents of a woman always kissed her and told her they loved her just before they hit her with a stick on her bare legs, then in adulthood she might flinch when someone kisses her and tells her they love her. In addition, we intuit what we cannot perceive directly; we don't see every angle of the things we perceive, but we fill in the blank spots intuitively. If there is a box in front of me, I can only see one side and part of another side, but I cannot see the opposite sides. So, I fill in the other sides and "see" a whole, complete box. In the same way, we make meaning of situations by filling in the sides we cannot sense directly. Unfortunately, we often imagine things wrongly, and that is where people often misunderstand one another.

Contacting is important to meaning making. If we have a poor connection with our current environment, we will have an impoverished sense of the situation. We won't feel it, taste, it, see it, smell it, or hear it very well, and because of that our perspective will be faint. We will be stuck in vague sensations, not able to quite figure out what our experience is about.

Imagine that you walk into an art gallery and turn the corner. Suddenly, you find yourself with your face very close to a painting. All you can see are blurred things. So, you back up, and then you see brush strokes and places where color distinguishes shapes. You back up again, and again, and then suddenly the picture comes into focus. Now, you actually see it, take it in, and have a whole-person experience of it. You feel excited by the colors, warmed inside, and happy. You recall when a similar process the week before brought an attractive person into view. You recall your first lover. You look at the painting, and now you see the brick wall upon which it hangs and the lighting above and around it, and it reminds you of a coffee shop you like, and then you feel hungry for a cup of coffee. You have a decision to make on the basis of your experience and what you want. Because the contacting has been focused, the relevant values of being in an art gallery or going for coffee are clear, and you choose which one you want. In contrast, a person with poor contacting skills does not meet the environment well, does not stay with the painting or make the effort to "back up," and then doesn't get to what he or she wants, because he or she never forms clear figures of interest that might pose a choice.

Psychotherapists work with the meaning-making processes of the client in various ways. Some go for the developmental issues in the background of the client's current and foreground behaviors. Some work with the cognitive aspects of meaning making in the implications of what clients believe to be fact. Some observe the contacting of the client. Most therapists develop a working relationship with the client on their ways to the other methodologies in their approaches. All of this creates experience for both the therapist and the client, and their respective meaning-making processes interact. That interaction is embodied and extended. The therapist speaks into and through the client, and the client does likewise into and through the therapist. This is not ventriloquism; it is relational process. It is like thinking through the keyboard, and that is why people are often helped simply by meeting with a therapist and speaking freely about themselves and their situation. The speaking through one another, the dialogue, creates new experience that affects meaning.

When I meet with clients, I make every effort to be *with* them. I make and hold eye contact. I use tactile references and metaphors in my speech. I tell them I can hear them, or I tell them I am having a hard time hearing them. Phenomena are appearances—something appearing. So working with such an appearance becomes a matter of showing—showing the appearing of the client to the client. I do not tell clients my interpretation of them unless I own that relationally *as my imagination* or my curiosity. "I notice your chin quivering, and I imagine you are feeling something right now; is that right?" "I notice your chin quivering, and I'm wondering if you are feeling something." Often I don't even get to my imagination, because when I simply notice an appearing, some manifestation of the client, in a way that shows it to the client, the client is suddenly immersed more clearly in it. It's as if someone stepped up to the client in the art gallery, took him or her by the arm, and backed him or her up so that they could really see the painting. My observing and my curiosity are ways in which, with reference to the picture of the client, I back up from it and try to gain clarity. Together, the client and I are constantly moving forward and backward, stepping to this side and that, walking around one another, and making meaning out of what is happening between us. That meaning relates to other experiences that we've each had. It either relates directly or is colored by extra-therapeutic common factors in each of our lives. We meet in a two-person situation that is actually a subset of overlapping and larger spheres of influence, larger fields, and more complex situations, and it is what we do with each other, as we extend into one another, that makes a difference.

IMPLICATIONS

As in other considerations, the implications of subjective experience and meaning making for spirituality can be understood as the consequences of process and of relationship. Religious processes contribute to the significance of spiritual life. Likewise, relationships relevant to religious experience can change the direction in which a person is going.

Process

Imagine that on two successive weekends you attend two different churches. Church A is an Anglican church in a major city, and church B is a nondenominational church meeting in a suburb of that city.

At church A, you arrive and walk up the steps toward two large, wooden doors stained dark brown that open to the sanctuary. Inside it is dark, and you have to stop for a moment for your eyes to adjust. You take off your hat. You receive a program from the greeters, and then someone takes you down the aisle toward a pew. Everything is quiet, still, hushed. Overhead large, wooden beams support an array of candles. Filtered light comes through the delicate stained glass panels depicting scenes from the Bible. The altar is in the center of the platform ahead, and when you reach the pew where you sit, you realize there is a kneeling rail at the foot of the pew in front of you. No one is talking to anyone else. People are quiet and alone in their thoughts. The organ begins to play, and it is soft music, but rich from the depths of old metal pipes. Suddenly, the volume of the organ increases and the pace of the hymn picks up. From the back, the voices of a choir can be heard. You turn to see a procession beginning. There is someone carrying a large Bible, another with a large crucifix on a pole, priests and attendants in robes, and then the choir. As they walk past, you can feel your heart beat faster. The sound of their voices is exciting, and it rouses you to sing with them. You feel moved by the lyrics, affirming that, indeed, God is a mighty fortress and a bulwark never failing. You feel hushed and more reverent as the choir takes its place up front and the priest comes to rest behind the altar. He speaks the words of a collect for reverence,[1] followed by several readings: one from the Old Testament Psalms, one from the Epistle to the Romans, and one from the Gospel of John. The choir punctuates each with a chorus. The congregation stands for a responsive reading of the Nicene creed, and you notice you are focused on trying to make sure you read the correct stanza. It's a bit distracting from the creed itself, and you notice you'd like to think about those statements in the creed, but there isn't time. You sit, and the choir sings a hymn that sounds very "classical," and old. You notice that indeed it came from the 17th century. The lyrics have several stanzas of mounting theological content, but the music is staid and not very rousing. Then comes the sermon, followed by another hymn and the offering. Everything is done with solemnity, and it all comes and goes with precision, leading to a predictable ending 1 hour after beginning. The choir and the priests go out as they had come in, and from the back of the sanctuary, the priest utters the benediction. The people leave quietly, not stopping to actually engage one another until they have exited the sanctuary.

At church B, you arrive at a school gymnasium. People greet you at the door with a smile and a hearty welcome. There is no program. There is no one to show you where to sit. You wander into the expanse of the gym and notice chairs arranged facing one direction where a large sound stage has been created. All the lights are on, and it's bright in there. Several microphones on stands, amplifiers, guitars, and a bass wait up front. There is also an electronic keyboard. Contemporary religious music is playing very softly over the sound system, but no one is paying attention to it. They are all busy greeting one another and catching up with one another's lives. There is a loud hum in the room from all that chatter. You see someone you know from work and wave. Suddenly, the soft music stops and a drummer begins with a loud, steady beat that echoes in the gym, and you can feel the bass drum shake your insides every time the drummer kicks it. People appear behind the microphones, and they are clapping their hands. Everyone joins in. The guitars and bass start playing, and the singers start singing a popular chorus from a contemporary Christian music artist. The musicians and singers make it their own. It keeps going and the intensity swells, and then they modulate the key and move right into a different one. This all goes on for about 30 minutes, and the intensity of the music is pumped up by the occasional praises of the worship leader who calls out directly to God and asks that the Holy Spirit come upon them all with power. The people are standing for the entire time, clapping their hands, and as the intensity increases, some of them start dancing, and they move out into the aisles for more room to do so. The pastor is one of the musicians; at one point, he walks from behind the keyboard and comes out front with a handheld microphone. He starts praising God. His voice begins to emerge from the choruses. Four men pick up a small pulpit and move it to the front, and the pastor sings his way to a place behind it. However, he doesn't remain there. He is moving constantly back and forth from one side of the sound stage to the other, looking into the eyes of the people close and sometimes smiling at this one or that one. His sermon begins without notice; it simply emerges from the singing. After a moment, the other singers and musicians realize the transition that has taken place, and they leave the sound stage to find a place with the other people. The pastor preaches an expository sermon for an hour, and then he begins to come to a close. But he cannot. Each time he seems to move toward an ending, some new association, some new exhortation, some new point occurs to him, and he cannot stop. Finally, at 1 hour and 15 minutes into his sermon, he grows quiet. The room becomes still. Someone has taken over the keyboard and is playing a hymn very softly. The pastor begins to cry. He is overcome with the beauty of God and the magnitude of God, and he keeps uttering the broken sentence, "I can't . . . I can't." Then someone comes forward to stand as if before an altar, but of course there is no altar. The pastor puts his head together with the man and they are talking for a while. The music continues softly. The congregation sways, and you hear people praying out loud from here and there in the room. Finally, the pastor looks up and he says, "I want you to receive our new brother." He mentions the man's name and says that he has just received the Lord, meaning he has just expressed that he wants Jesus to be his personal savior. The congregation breaks out in loud and spontaneous applause, the music picks up, and the pastor starts singing another chorus. The whole place joins in with him, and the room is once more charged with loud excitement. It is now close to 2 hours since you walked into church B, and the pastor raises his hand, the keyboardist plays more quietly, the congregation brings the singing down to the ground, and the pastor utters a benediction and wishes everyone a safe week. The service is over, but people remain in their places or walk over to others and start talking with them. The music continues. Gradually, over the next 20 minutes people straggle out of the gymnasium.

There is a process to each of those experiences, and the process contributes considerably to the meaning and spiritual significance of the respective experiences. For one, the quiet and intellectual nature of the service communicates great reverence—the *mysterium tremendum*. For the other, the familiarity and rousing excitement communicates the intimacy possible between oneself and God, bringing them into an excited adoration. The first was scripted, and the second used planned spontaneity.

But what kinds of meaning making goes on with the people in such experiences? Perhaps the first one speaks of respect and awe, or perhaps it speaks of deadness and irrelevance. Perhaps the second one speaks of encounter with God through the presence and movement of the Holy Spirit, or it speaks of emotional excess and disrespectful familiarity.

A psychotherapist might be working with clients around spiritual issues, and it is helpful to realize that there are different styles in church-life process, that each style reflects not only how the church meaningfully conducts its ministries but also how the client makes sense of the various things the church does. People will experience themselves differently as they engage in embodied contact, or withdraw from it, in the corporate activities of their respective faith communities. They may see people they know acting pious one day and behaving mercilessly the next. They may encounter spiritualized platitudes when people in the church get together only to feel curiously out of touch with them. They might hear religious jargon thrown around like spiritual shorthand, but not really feel they understand what is being said (or know it as others seem to know it). They may wonder whether it is all "real." If people pay attention, they often experience a kind of cognitive dissonance between the acclaimed "joy of the Lord" and the evident suffering and dysfunction in their daily lives, and this is something that psychotherapists must learn to put together. The client is not the only one making meaning out of the experience. The therapist will come to the point of asking him- or herself, "What is actually going on here?"

Relationship

If relationship is indeed a matter of contacting over time, then in terms of spiritual meaning making it's a matter of what is being contacted and what it's like to experience that contact. The experience of tapping into the monistic ground of all being in Hinduism (Brahma) is not the same thing as accepting the is-ness of life in Buddhism and developing Buddha mindfulness. Likewise, contacting the Native American Mother Earth and being grounded through attunement with the Great Spirit and identification with the natural forces of the world is not the same as submission to Allah in Islam.

Many people are depicted in the Bible as having direct contact with the God of Judaism. There is something to learn from each of them. They are Abraham, Moses, Isaiah, and Job, because each of them captures something of what it is like for any given person in contemporary life to encounter this same divine Being. People can look these figures up and learn more about their lives. I will not go into great biographical detail about them. Rather, I want to focus on what I regard to be salient features about the kind of relationship these people experienced with God.

It is said that Abraham believed God. How did that become manifest? He was living with his family in one part of the world. He was set there. Then God told him to pick up everything and leave where he was living. God did not just say, "You're living on 53rd street, and I want you to move to 23rd street." He just told him to leave. That would be like somebody telling you to get out of your house. You might want to know why or where you should go if you left that place. Abraham was not given that. He was just told to leave where he was. If that had been you, would you have wondered if you heard right? Or if you had even *heard* at all? Maybe you would have thought you had imagined it. Maybe you would have questioned that you might have had a wild and irrational thought that you really would not be wise to share with others. This was not the way that Abraham was thinking. He definitely *heard* from God, and he was definite in his response to that hearing. He sensed authority over his life in the contacting. Abraham had to have felt that he was in contact with a being (a) other than himself, (b) greater than himself, and (c) with authority over his life. He is regarded to be the great example of faith because he acted on what he was told.

Moses encountered God directly on many occasions, and the two of them had an intimacy with one another that was important, but the first contact with God was also dramatic. It left a memorable impression. Moses was drawn through curiosity to a bush in the wilderness that was burning, but not burning up. That is, there was something supernatural about what he observed. He was fascinated by it. The indication of contacting going on is that he moved toward the novelty to which he was attracted, and as he did so he heard from God, telling him to take off his sandals for the very ground upon which he was walking was holy:

> When the Lord saw that he turned aside to look, God called to him from the midst of the bush and said, 'Moses, Moses!' And he said, 'Here I am.' Then He said, 'Do not come near here; remove your sandals from your feet, for the place on which you are standing is holy ground.' He said also, 'I am the God of your father, the God of Abraham, the God of Isaac, and the God of Jacob.' Then Moses hid his face, for he was afraid to look at God.[2]

He was afraid to look, but he did not run away, and he stood his ground and carried on an authentic conversation with God. This is the passage that Rudolph Otto (1923/1950) pointed to in establishing the features of the numinous—that it (a) fascinates and attracts to itself and that it also simultaneously (b) makes one tremble in fear. In the life of Moses, however, he was not aware of an abstract concept (the numinous); these characterizations were aspects that emerged out of his contacting with God. Obviously, he also saw in God a being who had authority over himself; so, relationally, he experienced yieldedness and obedience.

Isaiah was a prophet of God, and so he not only had contact with God, but he was also God's prosecuting attorney, bringing God's case

against the people *to* the people. On the occasion of his commission-
ing, the interaction between them went like this:

> In the year of King Uzziah's death I saw the Lord sitting on a throne,
> lofty and exalted, with the train of His robe filling the temple. Seraphim
> stood above Him, each having six wings: with two he covered his face,
> and with two he covered his feet, and with two he flew. And one called
> out to another and said,
>
> > "Holy, Holy, Holy, is the Lord of hosts,
> > The whole earth is full of His glory."
>
> And the foundations of the thresholds trembled at the voice of him
> who called out, while the temple was filling with smoke. Then I said,
>
> > "Woe is me, for I am ruined!
> > Because I am a man of unclean lips,
> > And I live among a people of unclean lips;
> > For my eyes have seen the King, the Lord of hosts."
>
> Then one of the seraphim flew to me with a burning coal in his hand,
> which he had taken from the altar with tongs. He touched my mouth
> with it and said, "Behold, this has touched your lips; and your iniquity
> is taken away and your sin is forgiven."
>
> Then I heard the voice of the Lord, saying, "Whom shall I send, and
> who will go for Us?" Then I said, "Here am I. Send me!"[3]
>
> (Isaiah 6:1–8)

Isaiah evidently had a capacity to see, to perceive God. He had visions,
and he had conversations. On one occasion, though, it seems he had
a better quality of contact, because it resulted in his undoing. He perceived God as "holy." This is a term that in Hebrew signals apartness
(Brown, Driver, & Briggs, 1907/1978), and through that separateness
it denotes exaltation—being apart, in a class of its own, and above.
Isaiah's experience of God is an intersubjective one in which through
the contact he not only perceives God in a particular light, but he also
understands himself as in a relational perspective—as compared with
God. Compared with God, he is ruined because of his uncleanness.
Further to that, though, and in spite of it, God maintains contact (the

coal burns him clean), and then Isaiah's response is one of willing service. He wants to be with and serve this Being he has come to know.

Job is like a person who has always heard about Bermuda, and has seen pictures of it and talked with people about it, even people with all kinds of theories about it, but who has never actually been there himself—until one day he goes there and experiences it firsthand. He writes home and says to his friends, "I've always heard about this place, but now I've seen it with my own eyes." After losing his family and all he owned, and after enduring the counsel of his theological friends (who had all kinds of theories about why what happened to him took place), Job actually met God. We are not given the description of their encounter as in the case of Isaiah, but we are given the result:

> Then Job answered the Lord and said,
> "I know that You can do all things,
> And that no purpose of Yours can be thwarted.
> 'Who is this that hides counsel without knowledge?'
> Therefore I have declared that which I did not understand,
> Things too wonderful for me, which I did not know."
> 'Hear, now, and I will speak;
> I will ask You, and You instruct me.' "I have heard of You by the hearing
> of the ear;
> But now my eye sees You;
> Therefore I retract,
> And I repent in dust and ashes."
>
> (Job 42:1–6)

Job's reaction in one way is similar to Isaiah's and to Moses's. He repents, and it's like lamenting "Woe is me . . ." or hiding one's face in fear. Contact with this God puts one's own being into perspective. But there is more to it. Job is drawn to God like others in that he wants to ask God questions. Evidently, he senses that in relationship with God is to be found answers to his most difficult and nagging questions.

When we break contact with one another, one way that we can do that is to cut off the flow of information (as in open conversation), and then, in the absence of information, make up stories about the other person to fill in the blanks. We imagine things about them.

I once worked with a client who came to me precisely because she knew that I am a Christian. She told me that she was tormented by believing in God. She was sure that God found fault with her, that

God is a judgmental Being who expects more from people than they can give and that the whole thing is unfair. To me she was an uncommon mixture of what scripture calls a weak conscience (needing rules of conscience to which she could attempt to measure up) but a strong faith. What she believed about God, the kind of being that God is, did not accord with a careful reading of the Bible, but believe it she did. She could not shake that belief, and it was excruciating. She was caught in her imagination about God, and that imagination was cutting off actual contact with God. She was furious with God, absolutely believing that God exists. Her stance, her faith, her projection of reality was untouchable.

Because I believe in a God of grace and self-sacrificing love, of omnipotent power to turn even catastrophes to the good, and that God is oriented toward people (open for contact), I trust God to act in ways that go well beyond what I can do. I really believe that God will be present in and with the client in ways that I cannot, but that I am part of the process that is going on between the client and God. In working with this client I would often feel stuck, as if she were unreachable. The process of meeting with her developed to the point at which I tried an experiment (see Chapter 9 on the movement to enactment) in which I told her, "Well, if there's nothing you can do to please God, and no matter what you do, you're damned to hell, then why not just please yourself and quit worrying about God at all?"

"I can't do that," she said.

"Why not?"

She fumbled around with that one, seemingly demanding of herself to remain stuck in that tormented middle ground of feeling obligated to please God but feeling utterly incapable of doing so and being convinced she was going to hell.

The psychotherapeutic hour is a three-way field. The therapist meets with the client, and there is God. Some therapists will not be able to embrace this concept. They will make this into a useful fantasy or just the meaning making in somebody's phenomenal field, but they will not entertain the idea that God is an ontic reality.

What are the implications if God does exist? As I wrote in another place (Brownell, 2012b), they revolve around the contacting that a given person has with God. If God is immanent, present with, then even though we cannot perceive through physical perception, there might be other ways that we can come to know God through experience.

Perhaps it is a proprioceptive sense, like an inner impression, in which a thought comes to mind. Perhaps it is a sense of foreboding. Perhaps one looks back and begins to see a consistent kind of experience. I know, for instance, that every time I get behind in a writing project, my case load will shrink to create more time to write. It's been consistent. So do you rationalize that away as pure coincidence, or do you accept it as something more? I have learned that prayer is a dangerous tool, because God may answer the prayer in a way that I did not expect. The point in sharing these examples is to try to communicate that I have experienced "push back" from a being I do not believe is indifferent to being known, starting from what I might call the beginning of my life with God, in which I asked Him to make Himself known to me on up to this day. He did make Himself known to me, and I have both read about his loyal love in the Bible and experienced it through various difficult phases of my life.

NOTES

1. A collect is a focused prayer.
2. Exodus 3:4–6.
3. Isaiah 6:1–8.

CHAPTER 9

Spiritual Work and the Movement to Enactment

*[F]aith is knowing, beyond awareness, that if one takes a step
there will be ground underfoot;
one gives oneself unhesitatingly to the act, one has faith that
the background will produce the means.*

—Perls, Hefferline, and Goodman, 1951/1972, p. 343

As I write this, I am also aware that in a few hours I must take a shower, get dressed in something that looks halfway like I tried, climb into the car, and drive to Cambridge Beaches resort and spa, which is located on the west end of the island, near the village of Somerset. That is where our office Christmas party will take place, and if I do not show up, the office manager will come get me. At least, she has promised to do that. Now, here is where I have to make a calculation. Do I believe that she will translate her threatening words into action and actually leave the party to come get me? No. But do I believe that her ire would be unquenchable when we next meet at the office if I do not go? Yes. Most emphatically! So, I have about 2.5 hours left before I leap into action. Others will do likewise, and we will all show up and accomplish the things we have been talking about. It won't be scripted; it's not that kind of enactment, like acting in a play. Rather, this will be improv, and likely worthy of a skit on television.

The concept of enactment as used here is not the term as understood in psychoanalysis—the actualization of the transference, or the patient's efforts to persuade or force the analyst into reciprocal action (Hirsch, 1996). Rather, I am using enactment to indicate a deliberate

133

move to action from simply talking. It is experiential. Some therapeutic approaches, like gestalt therapy (GT), have made use of such enactment for decades, while others have done so more recently.

The movement to enactment is the transition from talking about something to the actual here-and-now occurrence of events that comprise one's sense of being alive. It is an embodied process and so involves embodied cognition; the way we move influences how we think (Thomas, 2013). It can also be conceived of as behavioral (Bennett-Levy et al., 2004), because enactment as described here is something people do. Finally, action such as this is related to the existential risk taking, the stepping out in faith that things will be okay, and that through such action, people will live a more meaningful life.

THE MOVEMENT TO ENACTMENT

Psychotherapy has been called the talking cure. That makes it sound like magic. I hear those words—"the talking cure"—and I imagine standing over the client, my hands swaying back and forth like waves on the sea, and uttering a mellifluent incantation. Actually, I don't believe talking "cures" anybody. I believe that talking is important as one way that people meet in meaningful ways, one way for people to understand one another, but talking itself, as we've discussed, comes in a context of so many other things that it's not just a matter of talking.

People have a common agreement that what others do speaks louder than what they say. In meeting with couples for many years, I have noticed a pattern that exemplifies this idea. The two will be moving through time in parallel with each other. They will be standing upright next to each other, in tandem with one another. Typically, the man is preoccupied with his toys and pastimes, and his partner periodically asks him for more time, more attention, and for him to make her a priority. He then says something like, "Okay. Sure." He spends a little more time with her for a short time, but then he goes back to his familiar pattern of not being available, of being invested in other things and other people. This goes on for a number of years, and then one day she is done. She tips over and falls out of tandem. She no longer asks him to spend time with her, and she begins to develop friendships and pursuits to make her life more meaningful, but these are all things that a single person might do. He senses the increased distance, the interpersonal space, feels he could actually lose her, and goes into high gear to attempt to save the relationship, often by calling and trying to set up couples counseling. However, she is done. She is emotionally flat, and when the two of them get into the office, he is very animated and showing a lot of affect, while she is reserved and noncommittal.

In this scenario, what each person does speaks louder than anything they can say. The man who spends more time away from his partner enacts what is important to him until he feels he might lose her, and then he goes into action. The partner who one day drops out of the partnership acts upon what she feels and thinks inside.

Such "doing" has been evident in psychotherapy in at least two major approaches: cognitive behavioral therapy[1] (CBT) and GT. Both use something they call "experiment." Experiment in science has been defined as a "test of cause-effect relationships by collecting evidence to demonstrate the effect of one variable on another" (Davis, 1999, p. 52). Most simply, two groups are treated exactly the same way but for one element present only in the experimental group, and then the two groups are compared to see whether there is any significant difference between them. If there is, then the effect is attributed to the element in the experimental group. Of course, it is more complicated than that.

In CBT, experiments are consistent with the hypothesis-testing feature of research in science, but there is another perspective on them as well. The two ways of approaching behavioral experiments in CBT are (a) to test a theory or hypothesis, even if loosely held as an abiding imagination in which one might ask, "Is it true that . . .?" and (b) to investigate or discover in which one might ask, "What might happen if . . .?" Thus, the systematic observation and experimentation in research-based hypothesis testing is augmented by a discovery-oriented approach in which clients and therapists have little idea of what might happen in the move to action but need to collect information in a careful fashion so as to learn from the experiment. Behavioral experiments in CBT are mostly ways of checking the validity of thoughts, perceptions, and beliefs, constructing new operating principles, and generating new beliefs.

Qualitative research data substantiate that people have a more comprehensive learning experience through enactment—learning by experience that tends to be holistic as opposed to learning terms, theories, and/or principles alone. The experiential element provides a more solid and robust experience that benefits a person by not just knowing about something through secondhand sources but by knowing for oneself as a firsthand source (Bennett-Levy et al., 2004).

For instance, Bennett-Levy et al. referred to a patient who believed that an elevated heart rate meant that she was suffering from heart disease. Several family members had had heart attacks. The patient feared any elevation of her heart rate. The therapist suggested that both of them run up and down the stairs, and the patient reported that the way she felt was similar to her panic attacks. She also noted that the therapist had the same results (elevated heart rate and higher rate of breathing). The therapist asked her several questions: (a) what sense did she make of the fact that both she and the therapist experienced the same physical sensations, (b) what did she think given that the symptoms of her panic attacks could be brought on by exercise, and (c) what sense did she make of the fact that she did not, actually, have a heart attack? The therapist explained that the experiment was carried out to see whether there might be another explanation for the symptoms she previously associated with panic attacks, but this was certainly to test the patient's hypothesis that she would have a heart attack. She was asked to reflect on the experiment even further or to try to replicate it with a friend and see what happened. The enactment in this case was both something she experienced in session with the therapist and something the therapist gave her, like homework.

According to current technology, people can find an "app" to conduct their own behavioral experiments or to do so in conjunction with the work they are going through with their therapists (the user can e-mail a list of his or her experiments to the therapist). The app in question here (and the technology changes so fast that the app may morph over time) is called "Behavioral Experiments–CBT," and it is made by Happtic. This app was created for the iPhone and iPad and can be found on iTunes. It allows the user to test the accuracy of limiting beliefs, try out new behaviors related to possible new beliefs, and then observe and evaluate the results. It provides a structure for people to explore and learn from their experience. However, if a person wants a low-tech version of this idea, then with paper and pen that person can do the following:

1. State the prediction or theory about how events might come about under imagined circumstances (my mind will go blank if I get in front of people to speak) or state the question of one's curiosity (I wonder how I might do if I had to make a professional presentation).
2. Describe the design of the experiment (I will volunteer to give a presentation to my class or group, and then I will do so).

3. Conduct the experiment (make the presentation, but do so with attention to the process and awareness of self in the situation).
4. Describe the results (although I was very nervous and felt like I needed to go to the bathroom, I did not forget everything; my mind did not go blank, and I actually felt more relaxed as time went on, especially when I was answering questions in a more conversational manner. I even forgot that I needed to go to the bathroom).
5. State a modified theory or belief about speaking in public (I can expect some performance anxiety to be associated with speaking in public, but I suspect that that is normal and might even be helpful to keep me animated and invested in what I am doing).

In GT, the experiment runs according to the second purpose mentioned above. Perls et al. (1951/1972) stated that psychotherapy is not the learning of a true theory about oneself, but a process of experimental life situations that are adventures—explorations of what they called the "dark and disconnected" (p. 266). Thus, in contrast to the first purpose in CBT, the experiment in GT is a phenomenological and existential inquiry or investigation. In the introduction to their book, the authors explained the strategy of doing experiments. They claimed that the clinical moment becomes an experimental situation. They suggested graded experiments that were not tasks to be completed. Rather, they explicitly asked,

> What is going on if you repeatedly try this or that? With this method we bring to the surface the difficulties of the patient. Not the task, but what interferes with the successful completion of the task becomes the center of our work.
>
> (Perls et al., 1951/1972, pp. xii–xiii)

In GT, a technique and an experiment are not the same thing. They may both be experiential, but they differ in that the technique is a fixed form and the true experiment is a creative novelty in which form follows function and the dictates of the current moment. There is, of course, the experimental use of technique, and this is where many people utilize the gestalt technique of chair work. In chair work, a person imagines someone not actually present or some aspect of themselves currently split out in a polarity (my weak and shy self talks to my frustrated and angry self), and in the process it is not simply a testing of theories or the gaining of knowledge. Rather, aspects of the person become more completely integrated. It's not just that the client gets to know him- or herself better; it's that he or she becomes more whole.

Whatever the experimental might be to any given therapist, it is also at the same time existential. For instance, although the founders of GT were not theists, they still held to an existential position that included a certain kind of faith. In their worldview, faith was conceived as "knowing, beyond awareness, that if one takes a step there will be ground underfoot; one gives oneself unhesitatingly to the act, one has faith that the background will produce the means" (Perls et al., 1951/1972, p. 343). Thus, faith became an instrument of knowing and an essential, supporting principle of contact (Brownell, 2008) that found affinity in Lewin's belief that science would persevere in its methods (Lewin, 1935) and in what the more contemporary phenomenologist Merleau-Ponty termed "perceptual faith"—the trust one has in his or her perceptions (Brownell, 2008). For these founders, experiments were not essentially different from the existential and experiential nature of therapy itself. The unpredictable nature of gestalt process is experimental; GT is a flowing process that itself exceeds the scope of a technique. "Both the basic gestalt process and experiment are built on action in the current moment that reveals persons and establishes experience of self" (Brownell, 2012a, p. 90; cf. Roubal, 2009; Wojtyla, 1979). Whenever any psychotherapist moves from mere talking into doing, he or she engages the client in the kinds of processes described here as being existential and faith-based, whether or not the therapist calls him- or herself an existential psychotherapist.

I once met with a couple who, when they presented, were obviously keeping a safe emotional distance from each other. Although they sat bodily next to one another on the same couch, they were on opposite sides of the room. They would not look at each other. They would not address one another. They each talked to me about the other. In working with the woman, in exploring what it had been like for her in that relationship, I made inquiry that made her lips quiver and tears form at the corners of her eyes. She sat quietly suffering, feeling the pain of their dysfunction, looking straight ahead, not even seeing me; she was so alone in her anguish. I turned to the husband, who was still looking at me, and I said, "Look at her." He blinked. I repeated, "Look at her," and he turned his head. I said "What do you see?" He gulped and could not find the words, but he reached out with his hand to touch her. Finally, he said, "She's crying," and she turned to look at him, at which time her crying became audible, the tears rolled down her cheeks, and she began to sob openly. She buried her face in his shoulder, and he put his arm around her.

Experiments were developed as enactments that heighten awareness, leading to learning and skill. They arise out of unique situations and are linked to current experience. They are related directly to the unique conditions involved between therapist and client. They require creative imagination and courage to be called into existence. Such enactment is always also an embodied process (Kepner, 1999).

> [The] self or "I" is an embodied self as well as a thoughtful one. We exist, love, work, and meet our constantly changing needs through our physical being and interactions in the world. Experience of our body is experience of our self. . . .
>
> (p. 10)

When the gestalt therapist observes the client to attend to the client's experience, it is to the body that such observation goes—that is, to sense embodied, nonverbal discourse. During experiment, that which has been distant through thinking about the situation becomes near through paying attention to the body and exploring what it is like to do this or that.

There is much the reader could learn about moving to enactment, different kinds of experiments, and so on. Let me end this brief description, however, by saying that the therapist can move into enactment by negotiating a bilateral experiment or by simply carrying out a unilateral experiment. In the example of the couple above, I did not negotiate anything. I moved intuitively into a unilateral experiment by telling the man to look at his wife. The negotiation is when a therapist suggests a move to enactment, suggests a behavioral experiment, and sets it up. The client has more of a choice, more time to consider whether or not he or she wants to take the risk. In unilateral experiments, the therapist may ask the client to do something, or the therapist may do something that creates new experience for the client quite apart from the client's choice about the matter. For instance, while working with people who have been treated badly, abused, neglected, or betrayed, I will, on occasion, allow my emotions to flow more freely than on other occasions. This is quite often the case when the client is cut off from his or her own affect. On such occasions, I will allow myself to tear up and cry, to say how sad I feel hearing what has happened to the client, and to be as present as possible with such sadness. I have also done a similar thing with my anger when I have sensed an outrageous injustice. This is also an example of how many of these ways of working with clients overlap one another, for the outrageous certainly has taken place in the overall situation the client brings into therapy, and once there, both through verbal and non-verbal discourse, I am engaged dialogically with the client, and both the client and myself, the therapist, are having our own experiences, making our own respective meanings, out of the encounter.

IMPLICATIONS

Once again, it's not simply that something has taken place, but what it means. It's the significance of events, thoughts, feelings, and experiences for both the therapist and the client, for both process and relationship with regard to spiritual and religious issues relevant to them both.

Process

One day I was reading about emotions and, without getting into the tallgrass of what I was reading, I wondered whether a feeling arises from within and is expressed through the face or whether one could actually change the expression on one's face and generate a feeling. So I went to the mirror in the bathroom and stood in front of it. Keeping aware of myself, I smiled broadly. Sure enough, I felt happy (not just silly!). So I took the smile off my face and I frowned forlornly, and then I no longer felt happy, but a bit sad. Now, I don't know why or how, but I just know what happened. I'm sure there are neuropsychological reasons for what I experienced, but there is a corollary for me as well in the spiritual life. When I pray, I have a different experience when I pray within myself to God, maintaining my outward silence, as opposed to when I speak out audibly in my prayer. When I'm with a client and ask God to help me understand this person, it would not be wise to do so out loud (and I don't), but when I'm driving alone in my car, there's no reason to keep silent. The praying-out-loud version of praying is qualitatively different for me. It grips me in my gut, and I often feel more in contact with God. It is not always like this. I have many times of soaring worship in which my heart is moved tremendously and I feel in tears while talking to God in the stillness of my mind.

Prayer is something I, as a Christian, do. There are various reasons that I do it. There is a purpose to it (Bounds, 1997) and there is power in it (Torrey, 2000), but these ways of talking about it are almost stereotypical code-speak in the Christian dialect. Mostly, Christians believe that talking to God about one's circumstances, struggles, desires, needs, and hopes will bring change. It *will* bring change, but it might bring change in the person who prays more than in the world in which that person prays.

This just illustrates for me that even though there is no one prescription for action that will always have a defined result, action of some kind is an element to one's spiritual life that takes it to a new level. The way a person practices his or her faith has an impact.

Biblical faith is composed of assent to some kind of proposition or fact and the action that is based on conviction that it is true.

> Now faith is the assurance of things hoped for, the conviction of things not seen.
>
> (Hebrews 11:1)

> So also faith by itself, if it does not have works, is dead. But someone will say, "You have faith and I have works." Show me your faith apart from your works, and I will show you my faith by my works.
>
> (James 2:17–18)

One without the other is not a complete understanding of what faith is; faith without the action that completes it is stillborn. Action is what actually completes one's faith. It's what we do on the basis of what we believe. Untested belief is not faith; it's just untested belief. Paul wrote to the people in Ephesus telling them that Christians are the product of God's artistry, "created in Christ Jesus to do good works, which God prepared in advance for us to do" (Ephesians 2:10). These "works" are works of faith. They are enactments that are based on a person stepping out to make complete what, up to the point at which he or she moves to action, are impressions, convictions, affirmations, imaginations, and inclinations—the beliefs that God wanted this or that to take place.

For a Christian, this is also wrapped up in two related considerations—love for God and obedience. Jesus indicated that if people loved Him, they would do what He said. God does not tempt people as Jesus was tempted in the wilderness. God does not say to people, "Throw yourself off this building and see if my angels keep you from smashing to bits."

Sometimes it's not because a person believes something specifically will result—that God has impressed upon them that it will. It's just that God wants them to do it. It's just that the Jesus who died for them, because He loves them, wants them to do it, and so if they love Him in return, they will move to action.

This enactment is integral to the process of sanctification. A person cannot grow in his her faith by simply camping out in the affirmations. It truly feels good to affirm the elements of one's doctrine, but what are their implications? If such and such is true, then what does that mean for how I'm living my life? What kinds of internal struggles do I go through just to move from the affirmations to the actions based on the affirmations?

It is a war. Paul wrote to the Christians in Rome and said, "For what I am doing, I do not understand; for I am not practicing what I would like to do, but I am doing the very thing I hate" (Romans 7:15). The process of engaging in actions that build up a person spiritually and for which that person does not condemn him- or herself is a struggle. I have worked with numerous people who did condemn themselves, and I have worked with numerous people who did not but should have. Paul was not talking about just living a life without regard to what God wanted; he was talking about living a life with the acute awareness of what God wants, but admitting that even in the very moment of doing something God would frown upon, hearing from God in a very faint reminder that He is there and has a standard and has a desire for that person, the person purposefully, willfully, and with complete awareness of what he or she is doing chooses to disregard God and go ahead with whatever it is that they know is not right.

For many these days, that is watching online pornography. It's like sitting at a campfire in the woods on a dark and cold night, watching the logs burn down to a brilliant orange and red in a shimmering bed of glowing coals, and reaching out to touch them even though everything in you says, "Don't do it." It's not that the person doesn't know he or she is going to get burned. It's not that the person doesn't know God wants better things for them. It's that they are entranced by the glow and there is some part of them that is determined to go ahead and reach for the embers anyway.

Paul wrote to the Christians in Philippi, and in describing what the process is like to be attempting to grow spiritually while at the same time caught up in this war within oneself, he said,

> just as you have always obeyed, not as in my presence only, but now much more in my absence, work out your salvation with fear and

trembling; for it is God who is at work in you, both to will and to work
for His good pleasure.

(Philippians 2:12–13)

Christians take solace in that they believe God is, indeed, actually at
work in them "to will" and "to work" for His good pleasure. So for the
psychotherapist working with someone of this religious faith, there
will likely be already some concept of the process of sanctification, that
is, this process of working out with fear and trembling. By the way,
"fear and trembling" is an idiomatic way in the Greek text of that time
to say, "with great care and concern," not that people are supposed to
cower in horror like those who quaked at Jonathan Edward's famous
sermon, "Sinners in the hands of an angry God." So the psychotherapist can engage the client along the lines that he or she is a work in
progress, and this idea is in keeping with the process view of psychotherapy itself ("two steps forward and one step back").

This idea of action being crucial to the quality of one's spiritual experience, I am sure, is present in most religious systems. The way to
such a country is through that country.

Relationship

The mark of a leader is that he or she has followers. This is a common
understanding, but the fact that someone has followers isn't enough.
People can feel forced to follow. Sometimes it's expedient in order to
get ahead in one's business. Sometimes the political situation requires
it. One can follow out of a sense of intimidation or obligation. The fact
that someone has followers does not mean that those followers have
personal interest, that there is something relevant and attractive such
that they just want to get into step with that person they find so com-
pelling. Both Jesus of Nazareth and Siddhārtha Gautama had this kind
of effect on people. They each had disciples who followed and were
taught a way of life, which was a way of doing things. They were not
just taught things to know, things to file away as religious facts like
dogmatic creeds. Rather, they were taught new ways to understand old
creeds. For instance, in the Sermon on the Mount, Jesus used a repeat-
ing formula: "You have seen that it is written . . ., but I say to you. . . ." It
was written not to commit murder, but anyone with anger in his heart
toward another is guilty of murder just as if he had physically killed.
The implication was to gain mastery over one's anger. It was written

that a person should not commit adultery, but Jesus indicated that if a person looked at another with lust, it was as good as sleeping with that other person. The implication was to gain mastery over one's passions. Buddha taught disciples to be mindful and to practice meditation by attention to breathing in and out, to one's postures (sitting, standing, walking, and lying down), which brings about the awareness of the presence of mind associated with the body (Batchelor, 2010).

Dietrich Bonhoeffer was a Lutheran pastor and theologian. He was a founding member of the confessing church in Germany, standing up in opposition to the Nazis in Germany during World War II. Following the biography of Bonhoeffer by Metaxas (2010), it was evident that something happened to Bonhoeffer when he visited the Abyssinian Baptist Church of Harlem while studying at Union Theological Seminary in New York. At the time, he was suffocating from the liberal theology he found at the university and at Protestant churches he visited until he went with a fellow seminarian to Harlem and came under the ministry of Adam Clayton Powell, Sr. There, Bonhoeffer discovered black spiritual music, the down-to-earth preaching of the gospel, and its application to the social issues facing black people in America. Through these influences, he became much more socially conscious, and he also seems to have undergone what some have called a conversion. He became less concerned with the dogmatics of theology and more concerned with the people in the churches where he anticipated serving. Although he had a chance to remain in America and be safe, he decided to return to Germany and to the people he felt compelled to serve. It was an experiment. It tested the theories of his friends that being in Germany was not safe, and at the same time it was an existential leap of faith for Bonhoeffer himself. Back in Germany, Bonhoeffer put his newly invigorated faith to work in supporting the confessing church and resisting the Nazis. He was imprisoned and eventually hanged because he had participated in a plot to assassinate Hitler.

It is here that perhaps it would be useful to realize that the person of the therapist, if there is any bond between therapist and client, will be relationally instrumental to the client. There would then be a relational influence not only between the client and current religious or spiritual leaders, but also between the client and the therapist. Therefore, the spirituality of the therapist is quite relevant.

But there is more to this than the historical influence of great religious leaders who started various religions and the connection between clients and their contemporary religious leaders. Jesus told His disciples that He would not leave them alone, that He would come to them, and the implication of scripture is that He would come to them in the person of the Holy Spirit. Thus, the Christian has a current, here-and-now relationship with God, with Jesus, through the presence of the Holy Spirit. Writing to the Christians in Galatia, Paul said, "If we live by the Spirit, let us also walk by the Spirit" (Galatians 5:25). Walking in step with the Spirit means being responsive, learning to discern the leading of the Spirit of God, and then stepping in right behind Him to affect one's actions in the world. Living that way follows the example given by Christ, because He said that He did nothing from His own initiative, but the words He spoke were the words given to Him by His Father and the things He did were the works He saw His Father in the process of doing, and in which He got into step with the Father to accomplish. So the model for the process of sanctification in the Christian life is relational and responsive to the person of the Holy Spirit.

Being spiritually sensitive, then, is not just a matter of enjoying the sunset or considering something mysterious and momentous. It is a matter of building a relationship with God through the Holy Spirit in which one learns to interact with a Being who cannot be seen, heard, tasted, touched, or smelled—God is not material. God is spirit, so one cannot perceive God with the usual senses, but God can be experienced, and one can learn to identify the touch points of one's contacting with God. The point here is that such a relationship is experiential in nature. When I talked with God and challenged him to make Himself known to me, it was an experiment that I walked out experientially, and I had an experience of God. I did not call it a behavioral experiment (I didn't know the concept then), but that is what it was. I had no idea what was going to happen, but I decided to stop pushing God away and take Him seriously. I would find out whether God existed for me.

Often, I ask people whether they can hear from God—what I mean is how sensitive they are to the ways in which God communicates to them. Everyone will have his or her own ways of hearing God. My wife is extremely sensitive in this way. She reminds me of a Biblical character who is frequently being told, "Get up. Go to this house and speak to these people." In her life, she frequently feels impressed to talk to someone, bring someone something, give away her belongings to others, help with food, etc.

Hearing from God in this way used to be considered a sign of psychoticism. Some people actually hear an audible voice just like a hallucination. The question of what is going on with that is important for the psychotherapist. Is he or she dealing with psychotic process or with spirituality—the process of relating to a divine Other? Is it just a matter of the client's phenomenal field, or is this something that transcends both client and therapist, catching them both up in the immanence of a transcendent Being—the ontic aspect of the pneumenal field? The person actually hears from God.

I have a confession to make. In a church that I served, I was experiencing quite a bit of conflict—the push for legalism that I wanted to resist, and, to be honest, my resentment and determination to win. So I began to preach messages directly related to the conflict. One day, a woman of low repute, someone thought to be rather limping in life, whose son was beginning to get into trouble in the community, stood up right in the middle of one of my sermons. I stopped, of course. What do you do with someone standing right in front of you and everyone looking at her? She said, "I don't know why, but I feel like God is telling me to say, 'How dare you use my Word in this way.'" And then she sat down. It cut me to the quick. I was immediately convicted and felt certain that I had been called out in front of my whole church by God Himself.

So the same question applies. Was this simply her phenomenal field and my phenomenal field interacting, or did the real God intercede in the ontic field of which we both belonged? I'm sure I know the answer to that. But the point in this context is that the woman responded and did not just sit there with that thought bouncing around inside her head. She acted.

NOTES

1. Obviously, action or behavior is an essential component of behavior therapy, but here it is assimilated to serve the cognitive process, thus, cognitive *behavioral* therapy.

PART III

Common Spiritual Issues Encountered in Therapy

These are narrative explorations. I know from experience that the issues in these stories are those that people encounter on a spiritual path. I know them because I have lived them and because I've been with people who have lived them. I am in these stories somewhere. So are the people I have known and worked with, but their names are changed, and some of the details of their lives are purposefully camouflaged so as to maintain confidentiality.

Maybe you know these stories because you've lived versions of them yourself, and so you might find *your*self in them somewhere. So much the better if you do, because all we have to offer the client is ourselves. Competence is knowing what and knowing how, which comes over time through experience and is also called wisdom.

This section is focused on Christian spirituality, because, as I've said before, it is what I know best. The reader from another religious perspective might be able to recognize the dynamics going on in his or her respective faith community. The psychotherapist working with clients from other religious traditions might have to study those religions more closely, but in many of the chapters ahead, I suspect there is a version of these issues in other faiths where both the process and the relationship involved in one's spirituality are relevant. What I hope to communicate in these chapters is what the Christian life is like so that psychotherapists can peer into it. For those who do not believe in God or do not follow Jesus, it may seem like foolishness (and the terminology at times might seem like a foreign language), but I would suggest that it is a "foolishness" they might want to learn about in order to be more culturally competent (so look up the terms). For those who regard themselves to be Christian, some of what I say in these chapters might seem off base or incomplete. That should be expected; how many different theological systems and stances exist? Just as this book is not a psychology of religion, nor a philosophy of religion, it is not a Christian theology of psychotherapy either.

CHAPTER 10

Living in the Present

There are really four dimensions, three which we call the three planes of Space, and a fourth, Time.

—H. G. Wells, 1895/2013, p. 2

For by one offering He has perfected for all time those who are sanctified.

—Hebrews 10:14

When I had been out of seminary for about 4 years, after I'd been part of the pastoral staff of a large church in Sacramento, California, I became pastor of a small Bible church in King City, California, at the southern end of the Salinas Valley. The town is situated between the Gabilan and Santa Lucia mountain ranges, bordering the Salinas Valley to the east and west. Under the valley itself runs an aquifer that provides ample water for irrigation, resulting in a very rich farmland where people grow vegetables. There is a garlic factory in King City, where garlic is dehydrated and turned into powder for sale as a seasoning. The whole place smells like garlic. It seems like it permeates one's clothing and gets absorbed through the skin.

One day I had Mark Platt, at that time the Associate Director for the Conservative Baptist Association of Northern California, come to visit. He met with me and my church, and he spoke in the services. I was dismayed at the time when he said, "You will have to be patient with Phil. He hasn't recovered from seminary yet." *What*, I wondered, did he mean by *that*?! I have since answered my own question. I was, as a saying had it in that day, so heavenly minded that I was no earthly good.

Living with a spiritualizing attitude is like having positional truth permeate one's clothing and absorbed through the pores of perception into one's version of reality. On the one hand, believing the truths that are stated positionally can bolster one's faith and be encouraging, but on the other, walking by faith can become a dodge, a way of not paying attention to what is going on around oneself and especially the nature of the relationships between oneself and others. It's a way of being so heavenly minded that one is no earthly good.

Positional truths are all those things in the Bible that are either (a) stated as if they had already happened when they haven't or (b) found in prepositional phrases in which a person is said to be "in" something or someone (i.e., Jesus). If the first, they have not yet taken place in anybody's experience (except in the mind of God). In terms of the language choice of the New Testament writers, it is a literary technique that puts emphasis on something. That something is stated in the past tense as if it had already happened, as if the writer is so sure of it that he used the past tense of the verb to describe it. But that puts the emphasis on something that is yet to take place. If the second, then one contemplates how one can be "in" something when one is obviously and physically not "in." The implication is that one is so closely identified *with* as to reside within the sphere of something or someone else, as in the case of being identified with Jesus. The way positional truth operates is that the believer is supposed to bank on something as if it were a current reality. What this does, however, is promote living in what some would call a fantasy. In fact, this fantasy for some people becomes a way of life that is an overspiritualized perspective. You could call it the positional attitude, and it's something that takes a person away from the present.

Consider three passages: one from Paul's letter to the church in Rome, another from his second letter to the church in Corinth, and the last from his letter to the church in Ephesus:

> And we know that God causes all things to work together for good to those who love God, to those who are called according to *His* purpose. For those whom He foreknew, He also predestined *to become* conformed to the image of His Son, so that He would be the firstborn among many brethren; and these whom He predestined, He also called; and these whom He called, He also justified; and these whom He justified, He also glorified.
>
> (Romans 8:28–30)

Therefore if anyone is in Christ, *he is* a new creature; the old things passed away; behold, new things have come.

(2 Corinthians 5:17)

But God, being rich in mercy, because of His great love with which He loved us, even when we were dead in our transgressions, made us alive together with Christ (by grace you have been saved), and raised us up with Him, and seated us with Him in the heavenly *places* in Christ Jesus.

(Ephesians 2:4–6)

In the passage quoted from Romans, notice that there is a tight chain of connected links starting from "For those whom He foreknew" and ending in "He also glorified." All the verbs (foreknew, predestined, called, justified, and glorified) are in the past tense.[1] However, if you consider what these words mean, that last one does not fit. It is possible that God foreknew people. He could have predestined them, then called them, then justified them, but if they are still alive and living in the world as human beings at the time of writing (as were the people to whom the letter was written), He had not yet glorified them. The certainty of coming glorification is encouraging, but if people live their daily lives thinking they have actually been glorified, or being so wrapped up in that coming glory that they lose touch with the daily grind, then that becomes a fantasy and a problem when it comes to getting along with others (because others are in the daily grind and often feel ground up by the behavior of the person in question).

There is another way of looking at this, and it harkens back to the difference between an ontic field and a phenomenal field. Positional truth can be actual in an ontological sense but not actual in a phenomenological sense. That is, *in* Christ, in a timeless now, in an infinite sense, in an ontic field that is "God-in," the justified could indeed be glorified now. Perhaps in a time warp, in a parallel dimension or membrane, in heaven, the justified are already glorified, but in the everyday world that is trapped in the sequence of actions that we know as "time," living people are yet to be glorified. In that world, there is misery, suffering, and brokenness that accompanies the sublime.

The Christian living in such a world is attempting to live by faith in an ontic field. Living by faith is not living by sight. There is a tendency to talk about such things as positional truth and to live by them so much that one becomes used to thinking in terms of things the way they might be in heaven but not in terms of the way they are in the world. The Christian who loses touch with that mixed reality, the one in which there is a calling and a commission to be in that world even while knowing that one's citizenship is in heaven, and who then lives in the fantasy, has become so heavenly minded that he or she is no earthly good. In the passage from 2 Corinthians, being "in" Christ has to be understood. How is one to understand this statement? Is it a matter of physical space or something else, like a perspective?

Everyone is situated. In any given room, one is here and another is over there. It provides difference of perspective, and people actually see the room differently. But what if one is in the room and another is outside the room? That is a larger difference in perspective and also a matter of physical space. It is in this sense of perspective that being "in" should be understood, and a lot of people understand this. Nicodemus made the distinction about this when Jesus told him that a person had to be born again, and Nicodemus said it was impossible because a person cannot, as it were, crawl back inside his or her mother's womb in order to experience a second birth.[2] So in 2 Corinthians, Paul was talking about an identification with (not a physical location inside)—belonging to, as when someone asks someone else whether they are "in" or "out" ("Are you in or out? With us or against us?"). If they belong, they call themselves by the name of the group, they have a group identity, and they are "in" the group. But this sentence doesn't just talk about being in some group of people who follow Jesus; it claims that if a person believes in Jesus, one is a "new creature" and that "old things passed away" and "new things have come." This is partly true now (or for the Corinthians when the letter was written to them) and partly not. When people are "born again," they are ontologically new; they become indwelt by God's Spirit, and so they are like Jesus in the sense that the hypostatic union consisted of two natures existing in one person. The person of Jesus was fully divine and fully human; that is the decision of the church and the theology of orthodox Christianity. In a similar way (not an exact way), the person who has believed in Jesus is in a hypostatic union as well; that person has the Holy Spirit and the human nature resident in his or her person. This is also the theology of orthodox Christianity. The problem is that the human being may have been redeemed from the penalty of sin but not from the presence of sin, and so the human being is still, in the present tense, in the current moment, a sinner. So not "all" of the old things have passed away, and not "all" of the new things have come. The person is, indeed, a new creature (and a perplexing one), but this person still does not measure up to the glory of God in daily living.

In the Ephesians passage, the terms "raised" and "seated" are in the past tense,[3] and in the context they are referring to the resurrection and the glorification of those who believe in Christ. So, here is an instance in which being "in" and having the language use be emphatic are both used to convey something that is certain but has not yet actually happened.

I like to pay attention to what is actually happening. In my practice of psychotherapy, I am interested in the process, and that includes both the process that the client is describing about his or her life and the process of the growing relationship between the two of us—the two people who are actually in the room together in the current moment.

I once worked with a family in California who homeschooled their five children. The father worked all day for an information technology company, and the mother taught the children, took them around to various activities in the community, and also attempted to build her own ministry of soliciting financial support from people to help needy children in other countries. He was overweight, but she was morbidly obese. She desperately wanted his love and attention, and she would weep from a deep wound that broke open during their courtship. He had abruptly one day announced to her that their engagement was off because he basically didn't like her, and he had gone back home to his parents, who lived in a faraway city. A few years later, he showed back up in her life to say that he believed God wanted him to marry her, but he admitted he had no affection for her. She accepted, concluding that if God wanted this, it would work out somehow. In their daily lives, he was cold and aloof. He volunteered at a local fire department, so often he would come home from his main job to put down his computer, change his clothes, and go out to the firehouse and clean equipment or otherwise talk with his friends there. When they attended church, they sat down to the front, and she would often be carried away with the hymns, singing loudly, raising her hands, and standing with her face to the cross and tears running down her cheeks. He sat with them, and he had friends in the church. He attended men's Bible studies and went on retreats, but he was not as demonstrative with what he believed as she was.

Through a series of circumstances, they decided to come to me for conjoint therapy, and at first his focus was on her incompetencies. What became apparent in our process together was his disconnection with his own feelings. In a popular way of putting things, he was all "in his head." There was no sympathetic vibration when she would weep in our sessions. It was actually as if he were bracing himself against it, and finally it came out that he regarded her to be broken and too emotionally excessive. The work in session was excruciating, because he was quiet and emotionally unavailable, and she was routinely breaking apart and bleeding emotionally all over the room. The old wound (he never loved me and he left me) was still a current reality.

This couple stopped coming after a while. He resented having to come in the first place, and she eventually wanted to stop because she found out that paying attention to what was actually happening in their relationship only made her feel bad, and she didn't want to feel bad. They continue in their daily lives, but when you talk with them, what you get are spiritualized statements about what wonderful things God is doing, about how all God's promises are reliable, and how good God is. What they do not address, or even seem to recognize, is their continuing relational pain, the way they lean on others for all kinds of support, and the fantasy that they are an exemplary couple and family.

Another couple was older when I met them. They lived in a comfortable home, and their children were grown. He was an intellectual involved in local politics, and he imagined himself to be a minister at large. He liked to collaborate with other men of vision and put together ministry-oriented projects that were always described as important and big deals and to which he would often give away his money and do so even to the neglect of his wife. Early on in their marriage, when he had wanted to be the pastor of a church, she had had her eyes on the practical necessities of raising young children. He felt at the time, and still feels today, that his wife was disobedient then and continues to be so, and that she disrespects his leadership as the man in the household. He believes she cost him an opportunity to become the pastor of a local church. Whereas he was living in the abstract and the ideal, she was attempting to live day-to-day in the mundane, even while both of them, to this day, still hold to a Christian faith. By the time I came to know them, she was attending a small but intense Christian community, and he was not really going to church anywhere. However, he loved to talk theology and would often pose provocative questions to see what I might say about those issues. No matter what I would say, he would then embark on long-winded theoretical monologues that would evolve into tangential and boring lectures, and she would zone out. If you stopped him long enough to ask her what was going on with her, she would say, "I'm just so tired of hearing him talk."

She wanted to do something that might better their relationship, because with the children gone, it was getting to be intolerable for her. Alone, she would complain about how horrible it was being married to him, but when in his company, she would go silent, withdraw, and wait on his speeches. She would not express her discontent unless prodded by me. They were going in two different directions—he into his schemes involving religious aspirations, and she into her spiritualizing about God even while she was also in touch from time to time with how miserable and lonely she felt in her marriage.

Are these easy pictures, polarities in stark relief? Are these people all wrong in regard to the things they desire from God or for which they praise God? Are they wrong for leaning on God for support? I do not believe so. God *is* faithful. The Holy Spirit *is* a comforter. I am sure that God is a refuge for them in the context of their relative pain and relational suffering, but the refusal to deal with "what is," and to avoid dealing with their brokenness by attempting to live in religious platitudes, with the illusion that they have it all together spiritually, is bad mental health and poor sanctification. God is glorified not by people hiding their hardness and unloving behavior toward others, but by transparency about what reality is in the current moment, and trust in Him, acknowledging that indeed we are broken, but indeed we are trusting, indeed we *are* broken, but indeed we are working on it.

WHAT TO DO

What can a psychotherapist do with such situations as these? In Part II of this book, I pointed to four elements present in most approaches to psychotherapy: therapeutic relationship, complex situational dynamics, the interpretation of experience, and the move to behavioral enactment.

In my approach with these couples, I affirmed that I was with them, and I used all the elements mentioned above. They knew that I shared their Christian faith. Some people don't know that, and I believe it is important with spiritual people to demonstrate one's awareness of spiritual matters and to show that they are meeting with a spiritual person who, even if he or she does not hold to their specific religious traditions, at least is sensitive to spiritual matters and respects the fact that they have spiritual commitments of faith.

The psychotherapist has to be able to be a real person about the issues that come up in therapy. So with these people (given their respective dashes into the fantasy of religion),[4] I felt it especially important
to be down-to-earth, to not indulge in the abstracts of theology, and to
talk about what actually goes on between them and between them and
me in session.

This involved observation or dialogue about the what and the how
of process. This was getting at how the people were making meaning
out of their experience. "What was it like for him to call off the engagement?" "What was it like for him to show up after no contact for so
long wanting to marry you . . ." ". . . and saying he felt it was God's will
for him to marry you?" "What is it like to see him give away money
for one religious scheme after another that doesn't seem to pan out
while you are struggling to save a penny here and there in order to
have enough to eat?" "What's it like to feel like your wife disrespects
you?" "What's it like to see her so demonstrative about Jesus?" "Have
you told him/her what you think? Would you do so now?" "Look at
each other when you speak." "What is it like to tell her/him that right
here?" "What are those tears about?" "What happens to you when
she cries like that?" "You seem surprised to learn that she feels like
this." I asked them to pay attention to what is going on between them
between sessions.

Therapy also involved consideration of the people with whom these
folks had built a relationship and the quality of those relationships.
The contact over time had resulted in a kind of relationship. "Who do
you think he is; what kind of person is he?" "How would you describe
your relationship with one another?" It also involved what God thinks
of how they are actually living with one another.

As I have indicated, therapy did not lead to what I would call a sat-
isfying result. Both these couples preferred the fantasy of religion to
the very difficult work of looking at the assumption they made early
in their relationship. For those who have practiced living in the fantasy
of religion, it is a constant necessity to call them down to the ground.
It is necessary to affirm that even though they believe in God and that
God has a heavenly purpose for their lives, it is still necessary to attend to the mundane things of life. The mundane and the sublime in
this regard is a false dichotomy, because people cannot be spiritually
mature without attending to the practical needs of those around them.
So how is a person doing that? What does it mean that God saved them
but then left them here in the world? What are they to do?

The same man who wrote to the Romans, the Corinthians, and the Ephesians about positional truths also addressed the practicalities of living in this world. He told the people in Thessaloniki that while he was with them, he had provided them with an example. He had worked and paid his way, and he told them that they were to follow his example:

> For you yourselves know how you ought to follow our example, because we did not act in an undisciplined manner among you, nor did we eat anyone's bread without paying for it, but with labor and hardship we kept working night and day so that we would not be a burden to any of you; not because we do not have the right to this, but in order to offer ourselves as a model for you, so that you would follow our example. For even when we were with you, we used to give you this order: if anyone is not willing to work, then he is not to eat, either. For we hear that some among you are leading an undisciplined life, doing no work at all, but acting like busybodies. Now such persons we command and exhort in the Lord Jesus Christ to work in quiet fashion and eat their own bread.
>
> (2 Thessalonians 3:7–12)

Now, the situation in that church was not just that some people were lazy. It was that they believed that the second coming of the Lord was so much at hand that to work would be superfluous. So they did not. They were caught in a spiritualizing attitude and the fantasy of religion. Paul told them to get real. He told them to follow his example, work, pay their way, and eat their own food. That is pretty down-to-earth. It is also an example of the fact that a dichotomy between the mundane and the sublime in such spiritual matters is a false dichotomy.

So what can a psychotherapist do with a client who is caught in the spiritualizing attitude and the fantasy of religion? Bring people back to the real world. It won't be a necessary violence against them as spiritual beings. You don't have to challenge their beliefs. All you have to do is talk about their daily responsibilities to themselves and those around them, to their families, to their partners in life, and so forth. You can do that by asking our own legitimate questions ("How do you put together loving your wife by neglecting your wife?"). I once had a client who was convinced that God wanted him to leave his current wife and establish a marriage with someone he regarded to be more spiritual. I asked him, "How do you accomplish God's will by breaking God's will?"

NOTES

1. ους δε προώρισεν, τούτους και εκάλεσεν· και οὓς εκάλεσεν, τούτους και εδικαίωσεν· οὓς δε εδικαίωσεν, τούτους και εδόξασεν (SBL Greek New Testament).
2. He understood that being "in" could not be a matter of one person being physically inside of another, even though he did not quite understand what Jesus was saying to him.
3. As in the Romans passage quoted earlier, they are in the aorist indicative, meaning both the simplest way of expressing an idea and locating it in the past with regard to time.
4. Again, this is not to say that religion is a fantasy, but to say that often people fantasize about religion.

CHAPTER 11

The Issue of Truth

What is truth?

—Pontius Pilate, John 18:38

I am the way, the truth, and the life.

—Jesus of Nazareth, John 14:6

Gant (1994) made an astounding assertion. He said that there resides at the core of any formulation of a normative psychotherapy a set of ideological assumptions that are taken as factual givens regarding what is to be understood as ultimate reality or "truth" in the world. "These core ideological assumptions can be seen to be Utopian truth-claims because they not only make specific assertions about how the world in reality is, but also how it, in the idyllic, can or ought to be" (p. 147). Gant offered an alternative to what he regarded as false truth assumptions underlying psychotherapy by offering the face-to-face encounter (Levinas, 1969) in which the psychotherapist breaks with the narcissistic assumptions in the imagery of order—any legislation or codification of imperatives—in order to simply dwell with the other person in the current moment of immediate contact.

He was dealing with an old problem and one that goes back at least to Biblical times. Consequently, there are many philosophical discussions of the rhetorical question Pilate posed to Jesus when he had Him in court, but Pilate was not actually looking for a philosophical debate, much less an actual answer. He was making a cynical statement.

The most common way of looking at truth is to say that it is what corresponds to the actual facts, to reality. For some, truth is that which fits best within a system of facts that cohere with one another; thus, truth is contextual. Related to the contextual idea is the one that claims that truth is constructed socially and so is relative to the social group that agrees to it. Still others would say that whatever works is true, but that we can't really be sure if something is ultimately true; we can just be sure that something doesn't work and is ultimately false.

When it comes to the issue of truth, religious people can be quite stubborn. The Bible, some would say, is inspired and infallible, meaning that it contains truth revealed by God and is, therefore, true in and of itself. Because it is true, it is trustworthy. People can put their trust in what the Bible says because it accords with fact, best fits the facts of history and of science, and is quite practical. Some have said that they do not need any books of science or philosophy because they have the Bible and that's all they need. I once served with a pastor who believed that the Bible had all a person needed in order to understand human nature. I think that while that is true in the large scheme of things, it is not true in the details. The Bible is no more a manual on psychology or psychotherapy than it is one on plumbing or electrical circuitry.

Related to the idea of truth is the polarity of right and wrong. Something is right if it is true, and something is wrong if it is not true. Thus, even though people used to believe that the earth was flat, that idea is not true, and they were wrong. It is an interesting phenomenon that people who believe in the Bible also believe that they are right about what the Bible means by what it says. The Bible is revealed truth. Thus, it is in itself true, and they are correct in their understanding of the Bible; so, they are right.

I came to maturity as a Christian while belonging to the Conservative Baptist Association of America (CBA). That is a pretty conservative group theologically, and when I went to one of their seminaries, I had to learn the history of the CBA. In the late 1940s, the American Baptist Association was sending out missionaries who could not in good conscience say they believed in the deity of Christ (and other breaches of orthodox theology), and the missionary society charged with sending them out began to have fits. A group was formed to attend to the situation, and the Conservative Baptist Foreign Missionary Society came into being. It started out of the desire to stand up for the truth, to differentiate from error, and to make sure that people being sent out as missionaries would be true themselves. Eventually, these people broke with the parent association and formed their own group, and they called it the Conservative Baptist Association of America. It came into being through conflict and the willingness to stand up and fight for what people believed to be true.

That is admirable, but in my experience of this group, it consisted of people who were bent on uncovering error, identifying it, and purging it. This often became identifying the people who were in error and purging them. I have also met people in the Southern Baptist Convention who believe it is their calling from God to tell people where they are wrong. Now, in identifying these groups I am not calling them out as being inherently bad. I am just telling things like they have been in my own attempt to be true. I also believe that there is a place for identifying error and setting crooked things straight, for rightly dividing the word of truth. So in the things of this chapter, balance is important.

There is a truth. Archer, Collier, and Porpora (2004) claimed that people commit an epistemic fallacy when they allow epistemology to completely swallow up ontology. Ontological realism claims the ontological existence of reality quite apart from anyone's beliefs about it. Following from that, something might be true in the sense that it belongs to reality even if people are mistaken about it, or even if they completely ignore it. They assert that the existence of God is a perfect case in point, making a distinction between what they call the transitive dimension, which is what people believe or their knowledge claims about what exists, and the intransitive dimension, which is the way the world is apart from our beliefs and assertions about it. These would also correspond to the phenomenal (transitive) field and the ontic (intransitive) field. This position is also called critical realism. N. T. Wright referred to this concept saying that he proposed a form of critical realism as a

> way of describing the process of "knowing" that acknowledges the reality of the thing known, as something other than the knower (hence "realism"), while fully acknowledging that the only access we have to this reality lies along the spiralling path of appropriate dialogue or conversation between the knower and the thing known (hence "critical").
>
> (p. 35)

In that way, one is a tad more humble about what the Bible actually means by what it says. God is inscrutable and unknowable but for revelation and the guiding work of the Holy Spirit. Thus, in dialogue with the Holy Spirit focused upon the Bible, the word of God, people should be able to come to a fairly consistent understanding of what it means, and if one takes a large view, that is what has happened over the centuries. If, however, you get into the minutia of various minor issues, then there emerge differences, and when people who care a lot about the accuracy of what they are doing in their Christian lives start talking about those differences, they usually don't take a reserved and tolerant approach. At least, people in the CBA did not.

I remember going to the ordination council of the man under whose ministry in children's work I interned while in seminary. There were a few questions about the big issues. But the process was also amply seasoned with esoteric questions that left me breathless at the time. (Is *that* what I had to look forward to?) I remember seeing men laugh because someone had asked something about ethical monism and there was humor in wondering how they would have answered, but there was also glee in recognizing an admirable stumper. After some time, I realized that the culture of the organization was one of contending for the truth, and if one was not searching for error to refute, one might not be doing his or her job. I grew tired of the conflict. When people are playing with the concept of truth, as if it were a game, or trying to destroy one another by catching them in a factual error, then the value of truth fades.

In psychotherapy, there are truths, matters of the ontic field that make a difference. A person either did or did not sexually molest his daughter. A person either did or did not start using a drug of choice again. A person either does or does not hallucinate. However, there are many more occasions in which it's a matter of the subjective experience and meaning making of the individual client. In such cases, it's more what a person imagines might happen because he molested his daughter, what a person knows about the influences that led up to his relapse, or what it's like to have to wade through the chorus of voices inside one's head in order to sort out what one set—the set the world says are real—have to say.

Many couples end up fighting about the situation in life that they share with each other. Imagine two people standing on opposite corners at an intersection. In the intersection, a car accident takes place, and a policeman asks each of them what happened. The first person says that the green car ran into the red car. When the officer asks the second person the same question, that one says that the red car ran into the green car. They hear one another from across the intersection, and they start arguing about which one of them was right. They haul out all their respective proofs. There is conflict. At that level, one of them might win the argument, but the other would either not think much of the other or not think much of him- or herself, having lost touch with his or her own respective version of reality. What we experience is what we know; it's our reality, and it's our truth. When a client comes for therapy, all he or she has is his or her truth.

When Christians come for therapy, they sometimes mix up their relative truths for The Absolute Truth, and then what complicates the therapeutic situation even more is that the psychotherapist has his or her own assumptions (Gant, 1994). Because Christians are also often steeped in the battle for religious truth, it is sometimes difficult to deal with this idea of relative truth. Sometimes religious institutional dogma, church policy, or pastoral preference is presented as absolute truth.

When I started working with one couple, it was for discontent between them. The husband was confused. He wondered if his wife had a strong will that defied his leadership in the family, and the suspicion of such a thing had begun after an unfortunate situation. In a rather successful church ministry in the Pacific Northwest, he was the worship leader. They had two young children. The pastor of the church expected all his staff to sit down front, along the first row. That was to include their wives and children. He wanted them all to look good. However, the children of the couple in question were a bit active, and so the worship leader's wife chose to sit a couple of rows back so as not to be a distraction. The pastor told the worship leader to instruct her to sit up front. The husband and wife discussed it, and she did not sit up front because she felt she needed to take care of the needs of her children as well, and he supported her in that decision. The pastor ended up dismissing the worship leader because, as he put it, the man did not show leadership in his own family and his wife had a rebellious spirit.

What was the truth of that situation, and what was the truth about this husband and wife? Was she rebellious? Was he a poor leader? She was certainly achievement-oriented and driven. She had an excellent job with responsibility, leading a team of colleagues. He was easygoing and more in touch with his emotions. He was sensitive.

He was demonstrably more spiritual than she was, and his sensitivity and spirituality made him an excellent worship leader. This situation was compounded by potentially three versions of reality: the husband, the wife, and the pastor. The pastor had authority in the church to advance his truth, and he did so. Since the worship leader was loved, the pastor called a church meeting to explain to the congregation why he had to fire the worship leader; he told them that the man's wife had been defiant of church leadership and unrepentant, and that the man himself lacked the leadership in his home (therefore failing to match the qualifications of an elder to be able to rule his own household). This was a way of managing a difficult situation, but it traumatized the couple, who felt betrayed and abused by the pastor. So what was the truth of that part of the overall situation? Was the pastor guilty of spiritual abuse (see Chapter 16)? Was the church a performance-based system or a grace-based system? What was the truth of the situation?

I chose to work with the couple following a largely dialogical approach. Accordingly, I shared my own curiosities as they arose—curiosity about how the husband and the wife experienced being in the situation, what they thought of the demands of the pastor, how they viewed each other, and what their values and priorities were as a couple and as parents. Through the dialogue, I investigated how each of them made sense of what had happened, identifying the confusion and suspicion that had been created in the husband's mind based on the pastor's version of reality made public in such a dramatic fashion.

A considerable degree of anger emerged from this process for both of them. The wife felt that there had not been an attempt to see her as a full human being, to appreciate her worth as someone with strengths, and to understand the needs of her family. She especially did not like being vilified and publicly denounced in the actions taken by their church. She was bitter and took the position of "having no use" for the people in that church. She felt betrayed by them. The husband felt disappointed that he had to leave the ministry that he loved so much. They both felt used by a pastor with a high profile in the community, someone who, on top of everything, seemed to be going for the right "look." That was disappointing to them.

This case brings to mind the issue of clients who come for therapy who happen to be what I call "professional Christians." I used to be one.

These are people who make their living doing what other Christians are supposed to be doing without getting paid for it. That is, perhaps, a crude way of putting it, but being in Christian ministry is a difficult life because of the two hats people have to wear. On the one hand, they are attempting to live and to grow like any other Christian, but on the other hand, they have to serve the church, lead in matters of ministry development, provide pastoral care for the people, and compete with polished religious leaders that are in the media. They have to look as if they have it all together, even if they don't. Not only do the ministers have to appear competent and exemplary, but their families also have to play their parts. The spouses are often considered co-ministers or oversee areas of church life all on their own. The children of these people are always being watched, and they have to measure up as well. Everyone has to look good. These people cannot afford to go through the normal growing pains of the Christian life, because they are getting paid to be perfect. While a certain amount of imperfection can be tolerated, it must look like a passing phase or a growth spurt and cannot become too distracting.

So truth also points to authenticity. A man is being true to himself if he says and does what accords with his values; a woman is true if her actions are consistent with her words. Although Jesus valued authenticity, advising people to simply say yes if they meant yes or no if they meant no, real authenticity is often difficult to come by in the church. To be authentic means that a person is on the outside like he or she knows him- or herself to be on the inside. Another word for this is transparency. What you see and hear from me is who I am. An authentic person is also coherent in regard to the match between his or her nonverbal and verbal discourse. That is, what you do does not give the lie to what you say. This also extends to intentional and conscious actions as well as unintended behaviors outside of one's awareness. If someone is scowling at you, but saying how pleased he or she is to see you, that does not compute. It is incoherent. Since we tend to read the nonverbal discourse as primary context, we usually make the verbal discourse either in sync or out of sync with the nonverbal, privileging the nonverbal as the more authentic.

Professional Christians have a difficult time being authentic with the people they serve in churches. I had one client, a female pastor who had been ministering in the same church for several years. She struggled with a codependent relational style in which she was over-extending herself taking care of others. She was leading in prayer meetings, Sunday School, preaching, visiting the sick, participating in association meetings, she was early to open the church, and she often baked food for the potlucks and tried to be an exemplary mother and wife. Her family regarded her ministry as her thing. They were not as invested in the church as she was. She wore herself out and became depressed. What was the truth of that situation? Did God really require all that from her? What was necessary?

WHAT TO DO

Sometimes, a psychotherapist has the opportunity to work with a religious system such as a church by working directly with its leadership. At other times, a systemic approach is what is needed, but it is not possible. Imagine the potential of obtaining the attention of the pastor who let go of his worship leader and dealing with his philosophy of ministry, his sense of needing to look good, and his performance-based approach in general. Is this simply organizational development, or is it a systemic approach to psychotherapy? If the field is all things having effect, if the situation is complex, then intervening in work with a specific client at the level of the field or system would still be considered psychotherapy. Multisystemic psychotherapy is a highly successful way, for instance, of working with juvenile offenders. It extends to situations where the truth is not so much a matter of one individual being "out of fellowship," as it is of the fellowship itself being out of order.

In the case of the worn-out pastor, I suggested that we try some experiments. First, I asked her to consider what she might do to be nice to herself, to take care of herself as if she were taking care of someone else. If someone else were worn out, what would she suggest for them? She suggested going to the spa. So I asked her to make space in her week, to let go of something in order to give herself some time in the spa. As it turned out, she had some vacation time coming, so rather than let go of some ministry responsibility, she let go of some domestic responsibility, informed her husband and children that they were on their own for a while, and then she booked herself into the local spa. She got a massage, and it felt wonderful to feel the tension in her body release. When we got together again and processed her experience, she said that she realized she had to be more "selfish," but she meant selfish in the sense of loving oneself. Jesus called people to love others "as" (i.e., in the same way) they loved themselves. She realized that she could not effectively love others unless she understood at an experiential level how to love herself. She further realized that she had just begun to learn how to do this and balance the other obligations that she felt.

The tendency in learning something new is to learn it in the head as a concept and then to live in the fantasy that one has actually made it a part of the procedural memory of one's life. That second part takes time and repeated experiment, putting into action and learning from experience in a holistic fashion that impacts the entire person and makes a lasting and memorable difference. Pastors routinely deal in "truths." They uncover them in scripture through exegesis, and they organize them into sermons and teaching outlines. When I was going through seminary, my experience was that of being challenged with new ideas and new information on a daily basis. None of it was presented as optional, as passing and irrelevant. All of it was given as crucial, as Biblical, and therefore as authoritative. Yes, I did not have the time to assimilate it all. Therefore, my seminary experience taught me to deal in truth, but not to assimilate truth and change my life so that I was living according to all the truth that I was being exposed to.

And here is a danger for professional Christians who deal in truth all the time and are responsible to deliver truths on a weekly basis. Scripture claims, "For as the rain and the snow come down from heaven, and do not return there without watering the earth," making the earth bear and sprout, furnishing seed to the sower and bread to the eater, "so will My word be which goes forth from My mouth; it will not return to Me empty, without accomplishing what I desire, and without succeeding in the matter for which I sent it" (Isaiah 55:10–11). One is either impacted by the word of God, allowing it to have an effect, or one braces oneself against it in order to delay, to dilute, to avoid, or to use it for other purposes. That leads to a hardening of the heart, and in terms of spirituality as relationship, it is a contact interruption between oneself and God. Professional Christians run the risk of becoming hardened and numb to God by their very work of handling His word in order to serve Him in the church. They have to learn to be selfish about their own spiritual lives, and so working with a professional Christian in psychotherapy can often be about what is needed as a priority to make sure that the professional Christian has an experiential relationship with God that is basic about how God loves them too and wants rest and peace for them too. The professional Christian is often too busy thinking about how to impart some decisive truth that will make a difference in the lives of others that he or she cannot appreciate the truth of God as it applies to themselves.

CHAPTER 12

Faith and Uncertainty

While certainty is beyond our reach, meaning—something far more valuable—is not. Meaning derives from a right relationship with God, based not on certainty and conformity, but on risk and commitment.

—Daniel Taylor, 1992, p. 94

Faith is often caricatured by people who regard religion to be an unsupportable shot in the dark, a cry for help against all reason for simple-minded people terrorized by superstition, the fear of spirits, or the demands of a punitive divine task master. If they consider faith as being something common to an authentic life, because in a sense one has to believe everything will be okay to take a leap in the dark, then they still regard religious faith to be something essentially different. Religious faith for some is irrational, whereas secular faith (I believe our government officials will act morally, I believe the economy will turn around, I believe I'll be able to have another Christmas with my family, I believe what I'm seeing right now is actually there in some form or another, etc.) has a reason. Merleau-Ponty used the term perceptual faith to refer to the belief and trust in one's perceptions, that they actually linked one up with the world that exists. He was not a skeptic who mistrusted and discounted everything, claiming there was nothing we could know because in some Cartesian-Kantian fashion we were cut off from things as they are and simply have to re-present them to ourselves in our minds (Hass, 2008). He claimed that "the radical skeptic borrows something from our experience, absolutizes it, then in his quest for complete certainty, he uses it to terrorize our experience of 'inherence in the world,'" an experience that Merleau-Ponty (1968; cf. Flynn, 2004, np), in *The Visible and the Invisible*, calls "perceptual faith." Inherence in the world means that we are situated, and Merleau-Ponty believed that we interact synergistically with the world through our lived bodies so as to jointly construct our perceptions. Although he would not have put it this way, such an outlook is a satisfactory ground for a critical realist perspective on life.

Just as there is reason to believe in something one perceives with the senses, there are reasons to believe in something one perceives by one's spirit. Spirit is the medium of communication with God, and spirit is the medium for perceiving existential meaning in this world. In Chapter 8 of Paul's letter to the Romans, it says that God's Holy Spirit testifies with a person's spirit that that person belongs to God. That is something one knows inside, and it is an experience.

When I was in the Navy as a neuropsychiatric technician, during the Vietnam War, I used to come home on occasion on the weekends. When I was at home, I would often argue with my mother, trying to catch her in an inconsistency and refute her faith in God. She had become a Christian and quit drinking. That part was good, but the Christian part just seemed so ripe for the picking because I thought it was nonsense. So she would often sit down with a big bowl of salad, and I would sit down across from her in the family room. Many times, Johnny Carson and the Tonight Show was on, and so we carried on our arguments in between laughter. But it was really no laughing matter. I recall one time I backed her into a corner, feeling pretty smug, and she responded, "Just leave me alone. I know what I believe." The sense I got of that is not that she had every argument down to refute naysayers, because I had successfully stymied her. However, in the face of no adequate retort or refutation of my point, she simply relied on her experience of God.

About a year later, I found myself talking to God. I won't get into what got me to that point, but at that point I had arrived. Not that I really believed. Not that I disbelieved. I said to Him, "If you are real, make yourself known to me." I told God that on my part, I would read a Phillip's translation of the New Testament that someone had given me. As I started to read, what I was reading started making sense. Whereas before that time I had laughed at the lyrics in hymns and found the Bible to be unfathomable, now, at that time, it seemed clear.

It more than made sense. I found myself enthralled, as if I were reading the best book ever written, and here is the significance of the experience: I believe God made Himself known to me. I have no other explanation for why it suddenly made perfect sense and for why it seemed to touch me deeply. This was not simply a cognitive idea that registered in my head, as if I were studying for a test. This was like contact with a person—someone putting two and two together for me in such a way that was astounding me over and over again—repeatedly and consistently. I read from Matthew all the way through Revelation. Somewhere in the gospel of John I asked Jesus to be my savior.

Through the course of events several months later, I began to feel as if I should go into full-time Christian ministry. I had been reading a book titled *The Late Great Planet Earth*, in which the author, Hal Lindsey (1970), laid out all the reasons why Jesus would be coming back imminently. As I asked God about full-time ministry, I also asked my minister. He told me that I would have to complete an undergraduate degree (at that point I had nothing since I had gone into the Navy right out of high school), and then finish seminary. All of that would take about 7 years. I felt God wanted me to do that, but I had to ask Him why, because I was certain that Jesus would be coming back before I would have time to finish seminary. All of that was about 44 years ago, and to tell you the truth, I'm not really certain when Jesus is coming back. Do I believe He *is* coming back? Yes. Do I know when? No.

Just so, there are many things in the Christian life that believers can be sure of, and there are quite a few about which, if they are honest, they cannot. That is the point of the quote from Daniel Taylor above. To be certain is to have confidence in what one believes, but a certainty itself is something somewhat different. A certainty is not a matter of belief, not even of belief that has its reasons. A certainty is a fact that is definitely and reliably true. It is something known to be so. A certainty is an artifact of the ontic field, but being certain is an experience in one's phenomenal field. The first says something is, and the second says one has strong faith that something is. Certainty can also be a state of mind based on feeling certain; thus, the people who persecuted Galileo around his hypothesis that the earth circled the sun rather than the sun circling the earth had certainty regarding their theory. However, since it was built upon a feature of the phenomenal field, it had no ontic standing. It was their truth, but it was not God's truth.

Doubt does not have to indicate the failure of faith or losing one's faith. It can indicate a ripeness for growth. If a person never doubted, he or she would never test his or her faith and find out if God were faithful and true (Guinness, 1976). Certainty in the face of untested faith is religious fantasy.

When I went to seminary, I was taught that the Roman Catholic church was heretical, that basically it was a religious deception, and that people who belonged to Catholicism were wrong—not just in error about a few things, but basically, ontologically, totally wrong. You might as well have said they were going to hell. So since I graduated from that seminary, when I began pastoring a small Bible church in King City, California, a missionary came through looking to drum up support for what he was trying to do, and I had him speak in the service. He presented me with his magnum opus, which was a theological refutation of Roman Catholicism. At the time I received it with appreciation, certain that he was correct. Then, one of the members of my church came to me and announced that she and her husband were returning to the Catholic church in town. I can remember to this day the two of us, who had been good friends up to that moment, shouting at one another across my desk, me wondering how she could return to the vomit she had escaped, etc., etc., and she basically telling me in colorful language to fly a kite. I think God must have been laughing His head off. And more so years later when I married someone who had converted from the Assemblies of God to Roman Catholicism and had taken me on a tour of the Vatican, including the crypts of the Popes, where I experienced a profound spiritual reverence, as if angels were standing right there, when people filed by the crypt of Pope John Paul II. I have since spoken with many profoundly spiritual and inspiring Roman Catholics whose faith in Jesus is every bit as vital as that of any Protestant I have known. Live and learn.

Not to have certainty can be troubling. We do not know the details of what comes next one day after another. We cannot be sure that our loved ones will share our faith. We cannot be certain that they will live long lives and prosper. My youngest brother was killed suddenly in an auto accident right after playing a concert at Disney World in Florida. He had a wife and young son. How do such things fit into the broad scope of God's wonderful plan for someone's life? There are just too many things that don't make sense and leave us wondering. We are finite and cannot tell the end from the beginning.

WHAT TO DO

A psychotherapist dealing with the anxiety of uncertainty with a person of faith does not have to search under rocks for some kind of unique spiritual intervention. People are whole beings, and so our spirituality is not compartmentalized and separate from the other aspects of our being. Thus, what the therapist would do in general for anxiety might suffice nicely when someone is perplexed, because they worry in the face of uncertainty about spiritually relevant issues. Often the client can put together what escapes the therapist.

For instance, one thing the therapist can do is normalize the experience. This is especially important if the person belongs to a faith community in which the public face on the spiritual life is one in which people have it all together, in which faith trumps uncertainty. In that kind of context, a person who is not certain is a person who lacks sufficient faith, a person who is not a "good" Christian. Since a simple assertion like "There is no such thing as certainty" might be met with resistance, the therapist might ask the client to engage in an experiment. Have the client follow the life of the prophet Elijah and write down all the instances where it looked like he was certain and all the instances where it looked like he was uncertain. Have him or her do the same for the man named Abram or Abraham in the book of Genesis. Have him or her do the same for the man named Peter in the New Testament, including where Peter is mentioned in the book of Acts. Ask whether any of these people were always certain. When it seems that they were certain, of what were they certain? Was their certitude supported by events, that is, was it proven?

Faith is the assurance of things hoped for and the evidence of things unseen, and faith is made complete in action. It is not assent alone, as in saying one believes *that* such and such is true. It must be made complete by what people do. It is what people do, on the basis of what they hold to be true, that can be described as faith.

In one church in Portland, Oregon, Imago Dei Community, their custom at one point was for people to come down front for communion, or to celebrate the Lord's Supper. This is where the believer takes a piece of bread and drinks a small amount of red wine or grape juice as an enacted remembrance of Jesus's death. In order to do this in this particular church, however, people would have to get up in no particular order and go down front. The rows were not all excused one after another as in some churches; so there was no social pressure to do it in order to just fit in. If a person went down front, it was a sign that he or she believed in what the bread and the wine/juice symbolized: Christ's body broken and His blood spilled, his life poured out as a propitiation for the sins of all mankind. It was a public profession of one's faith, and as such it was an act of faith in publicly identifying oneself with Christ. Thus, faith was made more certain in action. Action like that, based on what one believes, produces experience that is confirmatory.

No Christian living today walked with Jesus in Palestine, let alone perceived his pierced and broken body laid in the tomb or raised again a few days later. No one has certainty about that in the sense of an unquestionable artifact of the ontic field. It either did or did not happen. If it did not happen just as it was reported to have happened in the gospels, then it didn't happen at all, for that story is the asser-tion. There may have been a mere human who was named Jesus, and perhaps he lived and died at the hands of the Romans, but maybe he was married and had children, and maybe Mary Magdalene was his wife, etc., etc. These stand for a number of other alternatives that suggest that we simply cannot know for certain what actually happened—that Jesus was probably just another human being blown out of proportion over the millennia and fashioned by the needs of true believers.

Some people are afraid to think to all corners of the box in which they reside, and the psychotherapist can help them risk finding out what is there for them. This is not the same thing as intentionally chal-lenging the tenets of faith and trying to persuade a person out of their religion. If the phenomenological method of working with a client is to any extent the way in which a therapist works with his or her clients, then showing the client to the client can be helpful. If there is untested faith in one of those corners, the client might know what to do with that even if the therapist does not. If it is an appearing for the thera-pist, it can become a showing to the client, but the therapist must be very careful here not to inflict his or her own lack of faith (thus issues of religious countertransference) on the client, as if working out the therapist's unfinished spiritual business using the client as a tool of opportunity. It is strengthening to faith to consider challenges to faith, to work through doubt in the face of uncertainty, and psychotherapists working with people of faith can serve them by working the edge be-tween faith and uncertainty.

In my practice, one young woman began coming for a number of issues. She suffered from obsessive and compulsive anxieties. She was the longtime mistress of an older man and played second to his wife. She'd been abused as a child, and she had divorced from a very abusive and controlling husband. In the course of our work with one another, I asked her whether she believed in God, because she frequently referred to "the man upstairs." She would typically say that she did believe in God, but she would also assert that she wasn't a church-going type. One day while driving her car, she happened to turn on a Christian program from the Midwest United States, and the man was talking about forgiveness and how when someone has abused a person, that person needs to forgive them.

> She said, "He said, 'you don't want to,' and I said, 'Damn straight!'"
> She said, "He said, 'they don't deserve it,' and I yelled back, 'You're right about that!'"
> She said, "He said, 'they didn't ask you for it,' and I said, 'He wouldn't even think of it.'"

But she said that the man on the radio also told her it was the right thing to do and it would set her free. There was something about that radio broadcast that got her attention, and she said that from that day on she would listen to the broadcast. Somewhere along the line, she started hearing from God, in soft impressions, saying that she needed to do this or that act of kindness toward those who had mistreated her, and she began arguing with God, talking back to Him. She said that He just gently kept stating she should take a shawl to this one or bake something for that one. And so, eventually, she started doing those things. That is how she slid into a conversational relationship with God.

Gradually she also started talking with Him about her compulsions and anxieties. At the time of this writing, she is still battling them, but also at this point she is taking them to God for Him to deal with, and it's resulting in more peace. She has confidence in Him. She trusts God. Is she certain? She is certain there is something going on, and she believes she is in touch with God. Is God or anything close to theology a certainty for her? No.

My role in this process was to be transparent myself with my understanding of God whenever she would bring God up in the course of our dialogue. At times, I had also talked about forgiveness and having a conversational relationship with God, but these were things that seemed to roll off her, and I let them go. However, when this new dynamic entered the process, I supported it and got into step with it.

This is an example of how God, present and at work in the ontic field, becomes an experience for people in their phenomenal fields. This is an immanence of transcendence that cuts across both the ontic and phenomenal fields in the person of God who is both transcendent and immanent. In terms of psychotherapeutic outcomes, God's providential intercession with people is an extra-therapeutic factor—one of those things that accounts for about 40% of the outcomes in psychotherapy. I could not have orchestrated or brought about the experience and change my client experienced. This kind of thing is something only God can institute. However, it is something in which the psychotherapist can participate.

Contact with God, like the figure of God Himself, is similar to James Stewart's Pooka friend, Harvey, in the movie of the same name. He is outrageous, nobody else can see him, but he has the power to stop time. Stewart carries on conversations with Harvey and tries to introduce him to the people he meets. Harvey, in that film, is certainly a feature of Stewart's phenomenal field, but is he actually present in the ontic field? That is the enigma posed in the film, and with regard to the person of God, that is the uncertainty present in the lives of both client and therapist.

CHAPTER 13

Communal Belonging

We do not want churches because they will teach us to quarrel about God.

—Chief Joseph, Nez Perce, in Nerburn, 1999, p. 32

In Bermuda, up on a hill in the town of St. Georges, there stands a monument to the sentiment expressed by Chief Joseph. It is called "The Unfinished Church." St. Peter's Anglican church was begun in the early 1600s when the world heritage site of St. Georges was founded by the British. In the 1800s, a hurricane damaged St. Peter's extensively, and its members decided to build a new church. They chose a hilltop about a 15-minute walk up the hill from where the original church stood. They began building in a Gothic style, with tall stone towers and huge windows. But the church members began to argue about various things, and some began to think that spending money to repair the original church was a better idea than completing the new one. The church ground to a halt in conflict, and the builders of the new church could never get it together enough to complete their work. The old church was indeed repaired, and today it is a beautiful historical site with part of it dating back to the 1600s. The "Unfinished Church" has become a landmark. Its roof is gone, and there is no glass in the windows. The floor is grass. It is a spectacle, a tourist destination. For anybody who knows anything about what church life is like, it is also a clear indicator of what can happen when things get out of control in a faith community. The Biblical concept of the church, that is, the model of how it's supposed to work, is not, unfortunately, how it often does work—at least not obviously so.

Communal belonging is not simply a matter of communal living, nor of communal gathering. Sometimes people rub shoulders with one another, but they clearly do not belong to one another.

In May of 1970, four students were shot dead on the campus of Kent State University by the Ohio National Guard. At that time, I had just moved into a house atop a mountain where Skyline Boulevard skirted the Redwood Regional Park in the Oakland Hills. Several students attending the University of California at Berkeley were also living there. We used to have our meals together in the evenings, and it felt like a commune. It wasn't really a commune, because we each definitely had our own lives, but we each paid rent for our respective rooms, and we often sat together in the living room discussing current events. These students in turn had their friends over to the house, because they were involved in student protest organizing in connection with the Vietnam War. The shooting at Kent State sent them all into a furor. At that time I had just gotten out of the Navy, having taken care of combat veterans returning from field operations in which they had developed some kind of psychological or neurological disorder. I was not a student; I was working at a local psychiatric hospital, but I was accepted in the house. I was not part of the student organizing, however. I was clearly not one of them, but with regard to the house, I was welcome.

The way it is in the church is that people can be living together in the sense that they all come on Sunday, they may give their offerings, and they may sing the songs and even help out in the Sunday School; they are welcome, but they're not really "one of us."

There are two ways of looking at Christian community. One is at the organization with a building that is found at a certain address and has a name like "Ebenezer Baptist Church," "Apostolic Brethren Tabernacle," or "First Presbyterian of This or That City." It is the local church. It is the church that functions like a distinct group, but it's actually a subgroup of the second way of looking at Christian community. The second way to understand it is to say that the actual organism consists of all those who have an experiential relationship with the risen Jesus through the Holy Spirit wherever they may live. They are found all over the place.

So it is possible to join the organization without belonging to the organism. Bermuda affords such a possibility, because it is culturally Christian. Sixty-five percent to 70% of the Black population of Bermuda attend one of the African Methodist Episcopal Churches on the island. Most of the White Europeans or North Americans, who comprise about 30% of the community, attend Anglican or Episcopalian churches.

A large number of the Portuguese community attend Roman Catholic churches. There are churches all over the island, and Bermuda is one of the most highly "churched" countries in the world, with a very high per capita church presence, but it could be said that a majority of the people in many of these churches belong to the organization but not to the organism.

The New Testament describes the church as the body of Christ. Jesus is the head, giving direction, and then there are many and diverse parts of the body, all functioning for the common good. No one part of the body can function as the whole body, and every part of the body is needed. All these various parts are people—not cogs in a machine, but more like cells in a living body. The Bible describes these parts as hands, ears, eyes—body parts each having been imparted with some strength or ability that allows them to contribute with effectiveness. So there are varieties of these gifts, varieties of programs or ministries in which they can be put to use, and varieties of effects when strengths and abilities are in play (1 Corinthians 12: 4–11). It is the picture of a complex, adapting system, but with directed intentionality.

Like many aspects of spirituality and religion, the faith community can be studied as a social entity apart from the religious consideration. An example of this is the work of Erving Polster (2006, 2009a, 2009b) in his suggestion of life focus communities. Polster has had a long-standing interest in faith communities and how they work. He has studied them from a social–secular perspective and attempted to understand what they are and how they work—what their "active ingredients" might be. Concomitantly, he has suggested that the next developmental stage for psychotherapy is to move outside the one-to-one meeting as part of mental health care and into life focus groups that provide what can be found in faith communities, but his view is not really a spiritual perspective. It's a growth-by-group perspective in which he redefines the sacred and suggests that life focus communities might provide alternatives to religious sanctimony and traditional psychotherapy. Polster claims that the four attributes of the sacred he believes to be active in both religion and psychotherapy are amplification, symbolism, sanctification, and an indivisible union with otherness. Amplification can be understood as making things larger than life, symbolism is what it sounds like, and sanctification is setting some things aside to designate them as dedicated for specific functions (such as a special room or building in which to meet). The last item, indivisible union with otherness, is not communion with an ontic Being known as God; it is simply feeling close to something that a person experiences as significantly beyond him- or herself. This could be the sunset, or it could be another person, the community itself, or it might be the idea of God (without any ontological claims about the presence of an actual divinity). These things could be understood to comprise key elements of spiritual community, but if so, the deconstruction and reconstruction of what constitutes the sacred would be purposeful escape from what many call fundamentalism in order to embrace something less "supernatural" and more appealing to liberal theology and secular worldviews.

In all of this, though, the main idea is that of belonging. Sometimes, you just get the impression that you're in the wrong place and do not belong.

When I was living in the San Francisco Bay area, I bought a guitar and for a brief while took lessons at a local music store. My guitar teacher was Rick Bockner, who played guitar for a band called Mad River. He was amazing. He played ragtime guitar—an alternating bass run finger-picking style with counterpoint melodies finger-picked on the higher strings. (If you can find their two albums anywhere, the guitar work is hypnotic!) Mad River had moved out to Berkeley from Antioch College in Yellow Springs, Ohio, and they had come to the attention of the writer Richard Brautigan. He introduced the band to the hippie culture, and the members became friends with established people in the music scene of that period and place. One day Rick invited me for a potluck dinner at the house where he was living with his friends, and I went. Members of the band called Country Joe and the Fish showed up as well, and I recall playing darts with their drummer, but all those people knew each other quite well. Although they were all nice, welcoming, and generous, I just did not feel like I belonged. I imagined they wondered who I was and what I was doing there. I knew quite well I was not in a band. I did not even have long hair, and I was in the military, of all things. I felt like I stuck out and had a circle drawn around me in a test of which of these things do not go with the others. I remained briefly and then made an exit.

The sense of belonging in spiritual community affects a person's ability to participate, contribute to others, and feel appreciated, valued, and accepted, which in turn affects one's appraisal of religious experience and the truth of spiritual assertions. Shame is what gets in the way of such belonging.

Shame and guilt are self-conscious emotions (Tangney & Fischer, 1995; Tracy, Robins, & Tangney, 2007). Guilt is the sense that one has done something wrong, and shame is the sense that one *is* something wrong—that one is defective and unacceptable, despicable, unworthy. That is what I felt like at the potluck dinner (unworthy), even though no one said anything like that; it's what I imagined, and when people are in the grip of the self-conscious emotion of shame, it is likely that others have not done as much to generate that experience as the subject him- or herself. The self-conscious emotion is an attribution, a sense of imagined judgment on the part of an internalized social audience. If someone feels guilty of a transgression, he or she can make amends; he or she can return the stolen money, pay the parking ticket, apologize for careless words, and so on. However, if someone feels shame, there is nothing that person can do but cease to exist, and so the overwhelming experience is one of wanting to escape the situation, disappear, and, as much as possible, cease to exist (or at least cease to exist for the immediate group of people with whom one happens to be).

People need a place to call home and a sense of belonging to help facilitate good mental health. In research on recovery communities embedded in complementary service provision systems, it was found that a physical environment could provide refuge from homelessness, drug activity, and violence; the social environment in such communities could provide a place of belonging with peer support for mental health and recovery from substance abuse. The research found that such recovery communities needed to be holistic in order to address numerous and complex needs that go beyond attempts to reduce psychiatric symptoms, substance abuse, or the effects of traumatic experience (Carpenter-Song, Hipolito, & Whitely, 2012). These things are also true for spiritual community. The sense of belonging, that one has found a spiritual home, is more than just another node in one's support network. It can become the most significant means of support in and of itself; so anything that interrupts that sense of belonging, from a spiritual perspective, ought to catch the attention of the psychotherapist.

Somewhere in my journey as a clergyman, I ran across a person whose concept of ministry had implications for the church. He regarded the church as a hospital for injured and sick souls. That is a nice ideal, but it takes quite a bit of nerve to try and pull it off. That is because the lost, the broken, the maimed by life, and the very people who need such a spiritual hospital are often the unkept, unclean, and unruly that don't look good on Sunday morning. The church could be a recovery community not only for those suffering from mental illness but also for those suffering from a sickness of spirit, but not if someone is communicating to them that they don't belong.

When I was on staff at a large church in Sacramento, I helped create what we called "special ministries" to the disabled. That was because one of the children in the church had spina bifida, and his mother came to me dismayed. Her son was being shoved off into a small class with two intellectually delayed children, and he was not learning anything. Worse than that, he felt misunderstood and rejected. Her complaint touched me, and together we decided to attempt to create a ministry to address the problem. We brought in Joni Eareckson Tada for a weeklong conference on creating ministries for disabled people. Joni had become a quadriplegic when she fractured her spine between the fourth and fifth cervical vertebrae; she was paralyzed from the shoulders down, but she had learned to paint by holding the brush between her teeth and gained some fame for her artwork. She had also dealt with her injuries and sadness through faith in Jesus. That developed into a successful radio ministry titled "Joni and Friends." During the week, we would roll paralyzed people down in front where they could hear Joni better, see her up close, and interact with her. I was troubled to learn that some people in the church thought having all those disabled people right down front, right in front where they could be seen, was a bad visual, and they wanted us to move them to the back of the church. I laugh now to recount it. Those people just did not understand. If you want to communicate to someone that they belong, then accept them and put them right next to you, right down front or wherever they want to be, and if you want to communicate that they do *not* belong, then send them to the back of the room.

WHAT TO DO

My daughter lives in Portland, Oregon. One year, while visiting with her, she said, "Dad, I have a church I think you'd like. We should visit there." She had visited this church and found it to be interesting. So I went with her one Sunday morning. There were between 200 and 300 young people there, about the same age as her. They would have been students, and other people trying to get a start in life out on their own as young adults. These were the demographic I would have salivated over when I was in the ministry. I joined in the music; they had a band playing contemporary Christian music, even music that was "converted" from secular to serve the purposes of worship. I kept looking for the gimmick, the hook that would explain what all those people were doing there.

I waited for the sermon, figuring it would be watered down and insipid or laced with buzzwords. It wasn't. The Pastor preached for about 40 minutes, and his message was solid Reformed theology. The man himself came out in shorts, with a bit of a gut, and goatee. He was intelligent and had a great sense of humor. He was personable and rather down-to-earth. I would have called him "real." Whenever I am in Portland, I try to attend that church, because even though I am not a regular attender or member, I feel like I belong. It feels like home to me.

That is quite different from other churches I've attended faithfully over time but never felt like I was one of the "in crowd." These were places where it felt like there *was* an "in crowd." They had privilege. They set the tone for others. Theirs was a dress code, and their attendance was the norm. There were also raised eyebrows for lack of performance, and the people raising them were the ones who laid down the benchmarks for acceptance or rejection of others. These other places may indeed have been home for other people, but they did not feel like that to me.

That sense of belonging is something a therapist can address directly without it becoming overly spiritualized. The therapist might inquire into the phenomenology, the subjective experience, of the client who is struggling with belonging at church, the same way, perhaps, that he or she is struggling with belonging in life outside of church. The therapist can ask whether that experience reminds the client of any other time in life, getting back to important developmental themes, and then begin to work with attachments or other relationship issues as they manifest in church life.

The therapist can inquire into the process by which the client is attempting to navigate entrance into any given church. This could take a solutions-focused approach in which the therapist asks what the client wants to accomplish, and then therapist and client together generate a plan to attempt to achieve it. Quite often, churches will offer an inquirers' class or a new members' class to introduce people to what the church is about, its emphases, and its opportunities for growth and service. These are good kinds of small groups in which people can make lasting and meaningful friendships. Does the client have enough internal support to ask relevant questions and to engage the staff of the church in authentic dialogue about what he or she wants in a church? People looking for a church should be encouraged to "interview" relevant people from that church, including its pastoral staff members, to see what kinds of influences might become important over time.

Part of the process of moving into a faith community would, of course, include asking God where He wants a given person to attend. For a Christian, sensing that God is in a given place can make all the difference to feeling like it's a place where one belongs. So one starting point with a client who is presenting with a discouraging sense of not belonging at church is to ask the client, "When you talk with God about this, what do you get back?" Then, the therapist might listen for what the client actually gets back, respecting it as possibly being more than the client's fabrication.

Sometimes it's not a matter of having failed to push the right buttons or meeting with the right people. Sometimes a person just really does not belong. When I was in seminary, one of our assignments was to go to some group of people and "witness" (which means to present a gospel message with the idea of sharing with others what one believes Jesus to have accomplished in one's own life). I decided to go to the Krishna Temple that existed just down the street from the seminary. The people opened the door to me without hesitation. I told them I just wanted to meet with some people and ask some questions. They brought me into what I might call their "sanctuary"; it was a large room, bare, with a statue at one end and another at the other. While I was in there, people brought cooked food and placed these before the statues, devoting the food to these gods. Then they brought me and the blessed food into a common room, and there ensued a discussion. They kept pressing me to eat the food, and I felt weird, knowing it had been devoted to what I regarded at the time to be false gods. So I kept telling them I wasn't hungry, and they kept trying to get me to eat. Finally, it came out that they believed that the food, having been devoted to their gods, was then potent to bring a person to spiritual enlightenment or "salvation," to use a Christian concept. I realized that the doctrines we were discussing were at such odds with what I believed as a Christian as to pose an impossible divide. Eventually, I left, realizing how difficult it was to even have a common vocabulary upon which to base a true dialogue.

In such cases, a therapist can offer support for disengaging and choosing to reject that faith community as one's own. In such cases, it's that the goodness of fit is not there, and it's not that the client is defective or "wrong." It's just not a good fit. Such is the case when a person encounters something so at odds with their beliefs and values that they might realize that they truly do *not* belong.

CHAPTER 14

Dissatisfaction With God

A belief is a lever that, once pulled, moves almost everything else in a person's life.

—Sam Harris, *The End of Faith*, 2005, p. 12

There are lots of people out there who have been brought up in some religion or other, are unhappy in it, don't believe it, or are worried about the evils that are done in its name.

—Richard Dawkins, *The God Delusion*, from the preface, 2006, p. 1

Imagine that you are a cat. We serve four of them in my household: two indoor cats and two that come and go but are part of our family. Did you notice I said that we serve them? You don't own a cat. A cat decides whether it wants you and will bless you with its attention. If you call a dog, chances are it will come. If you call a cat, chances are it will not. Then, at another point, it will show up and demand that you stop whatever you are doing and pay attention to it, feed it, change its litter box, let it outside, or other such things. One of our cats lets me know it's time to stop writing and go to bed by jumping into my lap, running across the table where my laptop sits, jumping on the back of my chair, putting its front paws on my shoulder, and then leaning over to look at the computer while rubbing up against my neck. No matter how hard you imagine being a cat and having people serve you at your whim, you cannot really understand what it is like to be a cat, because you are stuck with your experience of being human. However, in one respect we are similar to cats (and dogs too for that matter). When my cat leans over to see words forming on the screen of my computer, it cannot really understand what I am doing. It does not know the significance of my writing, nor that the time for writing makes its own demands on my time, energy, and attention. All it knows is that I am not doing what it wants me to do, and in this respect human beings are exactly like cats with reference to our understanding of an infinite divine Being and the dynamics of our relationship with that Being.

I used to be a dog person. When I was growing up, we had dogs. When I moved out on my own, I got myself a puppy and raised her. When I got married, we had dogs. It's too expensive to have dogs in Bermuda, so we got cats, but I used to be a dog person. One day I was reading, and I looked up to see my dog looking at me. It suddenly occurred to me that my dog might be in wonder about me as I am often in wonder about God. "What is he doing?" "Why is he just sitting there with that thing in his hands?" "When are we going to go running?" My dog has no frame of reference to understand "reading." It cannot look at symbols such as letters in something called an alphabet that are arranged to communicate descriptions of life, explanations of thoughts, or conjure up word pictures like poetry that fall upon a person with meaning like a predator upon its prey. The dog simply sees a person looking at a book.

I am the dog, and God is the person reading a book. His capacities are so far beyond my own that I don't even have an adequate frame of reference within which to understand them. In some things, because according to Christian theology human beings are created in the image of God (*imago dei*), I can attain a rudimentary understanding of who God is as a being and what God is doing, but it is a limited scope and depth that is possible. It is enough to believe that God is and to put my trust in Him, but it is not enough to resolve all the complexities and enigmas that I encounter in life.

God does not do what He does on our time schedules or in the ways we expect or want Him to. We cannot appreciate his timing, fathom the power at his disposal to accomplish what He has determined, or understand His ability to attend to every aspect of life, working the complex situation from multiple directions, for multitudes of people at the same time rather than attending to one individual's needs in a simple line of cause and effect. I accept that. It is part of my understanding of the relevant differences between myself, a finite creature, and God, an infinite creator.

For some others this will not suffice. They are like the cat who might say, "The man isn't acting like I want; so he doesn't exist," or the dog who might say, "The man doesn't make sense to me; so he doesn't exist." This position has baffled me in the people I know who embody it (and they would be quite offended at being compared, even poetically, to dogs and cats!).

One of my friends, a professional colleague, came from a Jewish family that suffered great losses during the Holocaust. As a young man, he converted to Christianity and took part in evangelistic street ministries, but he became increasingly troubled by what he saw as inconsistencies between doctrine and life. How could an omniscient, omnipotent, and loving God tolerate such horrors, cruelties, and evils as actually exist in the world? Or, as Elie Wiesel (1985/2006) put it,

> We believed in God, trusted in man, and lived with the illusion that every one of us has been entrusted with a sacred spark from the Shekhinah's flame. . . . *That* was the source if not the cause of all our ordeals.

My colleague and friend is a considerable treasure to me. At one point in our relationship we were fierce antagonists, but he has the capacity and interest to abide with a person through the exploration of difference, and where there is the will to meet in dialogue, he is present. Whenever I have the chance to interact with him, I feel like I am peering into a strange perspective, and because I value the man and his intellect, I find myself drawn all the more to trying to understand that perspective.

How could a thinking person demand that an infinite God who is unique and in a category all His own, with abilities and characteristics so far beyond *our* own, make complete sense or yield to whatever he or she wants? God's "volume" exceeds and overflows my capacity, and yet God is this saturated phenomenon (Marion, 2000) that overwhelms my usual ways of knowing and meets me in His presence. To me it is entirely logical and consistent that I would *not* be able to comprehend everything to my satisfaction and that I *would* find various things about God and what He does to be mysterious, enigmatic, puzzling, and troubling. But then, I would be approaching the issue from a position of belief, while my friend would be approaching it from a position of disbelief. What got us each to these relative positions could be explored, for faith is a developmental process (Fowler, 1996), but in the current moment, when these two worldviews collide, there is a starting point to be considered. The one accepts that there is a God who cannot be exhaustively figured out, and the other demands complete intellectual satisfaction before it will yield to the ontic existence of God. It takes a breach in the wall of that anti-God edifice for such a person to open up to the possibility of God (Flew, 2007).

My friend, though, does not believe in God. To say that he became dissatisfied with God is to put it mildly, because to be dissatisfied with something is to believe that it exists (one is just annoyed with it); he rejected the ontological possibility of God. He identifies as an atheist.

Many of the people who come to me for psychotherapy do not mention God or spiritual issues at all. These are not salient factors for them in the situation as it presents itself. Some identify themselves as atheists, and for them spiritual issues would be not simply irrelevant but inappropriate. For others, though, they are dissatisfied with God. They have been brought up in a religious community of some kind, but their beliefs have been challenged by life, and they are in the midst of a developmental transition with regard to their spiritual lives.

I once accompanied a man to visit his dying mother, who was in a convalescent home, suffering in her dying. He was a successful man, a vice president at an aerospace corporation, and he was used to traveling internationally to negotiate contracts between his corporation and others. He was an intelligent and highly responsible person. He worked with goals and the plans to achieve them, and on the ride back from his visit he grew increasingly troubled. With emotion in his voice, he said, "Why does she have to suffer like that? And *don't tell me* it's all part of the grand design!" This man identified as a Christian and had served as treasurer on his church board, but he was very dissatisfied with the way God was treating his mother.

For other people, the banality of suffering, oppression, injustice, and terror cancels out the possibility that a just and loving God could be anywhere nearby. How could God allow it? If God does allow it, then *that* kind of God does not deserve worship. Why are not things better in this world if God exists and cares about people? If God so loved the world that He gave His son to save it, then why isn't it doing better? Is this "salvation" practical or even worth having?

I had no answer that would take away the man's pain about his dying mother, and I have no answer that will satisfy people who see cruelty and evil apparently unaddressed by divinity. Their dissatisfaction with God is unhappiness, disaffection, and disapproval. It is often seen in spiritual dullness and malaise, because the dissatisfaction, like unaddressed doubt, is never dealt with and worked through to either a strengthening of faith or a complete disillusion and rejection of God.

These people are unhappy. It is a form of spiritual depression. The joy they once experienced in their relationship with God has receded. They don't "go out" and "do anything" with God anymore, because they don't trust Him.

Passion for God in such people has waned. They do not yearn for God, because they have lost respect for the kind of person God is. It's like finding out that your hero is a child abuser.

These people do not agree with the way things are going under God's administration. They believe there must be a better approach, a means by which injustice gives way to equity, misery and wretchedness yield to relief, disease succumbs to health, fragmentation unifies in wholeness, and disturbances of the mind find peace. They don't look to God for these things, because they don't believe God has the ability to organize a new life and a new world.

They believe in God, but they are dissatisfied with Him. In that state of discontent but not outright rejection, people do not fully integrate their religious and spiritual worldviews into their respected worlds, and religion floats free as virtually the same thing in all cultures. It is there like the hum of a city that is barely heard, and the price is that religion "is reduced to a secondary epiphenomenon with regards to the secular functioning of the social totality" (Žižek, 2003, p. 3).

WHAT TO DO

When I first came to believe in Christ and realized that I was in touch with God, it was both potent and calming. I experienced a peaceful euphoria, a settled peace, the sense that all things are as they should be. God was in control, in the process of working things out, and I was part of that. The sting of death, the fear of the outcome, the worry over whether other people might accept me, like me, want to be with me, and so forth gave way before the contentment that came from knowing that God would be with me and nothing could separate me from Him, but my sense of God and what He was doing in the lives of people was still small.

We walk *through* the valley of death, not around it. There is a lot more to living the Christian life than might appear at first glance, and it takes time to learn that suffering and confusion, difficulty and challenge are actually essential aspects of the Christian life. Thus, early on in my Christian life I felt God's presence, and it was exhilarating; I received immediate and dramatic answers to my prayers. However, as time went on, I experienced less of the spiritual "high" and more of the slog of walking without hearing from God, without the reassurance of his conscious presence, and without the excitement of new insights gleaned from the scriptures. There have been times when my prayers have seemed to fall dead at my feet, and there have been times when I suddenly realized that He had answered a prayer in a way I had not expected and in a way that took years to set up. So I learned that the process of my relationship with God is much more complex than I had imagined at first, and it really does feel sometimes like I am walking through the valley of death. What I know is that I am walking through this life, and it has its mountains and its valleys. As such, I prefer to be real about the process, both with myself and with others. It's okay to be dissatisfied at times. It's honest.

I come back here to one of the basics of psychotherapy: it is the client's work. It is the client's life, and it is the client's way of making meaning out of his or her experience. Spiritually, it is the client's processes of such things as racing past, doing, assuming, and reacting (among other things), or standing still, watching, waiting, observing, and responding (among still others). It is the client's relationship with God that is in question, and if, indeed, there is a God, then that God is an aspect of the ontic field and can break forth in the client's phenomenal field, but it will not be because the psychotherapist conjured Him up, said the magic words, asked the right questions, used the correct intervention, made the cogent interpretations, or suggested a reframe of the situation. If spiritual phenomena are appearances, then the work of the psychotherapist is to show these appearances to the client.

Is the client disillusioned? Show it. Is the client treading water in his or her religious experience because he or she does not see the practicality of depending on a God he or she does not trust? Show it. Has the client lost his or her spiritual passion? Show it. The client may be able to tell the therapist that he or she is without zeal, but the client is probably not paying close attention to just how and in what ways he or she has become dissatisfied with God. Show off the appearing of the client's dissatisfaction with God through dialogue in which the therapist discloses the affective impact on the therapist of being with the client or in which the therapist makes observations and follows his or her curiosities about what the client is doing (or not doing) and how the client is going about it. Show off the client's dissatisfaction with God through experiments that put the client's relationship with God on the line or that explore the value of the spiritual disciplines the client does or does not practice.

In a real sense, the therapeutic meeting is a fertile ground, and the therapist can plow that ground, perhaps plant and water some seeds, but the growth belongs to God, and that growth is the territory of the relationship that the client has with God. It's between him or her and God. Furthermore, the therapist has a part in the life of the client, but the therapist does not have the whole of that life. It may be enough to bring into clear focus the nature of the dissatisfaction with God, with spirituality as a way of life, or to expose the premises upon which a person has been operating in his or her approach to religion.

Some therapists might approach this differently. They might diagnose a symptom or a problem and then proceed to reduce the symptom or fix the problem. For such, it would seem paradoxical to simply make more clear the existence of the situation, its features, and its connections.

I know that in psychotherapy in general, it does not work quite as well for me to tell the client what's what as it does for the client to come to the realization on his or her own. Of course, it is not entirely on "his or her own," but the client has to have the light bulb go off within him or her, or just hear ideas and theories from the therapist as part of the same noise of life that evokes obligation, more confirmation that he or she is defective, hopelessness, and shame. When the client really hears the therapist, it's like the client puts some pieces together and hears the bell that cannot be forgotten. It is the same with spiritual matters, only in terms of the Christian life, the client must hear from God on the situation. The secular psychotherapist might say that this is nothing more than what usually happens in psychotherapy, for it does seem as if an "aha" from God is the same as an "aha" from the therapeutic process apart from God, but in reality, these are different kinds of phenomena—related but distinct.

Since the client must hear from God, one of the aspects of psychotherapy that might be explored is how the client does hear from God, or put another way, in what ways does the client have a dialogical relationship with God? *Can* the client hear from God? Has the client ever heard from God? Does the client even know what that means, or when you ask whether the client can hear from God, does he or she just look puzzled? For a client to conduct an authentic conversation with God in which he or she expresses the dissatisfaction that plagues him or her can be a healthy thing. It can evoke unexpected emotions.

I once conducted an experiential workshop at a professional conference in which I invited people to come and address their unfinished business with God. At first I said to the people gathered, "Imagine that God is in the center of our circle. Whatever God is to you, imagine that that is in the center of our circle. Can you sense God there?" Then I asked them to share what that God is like, which they did in a round. And then I asked them to address that God with whatever comes up for them that might be something unfinished between them and God. In one sense it was an empty-chair experiment, but in another, perhaps God, an aspect of the pneumenal field, was actually there and conducting His unfinished business with each person.

CHAPTER 15

Rigidity and Legalism

Six days. They should have finished in two. Talk, talk, talk.
Did you ever hear so much talk 'bout nothing?

—Juror #3, *Twelve Angry Men*, A script
by Reginald Rose

I find it ironic that in courts of law there is a great amount of verbiage when attorneys attempt to win their cases. Testimony and evidence is brought in for all to hear until it all becomes tedious. As Juror #3 says, in the classic movie *Twelve Angry Men*, "Talk, talk, talk. . . ." However, when legalistic and rigid people talk, they tend to be terse and blunt. They say, "No." They mean, "It's not allowed, and you should know better."

In Chinese philosophy, legalism is a term indicating a focus on laws, methods for employing them, and the legitimacy of the roles of law enforcers. Legalism in the West denotes a concentration upon the abstract logical reasoning involved with the analysis of legal texts, quite apart from any concern about the social contexts in which those texts are applied. In issues relevant to psychotherapy, the discussion blends these two perspectives to address the relationship between human rights and mental health law (Weller, 2010). Legalism in Christianity refers to the thinking that adherence to the law is sufficient to obtain salvation or spiritual benefit. By extrapolation, it extends to an out-of-balance preoccupation with the rules, the standards, the laws, and their performance-based systems for applying them in social situations, including, of course, the church. While it might sound at times like a lot of talk about nothing, when legalism manifests in the spiritual community, it is not about nothing. It's about expected behavior and the consequences of not measuring up.

Legalism is often experienced as rigidity regarding expectations that manifests in binary appraisals of people. While rigidity is not strictly a spiritual problem, rigidity and legalism are problems to spiritual people. They often inhabit a woodenheaded literalism in interpreting scripture. For instance, one woman in a church I pastored was determined to have me preach against women taking authority in the church. She had read in the New Testament that women of that day were to wear head coverings in order to show deference to men; so she believed that meant all women in this day should do the same. When I did not interpret the scriptures to require head coverings in the contemporary church, she made some for herself and her daughters, and then marched the family down in front of the church for all to see. Her nonverbal discourse was condescending and judgmental (and ironically defiant to my authority as the pastor—and a male). By her actions and her speech, she implied that her rule should stand for all others as well, and I, as the pastor, should make it so.

One of the ways legalism can be identified is by the adamant insistence that someone's "should" or "ought" be applied to others. Depending on the ways in which people align with the legalistic stance, the binary toggles between good and bad, acceptable and unacceptable, and even between Christian and non-Christian. The judgmental appraisal results in social–relational consequences.

These binaries are polarities, or the extreme and logical ends of given continuums of any kind. A polarity is a reduction, a simplification of an otherwise complex field down to a choice between this and that— black or white, wrong or right, in or out. When someone sees a situation in this way, he or she will usually identify with one end of the polarity and alienate or reject the other. Dealing with binary configurations leads to an efficient expenditure of time, energy, and resources.

Binary appraisal of people in terms of spiritual dynamics takes place in three ways. In the first, a person has clearly transgressed God's law. The Bible indicates that murder is a sin, and if someone commits murder, then that person is no longer innocent of murder but guilty of murder. It's a binary, and the toggle switches. There are numerous dividing points that can result in these kinds of scripturally based binary appraisals.

The second way in which binaries toggle from one polar opposite to the other is when there is no explicit Biblical injunction but the inclinations of people rule. This is where a person goes to R-rated movies and drinks wine with meals (this person may arrange his or her hair in a certain way, wear cosmetics or jewelry, and wear clothing deemed to be immodest; might read the "wrong" translation of the Bible; might attend the wrong church, etc.); they are regarded to be "carnal" or "worldly" as opposed to spiritual. This is what Jesus was referring to when He chastised the Pharisees for loading down the people with extra burdens by adding layer upon layer of man-made laws. This kind of binary appraisal has its basis in the cultures, interpretive inclinations, and preferences of people.

When people stand on the laws evident in scriptures, and so emphasize where people are either wrong or right (to the neglect of a grace-based attitude in which they might emphasize where people are loved and accepted by God on the basis of Christ's atonement), that is a legalistic attitude. When people set up extra rules, those that go beyond the ones obviously found in the Bible, and then hold rigidly to their applications, this is called legalism. Both totalize people and constrain them, and they contradict the freedom Christians have because God has forgiven them—transferred them from a performance-based economy to a grace-based economy. "Sin" no longer has any sting for people free in Christ, but people who are legalistic seem to prefer the stinging and being stung.

I used to entertain door-to-door evangelists more than I do currently. One day, a couple of people from the Jehovah's Witnesses came by. They wanted to talk with me and get me to read their literature. So I figured it was like the spider saying welcome to the fly, and I let them in. We spent a couple of hours talking, and they came back for another visit. Eventually, I tried to pose a contrast between what they seemed to be saying and what I knew of Christianity. It was precisely this business of living by the law or living by grace. They could not believe that God would simply forgive all sins for all time (based on Christ's death). They believed that my past sins could be forgiven, but any further sins would come under judgment. Now, I don't know whether these people accurately represented the doctrines of that group, but when I pointed out that the Bible says we are saved by grace through faith in Christ's death, and that Christ died once for all, they said that they believed too—they had faith. They said that they believed that they would be saved by following the law; their faith was in the law, that if a person were to follow the law, God would accept them. To me, that announced the point of impasse, and we ended our meetings.

The law in Christianity does not save; it kills. That stands for the Mosaic Law given in the Old Testament, and it stands for the man-made laws Christians put on themselves when they try to accomplish their own salvation. It comes from, among other things, an overworked but weak conscience.

A third way in which legalistic binary evaluations take place concerns the difference between a weak and a strong conscience. One might think that a strong conscience is the one that is demanding and punitive, the one that says "Thou shalt not." However, it is the weak conscience that makes up all kinds of rules by which it seeks to live. The strong conscience is much more free. The weak conscience is rule-bound and quite rigid, but the strong conscience is flexible and free from one-size-fits-all boundaries. The strong conscience is not antinomian, against all rules, laws, or boundaries; it is simply free to move this way and that as the situation dictates—to be considerate of persons and treat them as fellow subjects rather than to use persons as objects in order to maintain laws, and in terms of a Christian understanding of grace, the strong conscience is free to pursue novel experience, curiosity, interest, and pleasure without concern for breaking a religious rule. To put things in proper perspective, it is as Jesus told the religious leaders in Israel—the Sabbath was made for people, not people for the Sabbath. The strong conscience does not live by the law but by the Spirit, following the inward impressions that constitute a dialogical relationship with God. In other words, the person with a strong conscience knows that if something is displeasing to God, God will let him or her know about that.

> Therefore let us not judge one another anymore, but rather determine this—not to put an obstacle or a stumbling block in a brother's way. I know and am convinced in the Lord Jesus that nothing is unclean in itself; but to him who thinks anything to be unclean, to him it is unclean. For if because of food your brother is hurt, you are no longer walking according to love. Do not destroy with your food him for whom Christ died. Therefore do not let what is for you a good thing be spoken of as evil; for the kingdom of God is not eating and drinking, but righteousness and peace and joy in the Holy Spirit. For he who in this way serves Christ is acceptable to God and approved by men. So then we pursue the things which make for peace and the building up of one another. Do not tear down the work of God for the sake of food. All things indeed are clean, but they are evil for the man who eats and

gives offense. It is good not to eat meat or to drink wine, or to do anything by which your brother stumbles. The faith which you have, have as your own conviction before God. Happy is he who does not condemn himself in what he approves.

(John 14:13–22)

WHAT TO DO?

When the Chinese government sought to gain control of the nation's birthrate, they found themselves in conflict with the long-standing norms of Chinese culture (Peng, 2010). Ancestor worship and bloodline continuation had been potent drivers behind a larger birthrate than the government thought desirable. So, on the one hand legalism in the form of public policy dictated a smaller birthrate, while on the other hand a cultural legalism in the form of social expectations called for a larger birthrate. Studies showed that villages with strong kinship networks tended to have higher birthrates. The findings demonstrated the power of introjected values from social networks and the ability they have to bend the formalism of institutions.

No spiritual leader or psychotherapist can turn around an ingrained legalism by simply pointing it out and saying something akin to "Stop doing that." If there were compliance, there would not be a significant "turnaround" in the legalistic attitude; there would simply be the replacing of one rule for another.

In psychotherapy training programs, there is a tendency to introject the values and precepts of dominant trainers and/or the precepts of the program. One has to "get it right," and there is a great deal riding on the ability to present a picture of embodying the accepted set of values and competencies. It might sound like an odd thing for me to be saying, but even this book and what I'm attempting to communicate can be swallowed or introjected and then used in a legalistic fashion.

Gestalt therapy training institutes grew outside of formal academic institutions to create networks of stand-alone, postgraduate-level training institutions in which established and esteemed trainers held sway as de facto sages and protectors of the keys of the gestalt kingdom. Their power to elevate and demote people was unquestioned, and their ability to shame trainees for deviating from the acceptable vocabulary, philosophical perspective, and clinical concern has become one aspect in the dark history of gestalt therapy, acknowledged and addressed by contemporary gestalt therapists (Cole, 2013; Lee & Wheeler, 2003; Yontef, 1997). It is something requiring continuous vigilance.

This can happen in churches as well. I was sitting in a rather informal church gathering once in a large city, and the proceedings were progressing at their own pace until the pastor appeared. He emerged from a side door and walked in among the people of the congregation, stopping here and there to touch someone, smile at another, hug another, and all the time about two steps behind him strode a man dressed in only slightly less stylish attire, who carried the pastor's Bible and notebook. The picture of them together reminded me of the great hunter and his gun-bearer. The lord-on-safari walked ahead in his glory, and the servant walked behind carrying the lord's baggage. And God help anyone who might ask, "What does this visual communicate?" In organizations where there is an unhealthy confluence that resists difference of opinion, it is shameful to question authority, and in churches this is made more stubborn by the laminate of spiritual authority.

A psychotherapist can slow the parade down a bit and take each slide one at a time. "What do you see?" "What is he/she doing?" "What are other people doing?" "How does this affect you?" "What do you feel like when the spiritual authority acts like that?" "Do you feel like you could ever measure up or be 'good enough' in such a context as that?"

Frankly, I have a hard enough time feeling comfortable with the grace of God; it is totally undeserved, and I know it. I am keenly aware of my failings, and I don't need someone acting like they have it all together, making a display of themselves as "successful." I am also very tired of formula Christianity in which people are told that they can live the overflowing life if they just pray a certain prayer, memorize certain verses, witness to the unsaved, declare and agree with one another that such and such will take place, and so on and so forth. But what happens when the result is not according to the formula? Is it God who failed or the person who must not have worked the formula well enough? No, I don't need the lord-on-safari. I need the person who has got dirt on him- or herself just like me. I need someone who wonders and questions and struggles just like me, and so does the client. Psychotherapists who can present as whole people living in the real world in which Christians walk by faith and not by sight, in which we only see dimly as shadows on the other side of thick and wavy glass, these are the people who can establish helpful contact with the client and who can explore with them the many ways in which they do not feel good enough, or do not measure up. It is not uncommon in my practice to meet with people who tell me that they are not Christian, but when I inquire about what they actually believe, they believe in God, and they believe that Jesus died for their sins, and they are trusting that somehow, based on that, God might let them into heaven. What those people are telling me is that they don't believe they are good enough Christians, not that they are not Christians at all (but to them this amounts to the same thing, and to me that is a misunderstanding of what it means to *be* a Christian). They don't have it together like the people who go to church, and every time they go to church they feel this disparity between the good churchgoers and themselves. They feel shame in the simple presence of others in church.

I graduated from one of the programs accredited by the American Psychological Association (in accordance with Footnote 4 of the guidelines for accreditation) to train psychologists to work with peoples of faith. As such, it operates within a Christian university and attempts to integrate Christian theology and values into its training of psychologists. In my cohort of that program, one student became overwhelmed by the unreasonable demands of her first practicum, and she did not handle that well. Instead of self-regulating and bringing the impossible demands of her site to the attention of her student and faculty supervisors, she attempted to do the impossible, became anxious, and began to manifest symptoms of dissociation. In fact, she had a history of abuse as a child, and when that was put together with her symptoms, the program leaders decided she should be expelled from the program. It was a binary toggle. It was perhaps a toggle that made sense and could be justified, but on the other hand, this was a program that was supposed to manifest, to integrate, and to represent Christian values. So what values were being represented in a shape-up or ship-out toggle? To me at the time, it seemed myopically legalistic. I understand the thinking, and I agree that programs like that have a responsibility to prevent psychologically damaged individuals from gaining positions of influence as psychotherapists in which they could do damage to potential clients, but on the other hand, what of the overwhelming model of Christian discipleship in which people are taken from broken and limping and built up in Christ? I struggled with the tension between these two values. It seemed that to more accurately represent Christian values there should be the ability to see the situation with more complexity and to respond out of a sense of grace and redemption. After all, in programs such as this, one of the core beliefs is the holistic nature of the person, and so the student was not only a soul to be redeemed, but also a mind, a spirit, a whole person to be reclaimed and refurbished. Did this not require from the faculty more than a simple "in" or "out" toggle? Was there not some middle ground with regard to this student, and was there not some appreciation for the complex nature of the situation in which she had found herself? Indeed, after consulting, it was determined that the student could take a leave of absence for a year, engage in personal therapy, and at the end of the year, with the agreement of her therapist, she could pick up with her studies. That is what actually took place, and it is an example of how spiritually integrative work in psychotherapy has to embody practical decisions and action plans that accurately represent a spiritual model.

CHAPTER 16

Abuse

Jacob started, smiled, and in a hoarse voice replied in a mixture of Yiddish, Hebrew, and Aramaic, "Pichapoil! Yeggar Sadussa! Otz koytzetz ben koytzetz." Bessie feared that Jacob might sabotage her spiritual rebirth just as he had her other plans and programs.

—Isaac Bashevis Singer, 1973, p. 141

That quote comes from a delightful story titled "The Bishop's Robe." It's about people who go off their rails spiritually, but it's told with a cynical perspective. The point of the quote goes to the issue of one person's influence over another. Ironically, "Bessie" ends up killing both herself and Jacob in the end (hope I didn't ruin the story for anyone), and that also points to the fact that when one person abuses another, he or she usually doesn't see it that way. This is not just the twisted justifying that a person does in order to make it okay to abuse another; it's a blindness toward the situation of the other. It is being absorbed in one's own hunger to the point that a person doesn't actually enjoy the taste of what he or she eats as long as he or she can be eating. It's the eating that matters. To taste something means to actually take in and appreciate the uniqueness of that which is eaten. It is contacting. It is meeting the other and being able to tell the difference between sour cream and whipped cream, between spinach and kale.

This chapter divides into a consideration of two kinds of abuse: abuse that takes place within a church and abuse that takes the place of a church. In the first, the pastor is usually unaware of the abuser, and in the second, the pastor often *is* the abuser.

ABUSE IN RELIGIOUS COMMUNITY

When I first came to Bermuda, I used to ride the bus into town from a guesthouse on Southshore Road. Every day, it took a particular turn and went right past a certain church. Every day, I would be praying, "God, where do you want me to go to church here?" One day the light bulb went off. "Duh. Okay, I'll go there."

The next Sunday I caught the bus and got off just before the turn at the church. I walked up the hill and entered the sanctuary. As the service unfolded, it felt like I had stepped into the Twilight Zone. The church was exactly like the one I had served in California as the Minister of Children on a multiple staff. This church was quite a bit smaller in attendance, but still quite full. The order of service was the same as in California. The hymns they sang were the same. The remarks in between sections of the program were the same. The way they took the offering was the same. The choir sang in the same spot. It was like the previous 20 years had not even transpired.

After the service, I was greeted by some men, and one of them invited me to attend his men's small group, so I accepted. I got to know this leader well, and one day he introduced me to a woman with whom he worked. She was the mother of two young girls, and I often saw her at church.

This church was rather rigid and legalistic. In a subtropical climate, for instance, they insisted that people singing in the choir up front not wear open-toed sandals. Of course, all the males had to wear ties, and all the females had to wear dresses. There were other evidences of a rule-bound system, and I eventually decided to look for another church. After I had found one and had settled into my private practice of psychology, the woman who worked with my friend contacted me. She wanted to come in to talk about something.

Amy had grown up with a secret. In Bermuda, people call child sexual abuse being "interfered with," and Amy had been interfered with. It was someone in her family, and she had been too ashamed of it to ever really deal with it, but she knew she never wanted anything like that to happen to her daughters. So, she was very protective of them.

In the church where I had first met her, her mother had remarried a man, an older man, when Amy's older daughter was 8 years old. The man was a leader in the church, a man well-respected. He would routinely stand up and give public testimony, sounding righteous, affirming spiritual truths and good deeds among the membership. He also became a trusted member of their family.

When Amy's older daughter, Suzanne, was 9 years old, her step-grandfather began interfering with her. At first he would tickle her, and his tickling became so intense that she would laugh but only want to get away. Then, he began fondling her emerging breasts with his hands and then with his mouth. Her first kiss was with him, as he stuck his tongue into her mouth. She felt strange about what was happening, but she thought it was her fault, and the behavior went on for 4 years, until she was 13. She prayed every night that God would forgive her for her sin. She kept it all a secret, because the man was so respected in the church, and on the outside she tried to look normal. As she got older, though, she tried to eliminate time alone with him, something her grandmother, however, encouraged. He would take her snorkeling only to touch her body under her swimsuit. He taught her to play solitaire on the computer so that he could sit behind her and fondle her breasts or put his hand down her pants. He took her grocery shopping and sent her grandmother into the market so that he could molest her in the car in the parking lot.

When the man moved on to attempt to fondle Suzanne's younger sister, that girl told her mother immediately. Amy asked Suzanne whether the man had touched her, and Suzanne denied it. But her mother kept insisting that if it had happened, it would not have been her fault, and so eventually Suzanne broke down and told her mother everything.

Then Amy went to the church; she went to the pastor and wanted her pastor and her church to do something about the man being in a position of leadership when he was so obviously broken. They did next to nothing. The pastor met with the perpetrator, and the man confessed to something but largely concealed his activities and minimized what he was admitting to. The pastor took the position that the man "confessed." The church decided to conduct "discipline," and so they had him stand one day in front of the congregation. The leadership explained that they were conducting discipline. The man said he had sinned. The church pronounced forgiveness on him, and the man sat back down. That was the end of it. There was no detail concerning the nature of the man's sin, and thus no real accountability to the church body. From that point on, the church leadership closed ranks and cut off any further discussion, claiming they had dealt with it, conducted discipline, and the man was forgiven. They wanted no more talk.

In fact, though, like many sex offenders he minimized his behavior, equivocated, and used the system to conceal his actions. No one ever pushed to get the details, even though Amy tried repeatedly to meet with leadership and provide them. They did not want to hear it, and the perpetrator certainly just wanted everything to go away.

Amy eventually left that church. She could not stand seeing her daughter's abuser looking smug and talking in spiritualized language, while she knew that he had done what adult offenders usually do. In fact, he never got treatment for his offense, even though he eventually spent about a year in jail because Amy and Suzanne went to the police.

The spiritual ramifications when trusted religious leaders use people for sexual gratification are enormous. The stories of abuse of young boys by Catholic priests exploded in the news a few years ago, and the problem became widely known. Gartner (2004) described how children abused by spiritual leaders can develop a crisis of faith, believing that somehow they have betrayed God. There is also a problem of the heterosexual abuse of children and adults by clergy of all denominations. Even when it looks like an adult is giving consent to a sexual relationship, there is an influence differential that gives the pastor or other religious leader an advantage. To take that advantage and use it for personal gain is abusive.

In the case of Amy, she experienced a loss of support from trusted friends and church leaders. Her mother supported her stepfather, the abuser in this case, and Amy's need was for the psychotherapist to listen and not only provide general support but also to put into perspective the actions of church leaders. This raises the need to become familiar with ecclesiology—the study of the church. Or at least, if not to understand church history, to understand how the polity of various churches operate. The defensive actions of church leaders, who just want to make something distasteful and embarrassing for the church go away, and who tend to shove the abused under the rug, become abusive in and of themselves (see below for a discussion of spiritual abuse).

Some churches are part of denominations, and their governance actually comes from high up in a structure that might find top-level leadership living far away. For instance, in Bermuda, one church belongs to an organization headquartered in Canada and another belongs to one located in England. Still others are influenced by associational ties to governance in the United States. For nondenominational and Congregationalist churches, the polity starts and stops with the local church itself. In those churches, if you want to go to the top authority, you'll find that person right there in the local community. Beyond that, there is the structure and there is the de facto influence. Opinion leaders may not hold official office but just be long-standing families who have been in the church for generations. These people often hold offices such as treasurer, trustee, deacon, or elder. In that sense, the local church is like a big family—often a dysfunctional family.

Psychotherapists can perform preventative and even ameliorative work in churches by meeting with church leadership to help train them in identifying and dealing appropriately with sex abuse in the church. Such things are best not hushed up. It is best to name what is going on and deal with it directly. That was Paul's approach when he heard about a man who was committing incest:

> It is actually reported that there is immorality among you, and immorality of such a kind as does not exist even among the Gentiles, that someone has his father's wife. You have become arrogant and have not mourned instead, so that the one who had done this deed would be removed from your midst. For I, on my part, though absent in body but present in spirit, have already judged him who has so committed this, as though I were present. In the name of our Lord Jesus, when you are assembled, and I with you in spirit, with the power of our Lord Jesus, *I have decided* to deliver such a one to Satan for the destruction of his flesh, so that his spirit may be saved in the day of the Lord Jesus.
>
> (1 Corinthians 5:1–5)

Often these days, a church can also opt in for training with a number of organizations that have come into being to prevent child sex abuse. One such organization is Darkness to Light (http://www.d2l .org), whose self-proclaimed mission is to end childhood sexual abuse through prevention, awareness, and education. They believe that when people learn the facts of childhood sexual abuse, that helps to prevent it. Knowing how sex abusers work, how sex abuse can find an opportunity, helps parents and concerned adults safeguard all concerned.

Actually, I know this because Amy grew through her work with me and through reaching out to others to learn more about the problem. Because of her own experience and that of her daughters, she became determined and came to believe that God had led her into a meaningful ministry for her life. She trained with Darkness to Light and brought the program to Bermuda. It has now reached the highest level of government

(I sat in a group in which the governor of Bermuda and his wife were in attendance), and Amy and her colleagues have been in numerous schools and government ministries. The sad side to this, however, is that whenever she and her colleagues put on a training event for Darkness to Light, they are always met with numerous people who come to them saying how they were abused as children and wondering how they can get help to finally deal with the aftermath of it through counseling.

Psychotherapists can find training programs to become more competent to help those who have been abused, but they may not include a spiritual component. Psychotherapists would do well to watch for damage to the spirit in people even if they do not identify as being particularly spiritual or religious. The spirit is where a person finds ultimate value and existential meaning in life. The spirit is where one finds ground for a peaceful process of living (in accord with Eastern religious or philosophical beliefs). The spirit is where one finds meaningful relationship with God, for the spirit is the medium in which one finds contact with God.

As mentioned previously, when Jesus met a woman at a well, she asked him whether it was right to worship God on a local mountain or in Jerusalem. He told her that God is spirit and people who want to worship God (i.e., to approach Him with adoring contact) need to do so in spirit and in truth. That is, they need to be authentic and contact God in the sphere of the spirit (meaning the inner person often also described as what a person thinks, feels, values, wants, and intends).

ABUSE OF RELIGIOUS COMMUNITY

Spiritual abuse takes place when a leader uses his or her position to control or dominate another person, often running over his or her feelings and opinions and disregarding what might happen to the other person's life—his or her emotional state and spiritual well-being. Power is used to bolster the position or needs of a leader, over and above those of others—often people who have come to them in need (Johnson & VanVonderen, 1991). "Spiritual abuse occurs when a leader with authority uses that authority to coerce, control or exploit a follower, thus causing spiritual wounds" (Blue, 1993, p. 12). Spiritual abuse affects people by making them extremely self-focused, "preoccupied with doing things right and keeping happy those who are in places of authority" (Johnson & VanVonderen, 1991, p. 201).

Spiritual abuse grows like mold in a petri dish where church ministries are highly programmed and there is an expectation of success on the part of top leadership. Every church has programming of some kind. It would be irresponsible to simply get up in the morning and say, "Well, I wonder what's going to happen today." On the one hand, that would be refreshing, because Jesus told people that every day has enough concerns in it and so the best thing to do is to simply live one day at a time. Practically speaking, however, we all live in a world that runs on the clock. We have numerous events that need to be scheduled, and so people expect that church programs will correspond to pinpoints on a calendar, and they need those pinpoints in order to coordinate and balance their commitments. Having said that, some churches are highly programmed, as if the church were a smorgasbord.

In Brooklyn, people hold what they call the Smorgasburg. It is the Brooklyn Flea and Food Market, and it gathers at Williamsburgh and at Brooklyn Bridge Park, Pier 5. Over 108 vendors bring their varieties there, and you can get everything from Asian hot dogs to "BiteMe" cheesecakes to Beet Ketchup to Umame Nuts. Such places are a lot of fun to visit. There is always a festive mood. The Saturday Market in Portland, Oregon, is like that too. You could spend the better part of a day there walking between the booths, up and down the aisles, dodging the roller bladers and skateboarders, and listening to the live music.

When the church attempts to be a one-stop spiritual shopping spot, though, things tend to go awry. On the one hand, people begin to view the church as a place to go to purchase something they need, and on the other hand, people get burned out trying to provide that experience. People shop for programming in the church that provides something for the children, the adolescents, and the adults. As if they were looking at a menu, they expect to be able to purchase spirituality with their attendance and their tithe, but spirituality doesn't really work that way. For the church leaders, the goal becomes getting more people through the doors of the spiritual market and getting them to keep coming back. It fits with the commercialization of spirituality, and leaders tend to evaluate the success or failure of their ministries by how complete their programming is and how well organized and efficiently it runs.

Early in my ministry, when I was in charge of a Sunday School of over 300 and when that included a nursery and the recruitment, training, and scheduling of teachers for classes from preschool to junior high,

I realized that no matter how efficient the program was, if there was not a proper focus, it would be a waste. Worse than that, it would be a distraction. Ministry is not program. Ministry is people. If church leaders value program and the things that make for efficiency and maximal programming above their people, they will tend to use the people to accomplish the programming. If they tell themselves they are fulfilling their ministry because they have created buildings and programs, they are like the rich man who decided to tear down his barns and build bigger ones only to find out he would not survive them.

Spiritual abuse takes place when people lose sight of the fact of grace and institute performance-based economies in order to achieve program objectives. Grace, however, is favor that has not been earned. It is gift, not wage. It depends on the giver not the receiver. A religious community that is built around the appreciation of grace can have programs and benchmarks, goals, and a value for efficiency, but all those things take second or third place to the people themselves. The programs are seen as having been made for the benefit of the people and not the people for the benefit of the programs. This is the message that Jesus gave the Pharisees in Israel when they complained that he was performing miracles and healing people on the Sabbath. Among other things, He told them that the Sabbath was made for the people. At other times, he told them that they were loading up the people with additional rules and demands for better performance, but not getting involved with them in order to ease their burdens.

One client came to me explicitly because she was confused about her spirituality. She was 24 years old when I met her and had grown up in a cult. That is what she called it. As a young child she had been raised by members of her religious community, which was a rural community in the Northeastern United States. She recalled being warned about the kind of clothes she needed to wear as a female and how she was to wear her hair. She was schooled in how to talk and what kinds of language were appropriate. She was taught that strict obedience to the commandments of God was the only hope of salvation. She had to eat foods dictated by the community, but it wasn't really the whole community making such decisions. Her parents were adhering to the values and behavioral dictates of one or two men. The community was protective and minimized contact with people who did not belong to the community. Things, however, were not absolutely closed off; she had to get an education, and eventually she decided to go to college. Gradually, she realized that her upbringing was unusual, and she began to question the teachings she had received about God (and other things). After college, she did not return to her community, and her relationship with her parents became difficult. She was regarded to have strayed. What she wanted from me was a sounding board while she worked through some of her dissonance. Did she indeed grow up in a cult? If so, how far off base were they and about what? Was all religion bogus?

She did not believe all religion was bogus. She wanted to have a good relationship with God, but she did not want that to be tainted by the stains of her upbringing.

WHAT TO DO

When I am meeting with a person in psychotherapy who has been abused in the church or by a church member who attempts to use the church as a shield against accountability, I do not really shift into some special approach all its own. I am still dialogical, and I still follow the person's subjective experience, including how they make meaning for themselves out of their experience. I attempt through our relationship and my contact with the person to show the person to the person. Thus, with one person who was sexually abused over the course of several years by her youth pastor, I inquired into what had happened and what it had meant to her. She had been told how precious she was to the man, and she had been led to believe that he loved her. When she spoke about the betrayal and the loss she experienced when he turned to others and then when he finally left the church and went somewhere else, she wanted to cry, but she could not fully let loose and do it. She had experienced periods of depression and collapse over the course of her life, and the central theme for her was the loss of this man's love. She knew he was a pedophile. She knew she had been used. She was angry and she was sad, but her emotions were strangled by the memory of her complete breakdown as a young child when he had left and her parents had not given her support. She never wanted to feel that bad again, but she did want to get better. We spent many sessions in that impasse. She also felt guilty that she had never been able to tell her story in an effective way so as to end his career in the ministry, where she imagined he was still having access to other children. We tried imaginal dialogues as behavioral experiments. Eventually she constructed a plan by which she hoped she could bring some closure. She tracked the man down to where he was currently living, and she got on a plane and showed up on his doorstep. She confronted the dumbfounded person, and although he did not crumble into a pile of dust as somewhere inside she wished he might, she found a resolution of sorts in the process. She was assured that he was no longer in a position to be able to abuse other children. She had told him what she thought of him. She had brought some closure to the unfinished gestalt.

There are approaches to the treatment of abused persons that accord with various clinical paradigms. People can read about them in the psychotherapeutic literature. With regard to spirituality and religion, it's important that the abused person is treated psychologically and also spiritually.

Someone who has been abused in a spiritual community needs to be able to distinguish between a sex offender and a spiritual leader. Not all sex offenders are spiritual people. Not all spiritual people are sex offenders. Sometimes a person serious about his or her spirituality is also plagued by sexual compulsion or deviant sexual arousal. It might seem like a spiritual person could never be a pedophile or have deviant arousal or compulsive sexual behaviors, but that is not true. Many genuinely spiritual people are also extremely troubled themselves. So the issue of sexual abuse in the church is not a one-person consideration. Self-medicating and addictive sexual behavior among Christians is common. Sexual offenders need to be forgiven, yes, but they also need to be taken seriously, because sexual offending is a stubborn dynamic that is often accompanied by paraphilia and other comorbid disorders. Where there is receptivity, the psychotherapist can intercede at the level of the offender. The offender needs to be relieved of his or her duties and treated.

When I am meeting with people in psychotherapy who are caught in abusive spiritual systems, or in a spiritually abusive relationship (because sometimes this comes up in that context as well), I try to keep myself oriented to grace. It is important, because abusive systems are legalistic and dispersed by grace. It helps to provide a reading regimen that counters the skewed theology of these systems. In terms of Christian religious communities, Table 16.1 provides a listing of books a psychotherapist might recommend as behavioral experiments in reading. The client and the therapist can discuss what the client learned from reading, and even if the therapist does not hold to the same Christian beliefs, the therapist can inquire what the client has read, what it means to him or her, and whether it has any implications

TABLE 16.1
BEHAVIORAL EXPERIMENT READING REGIMEN TO POTENTIALLY
DISPERSE SPIRITUALLY ABUSIVE THOUGHT PATTERNS

Title	Author(s)	Publisher
Knowing God (especially Chapter 18, "The Heart of the Gospel")	J. I. Packer	Downers Grove, IL: InterVarsity Press
Mere Christianity	C. S. Lewis	New York, NY: HarperCollins/ Harper San Franciso
The Myth of Certainty: The Reflective Christian & The Risk of Commitment	Daniel Taylor	Downers Grove, IL: InterVarsity Press
Your God Is Too Small	J. B. Phillips	New York, NY: MacMillan
The Subtle Power of Spiritual Abuse: Recognizing & Escaping Spiritual Manipulation and False Spiritual Authority Within the Church	David Johnson and Jeff Van Vonderen	Minneapolis, MN: Bethany House Publishing/Baker Publishing Group
Tired of Trying to Measure Up: Getting Free From the Demands, Expectations, and Intimidations of Well-Meaning People	Jeff Van Vonderen	Minneapolis, MN: Bethany House Publishing/Baker Publishing Group

for what the client has encountered in church or at the hands of any given spiritual leader.

There are, of course, certain passages of the Bible that the psychotherapist might suggest to the client, but these could be problematic given that within the context of the abusive system many of these may have already been cast or interpreted so as to serve the needs of the abusive leader(s). It might be best to start with one of the books listed in the table, and then deal with the verses that come up in the course of those authors' arguments. The chapter out of Packer and the book by Johnson and Van Vonderen are especially good. Explore what they mean to the client and any dissonance encountered as compared with the teachings he or she has been exposed to under the abusive system. Unless the psychotherapist has a background in theology and exegesis of Biblical literature, it might also be best to leave such things to pastoral referrals, and so gathering a list of such people would be wise.

CHAPTER 17

Spiritism, Spiritualism, and the Occult

Seeing a ghost in New Orleans is as common as having a bowl of gumbo. The question is not when but where to savor them both.

—Kala Ambrose, 2012, p. 1

Spiritism, spiritualism, and the occult often get mixed up. In fact, spiritism and spiritualism are often used interchangeably, with the most notable difference being that spiritists believe in reincarnation, while not all spiritualists do (Bragdon, 2004/2013). Both hold to a dualism between the material/physical and the immaterial/spiritual, with the spirits of various beings inhabiting both. Both spiritists and spiritualists believe that disembodied spirits (discarnates) can communicate and carry on relationships with incarnate human beings. While many spiritualists become fascinated by communicating with discarnates, they miss the work of personal transformation that is a benchmark of spiritism, especially as seen in the work of shamanic healers. Spiritists, though, are empowered to make their own connections with God apart from the work of priests or others invested with spiritual authority. It would not be a stretch to understand spiritism as a reinterpretation of Christianity, with its own explanation of the gospel and its own path through forgiveness, gratitude, and love leading to wisdom that eventuates in liberation. These are activities and processes in which human beings engage to attain "salvation."

According to the Spiritist Medical Association, spirit is defined as the intelligent principle of the universe, in a duality with matter, and individual spirits are the intelligent beings of creation, incarnate (embodied) and discarnate (disembodied). "These intelligent beings, then, are the individualization of that intelligent principle."[1]

From a Christian perspective, spiritists have made a science, with its own philosophy, out of wizardry and the occult. Occult science (Steiner, 2013) is built on two considerations: (a) behind the visible world there is another and invisible world that is hidden from the senses and any thoughts linked to sensory processes, and (b) it is possible for human beings to penetrate this unseen level of existence by developing faculties otherwise dormant within themselves. The attempt to lay hold of the spiritual world, including the spiritual beings and powers resident within it, for one's own purposes by means of various rituals and methods is attested in the Bible. In Acts Chapter 8, Simon Magus, a Samaritan magician, attempted to pay Peter money if Peter would show him how to bestow the Holy Spirit upon people with the touch of his hands. Peter told him he was way off base and that the two of them had nothing in common. He advised him to repent and get with God's program. In 1 Samuel Chapter 28, Saul consulted a medium, a spiritist, to call up the spirit of Samuel (who had died of course) so that Saul could consult Samuel about the future. The spirit of Samuel was angry with him for disturbing his peace and informed Saul that he would soon die. From this and other places, it is apparent that Christianity accepts a spiritual world resident with power and the existence of disembodied spirits. It is not the belief in spiritual beings who exist after death that is a problem in Christianity; it is the attempt to conjure them up and use them for one's own purposes. That is magic and witchcraft, which is consistently condemned.

Magic is what some people do to attract others' attention, snag their senses, and affect what they believe. Magic "can either bind the human mind and spirit by its own subtle power, or the magician can make the appearance of something wonderful and use that appearance to catch and guide the mind" (Greer & Warnock, 2010–2011, p. 26). Thus, magic is either the appropriation of supernatural authority over people, or it is a trick played on the senses in order to influence people by suggesting supernatural or miraculous abilities and events.

What the magician attempts to simulate, spiritists and shamanic healers attempt to accomplish in reality. For instance, a spiritist might use magnetic action through various techniques of hand passes, appealing to the higher spirits to help in a matter, and the spiritist believes that spiritual fluids are transmitted to the patient through such hand passes, absorbed through the energy centers of the body known as chakras, and then dispersed as vital fluids throughout the body.

A shaman deals with spiritual aspects of disease by traveling "outside of time and space into what is called 'nonordinary reality,'" which can be understood as a parallel universe. In that realm, the shaman meets "spirit helpers in the form of animals or human teachers," and these compassionate spirits "perform the healing work with the shaman only acting as a conduit or 'hollow bone.'"[2] Such energy medicine "is the application of energy healing protocols and techniques for the soul utilizing ceremony."[3] Such shamanic healing has been practiced by indigenous peoples in various parts of the world for centuries. "Through a change in consciousness, Shamans enter 'non-ordinary' reality to request healing and advice from compassionate animals, humans, and other spirits."[4] In core shamanism, the shaman enters a

> shamanic state of consciousness through listening to rhythmic percussion. He or she then journeys to the world of spirits and connects with spirit allies for healing work. These spirits are available to help everyone, and the shaman's role is often to reconnect clients with their helping spirits, restoring their personal power.[5]

Shamanic healers "track and heal emotional wound, unhealthy relationships, loss of personal energy and motivation, and any other condition that is addressable at an energetic level."[6]

Table 17.1 shows various modalities available to shamanic healers and their respective purposes as depicted by Robin Gress.[7]

There is a great deal more that could be written on this overall subject, because people over time have accumulated libraries of esoteric literature on these subjects. A thorough treatment exceeds the scope of this chapter. If the reader would like to learn more, I recommend the PhD dissertation of David Wilson (2011), titled "Spiritualist Mediums and Other Traditional Shamans: Towards an Apprenticeship Model of Shamanic Practice," submitted in Religious Studies to the School of Divinity, College of Humanities and Social Science, University of Edinburgh. Occult practices, in general, are regarded by many to be a legitimate aspect of mystical spiritual experience; indeed, modern spiritism is regarded to have emerged from the ground of Swedenborgian practices (also influenced by the practices of Mesmer).

TABLE 17.1
SHAMANIC HEALING MODALITIES

Shamanic Modality	Description
Soul retrieval	Through trauma, pain, abuse, or other loss, a part of the soul leaves the body. The shaman's job is to find the lost soul part and return it to the body.
Power animal retrieval	Shamans believe that we each have a spirit guardian that could well be an animal spirit and whose job is to protect and empower us. The shaman brings back to the client his or her power animal and shares with the client the gifts this spiritual ally brings to help the client.
Extraction	The shaman removes unwanted or misplaced energy from the client; this unwanted energy arises from negative thought forms like anger, jealousy, and envy. It can also come from curses and spirit possession.
Soul remembering	The shaman travels to the client's soul to discover features of the client's life purpose, including his or her talents, skills, and gifts, and how the soul wants these used. The shaman brings this information to the client along with a symbol as a reminder of who he or she is on a core level and the light that they carry.
Divination and dream interpretation	Divination is used to clarify issues, situations, and events that would be helpful and healing for the client. Dreams can be interpreted by the shaman or by the client with the shaman facilitating by re-entering the dream with a spiritual ally to ask for the meaning and significance inherent within it.
Ancestral work	The shaman communicates with the client's ancestors, offering healing and/or to be a bridge for information between the ancestors and the client. Types of healing that occur with ancestral work include the lifting of family curses, removal of unhealthy contracts, healing a deceased soul or group of souls in the family line, and assisting the client in the completion of unfinished business.
Psychopomp work	The shaman assists a person who has died to cross over to the light. Some individuals remain earthbound after death. Situations that keep an individual's spirit on earth after death include sudden and unexpected death, attachment to a person or family, or a strong desire to complete some remaining unfinished business. A shaman's job is to help that individual soul move out of this dimension upon death, and take it to the light.

Adapted from the work of Robin Gress (http://www.sacredshamanichealing.com/20-Modalities.html).

There is a difference within the Christian frame of reference between something that is an error, as in having something in one's theology out of balance, and something that is intrinsically evil in the sense that it presents a counterfeit soteriology (study of salvation) and alternative truth claims about God, God's nature, God's activities in the lives of human beings, human nature and its limits (or lack thereof), and the processes of relating to God. There is simple error (misinterpretation, for instance), but then there is also heresy (e.g., outright spiritual deception). If one believes in a spiritual dimension, a world in which malevolent spirits are at work to destroy or disadvantage human beings, it becomes a troubling preoccupation to be constantly worried about how the battle will be waged.

The therapist dealing with such a case is not just dealing with an individual client and what he or she believes, but also with that client's faith community and what it believes (and teaches).

WHAT TO DO?

Some Christians preoccupy themselves with the spirit world and feel they are in a war with spiritual forces. While that is the Biblical picture as well (with such examples as God confronting Satan over the life of Job on the one hand, and angels doing battle with demons in response to the prayers of human beings on the other), some people attribute feeling ill, having a bad attitude, feeling frustrated or blocked, not experiencing success, and finding oneself in conflict with others to the influence of demons. Expressions like "he's got a spirit of negativism," "she's afflicted with a spirit of weakness," or "there is a spirit of dullness dominating that church" are common.

Some Christian groups emphasize spiritual warfare, and have various strategies and tactics for conducting conflict with the spiritual forces they imagine arrayed against God and against God's people. While the ultimate example of spiritual warfare is the casting out of demons—exorcism—the lesser forms of spiritual warfare concern dealing with temptation and the siege of the spirit that comes from living in a fallen world.

Dealing with these kinds of things amounts to exploring what a client actually believes. Life is an interconnected set of phenomena such that issues of truth, faith, faith community, and the processes and relationships connected to these and still other issues are all in play at any given time. I had a client who came from an Irish Catholic background, but in his work around anxiety issues, he became interested in mindfulness, and from there he became interested in Eastern philosophy and religious thought. He visited an ashram in India, and he began to wonder about losing one's self in the wholeness of the universe, about that kind of enlightenment and spiritual accomplishment. So I posed for him the question,

> Which do you believe? On this side you have losing your self to the universe, which is an impersonal field, but on the other you have a personal Creator that redeems you from sin. To which one are you currently more attracted?

He could not say. He did not know. He was trying to take from the East and match up elements of that worldview with corresponding elements in the Western spiritual worldview. He was "in process" in his development of faith, because he was sensing that it is not sufficient to simply "believe that." He had to put his trust in something; he had to put his weight on it and believe in it.

In this spiritual warfare, Christians find themselves in a struggle for the minds of people. They are engaged in evangelism and apologetics, because they want to have an influence for God in the lives of other people. Of course, these activities can become obnoxious to people who are really not interested, or at least not in the same mindset. Because of the aggressive tactics of some Christian groups, some people either feel guilty that they are not doing enough (i.e., what they should be doing by way of sharing their faith with others or making cogent arguments for the veracity of their teachings) or they feel ashamed and turned off to their faith because of what they regard as the bad behavior of a few believers.

Psychotherapists do not operate primarily as theologians, evangelists, or apologists for any given spiritual or religious group. They may interact dialogically with clients around issues relevant to such fields, but the psychotherapist is interested in the client's interpretations and the implications of facts that the client might see.

I have often used imaginal experimentation to explore such things. With one client who was especially troubled by an overly oppressive view of God, including the fact that she felt no matter what she did she could never please God, I asked her to imagine what it would be like to just give up trying. The mere thought of it was not freeing; rather, it was abhorrent. How could I suggest it? It was more preferable to her to maintain seeing herself as unacceptable and miserable than to ditch her belief in God and her commitment to the existence she had with Him. Hers was a strong faith, but it was a commitment to a position of failure and unacceptance in which she believed God to be punitive and harsh rather than gracious and loving. I simply called attention to that and how miserable she felt with that kind of belief. To "correct" her with my own theology would have been to privilege my perspective over hers; however, working dialogically, I was free to say that I did not understand God in that same way. We experienced difference, and we were satisfied to take note of it.

I believe that a psychotherapist needs to know his or her limits as well. Whether this be someone who does not believe in God or is not interested in spirituality, or whether it be someone who has a theological limit that prevents him or her from moving into the area of the occult, for example, the therapist needs to be able to identify that limit and refer the client if needed. I am not willing to explore occult practices and engage in experimental séances and such. I find the thought of attempting to contact the spirits of the dead or to engage demons in any way, even to give them the gift of my awareness, to be detestable. It is a strong feeling that I know would not allow me to be authentic and available to the client. This is not the same thing as doing empty-chair work in the client addressing significant people who have passed on. I suppose this is because I am seeing that kind of work as being conducted in the phenomenal field of the client rather than in the ontic field of both client and therapist. For instance, when I worked with a client who had lost her baby in childbirth, we did some empty-chair work, and the client addressed her dead baby. It was helpful and moving emotionally, but I conceived of the client syncing up her split-off concerns about that baby rather than attempting to contact the spirit of the deceased child. For psychotherapists who do not want to work with spiritual issues in their clients who have spiritually related issues, I believe it would be to the therapist's credit to respond to the client ethically and refer him or her to someone who can be available for such things and respond ethically and with some degree of competence.

NOTES

1. From the website for the Spiritist Medical Association (http://www.sma-us.org/content/about-spiritism-0)
2. From http://www.lenaswanson.com/what-shamanic-healing
3. From http://www.explorespiritism.com/SCIENCE%20start.htm
4. From http://www.spirithealer.com/about/carlas-bio/
5. From http://www.spirithealer.com/about/shamanism
6. From http://www.maraclearspring.com/shamanism__soul_retrieval/
7. From http://www.sacredshamanichealing.com/20-Modalities.html

CHAPTER 18

Endings, Death, and Personal Eschatology

Death is still a fearful, frightening happening, and the fear of death is a universal fear even if we think we have mastered it on several levels.

—Elisabeth Kübler-Ross, 1969/1997, p. 19

When I was a corpsman in the Navy, I witnessed death. There was the classic boatswain's mate who, looking to be about 50 but actually being about 40, had traveled the seas and was an alcoholic with a liver that could no longer function. He was bedridden and would go in and out of hepatic coma. One day when he was in a coma, I was helping another corpsman change his bedding and give him a bath. Suddenly, he began that very noticeable form of breathing called Cheyne–Stokes respiration, and he died. It was a dramatic thing. The other corpsman and I were invited to observe the autopsy, which we did. It was a strange thing to be taking care of a character of a man, listening to all his tall tales one day, watch him die, and then be looking at his body splayed open on the stainless steel table the next. Then there was the man who had a heart attack, and we tried to save him with cardiopulmonary resuscitation. Then there was the fellow corpsman who ripped open a malignant mole and died of metastatic cancer, and there was the patient on the psych wards where I worked who went on liberty, climbed the Golden Gate Bridge and jumped off it. There were also my friends, my fellow corpsmen, who went with the Marines to Vietnam and died there.

221

I have watched people pass from living through dying to death. The lived body is animate. The dead body is inanimate. The person does not seem to be there.

When I was a young Christian, a woman a few years younger than I was introduced in church. She had a brave expression on her face, but she was not polished or used to speaking in front of people. She had cancer, and she needed a bone marrow transplant. At the time it was a new procedure and rather experimental, but it seemed to be the only hope for her. The church offered her a chance to give her testimony of faith that God would work things out. God would somehow find a donor. Sure enough, a few weeks later, it was determined that her younger brother could be such a donor and the procedure was scheduled. Everybody prayed for them both. After the procedure was accomplished, the church had the two of them up front again, and everyone was praising God for the miracle and the success of the operation. The younger brother was mostly silent. Actually, he was rather marginalized, because his sister had the greater story. After all, she was the one with cancer. All he did was supply some bone marrow. She was the one with the miracle remission and the testimony that God is faithful.

A few years later, she died. It was when I was in my undergraduate study with a major in psychology. At the university, one of the professors had had a heart attack and almost died. In the intensive care unit, he started contemplating his life. He came to realize how precious every moment is, and the reprieve gave him a new appreciation for living. He decided to start teaching a class called "Death and Dying." The main text was Elisabeth Kübler Ross's book by a similar name. That class became the most popular class on the entire campus, and on the first day of the class, I sat with the younger brother of the girl who died of cancer even with her brother's donation of bone marrow.

He was bitter. He was angry at the church. Not only had they marginalized him and made her into such a star, but they had given all the credit for the remission of cancer to God, which had left no recognition for him, and then she had died anyway. As people in the class went around telling reasons for why they had wanted to take the class, the focus came to him, and he told the story of the church event. He told how angry he was at God and the church people. He told of how he had never been able to get over his sister's death. He said he had signed up for the class hoping for some kind of closure on a family nightmare.

The first funeral I ever conducted was for an old family friend. When I was still about 3 or 4 years old, we lived in a semirural area on the growing edge of the city of Sacramento. There was an electrified barbed wire fence in the backyard that jolted me real good one day. There was Kenny, a country sort of character who chased jackrabbits away from his place with a rifle. There were his daughters who babysat for my folks when they wanted to go out to dinner. We all grew up, and when I came home from seminary and joined the staff of a local church, Kenny died. His wife asked me to do the funeral. I was petrified. However, I got through it, and I eventually of course conducted others. There was the highly esteemed attorney from New York who one day was found floating in the ocean. It was a mystery how he got off his boat, but his family came out from the east coast; they were all liberal Jews who did not seem to have much of a personal faith in God. There was also the local man who had at one time run for governor of his state. His funeral procession ran up and down the highway on the way to the cemetery.

When I was pastoring a small church along the Oregon coast, members of a large family, with quite a number of young children, rented a house that sat on Ocean Road, where the sand dune dropped off to the beach in the little town of Manzanita. It was a Saturday. I was taking it easy at our house about 3 miles back into the mountains, where the Nehalem River wound through the forest. I got a call that people needed some help. The children had gotten up early, like children do when their parents are on vacation and just want to sleep in on a lazy day. They had gone across the road and started playing on the beach, running up and down and splashing each other in the shallow spots where the water ran up the sand before receding toward the Pacific Ocean. Recent flooding had washed a number of logs down and into the sea, and a few of them had washed up on the beach. As one young boy, about 3 years old, was playing near one of those logs, the surf came up a little higher on the sand, lifted that log and rolled it right over the little boy, crushing him. The parents were distraught, and I met with them that morning to help process their grief.

By the time I was in my doctoral program I thought I knew about death. I thought I knew about grief, and I thought I knew how to handle grief. I had been with the dying and the grieving. Then my youngest brother was killed. He was driving a car on a freeway, and an old woman in another car, going the other way on the opposite side of the divider, died at the wheel. Her car swerved, crossed the divider, and struck my brother square. It ruptured a main artery in his neck under the skin, and while he was unconscious, he bled out on the spot. His wife called me on the phone from the hospital where their son was recuperating. She said, "Tim is dead." It bypassed my head and went straight through my heart. It cut the equilibrium from my body, so that I instantly began to tremble and moan. While I stood there trying to fathom what I had heard, I began to cry. It was uncontrollable, and someone had to take the phone.

We had grown up together in a family of five children. He was the youngest, and I was the oldest. Although he was a fraternal twin with one of my other brothers, he looked more like me. We both had sandy blond hair as kids. I am sure he was closer to his twin brother, but I always felt somehow connected to him just because we looked alike. Tim was a great storyteller, and he was a musician. We used to play in a band together, and we both became Christians about the same general time. When I was going through college and headed off to seminary, he was out on the road, playing 25 shows a week and living out of motels. He met his wife on the road, and they settled down finally in Florida, where Tim had just joined the staff of a church as their youth minister. Don't ask me why *that* was the perfect time for him to leave this earth and "go home," because I don't have an answer for that.

The theological study of endings is called eschatology, and it includes the end of times in the culmination of history when God brings it all to a head in the re-creation of the world and the personal end of times for each person when that person dies. As such, eschatology is a perfect reason for people to argue, because the arguments are about things that cannot be proven. The end of the world has not arrived yet, so we really don't know experientially how that takes place. The end of *me* hasn't arrived yet either, so I really don't know how that is going to take place, and further to that, although there are claims people have made that they have died and come back, the jury is still out on what those experiences are.[1]

Religious people have claimed to have received revelations and visions about what is to come in the world and also about what heaven is like or the life after death. These things can be troubling and cause anxiety. People have actually acted upon some of these scenarios, sold their belongings, cashed out their investments, and so on, only to discover that the date projected for the end of the world came and went, and the world was still there. Will there *be* an end? That is what the Bible teaches, but it doesn't give a date, and in fact Jesus told His disciples that no person could know that day, because it was hidden in His Father's mind. Nevertheless, people pore over and attempt to reconcile the books of Revelations from the New Testament and Daniel from the Old Testament. There are other passages in the Bible that are included, but those are the two major ones. Many times, the debates about the end of the world focus on teachings about what is called the rapture and the tribulation. Supposedly, all the Christians will be taken out of the world prior to a period of unsurpassed suffering, but that is not universally accepted. Some believe Christians will endure the tribulation along with non-Christians. These debates often simply result in acrimonious conflict.

The most common theory among Christians about what happens at death is that the Christian who dies goes immediately into the conscious presence of God. How that can be is debatable. Some follow a Cartesian split between body and soul, the material and immaterial aspects of human beings. In fact, some further break down the immaterial part of a person to distinguish between soul and spirit or mind and spirit, and then they claim that the spirit returns to God, while the body returns to the dust of the earth (Beck & Demarest, 2006). Many current Christian psychologists and philosophers hold to what is called a nonreductive physicalism (Murphy, 2006; Murphy & Brown, 2009), in which the higher complexity of mind emerges from the relatively lower complexity of brain; the brain engaged in the world through the body gives rise to the mind, which supervenes over the brain/body and exerts downward causation, directing the activities of the whole person. In that way of seeing things, which tends to be supported by neuroscience, the mind is dependent on brain activity. They are not the same, but they are linked. So what happens to the immaterial part of the person at the death of the body/brain? The mind could not exist. Is there, then, some way in which a person's spirit, for want of a better term for referring to some kind of ongoing consciousness, does go into the awareness of God's presence? Or does the person just cease to exist? Does the person wait for the resurrection in a kind of "soul sleep?" Does the person simply blend with one great consciousness of the universe (Atman assimilated into Brahman) as Eastern religious thought would have it? For all practical purposes, that would be the same as not having any afterlife at all (as the atheist would have it), because there would be no individual awareness of self.

WHAT TO DO

In Bermuda there is a gang war. Guns are outlawed on the island, but the gangs have them anyway. They assassinate their victims on buses, at night clubs, at church functions, and while they sit in their homes.

The assassins ride two to a motorbike, one a driver and the other a shooter. They wear black clothing, and black helmets with tinted visors. You can't see who the person is. They ride up, shoot, and ride away.

I routinely have clients who are related to these victims. Sometimes I have clients who are related to the assassins. One client started off naming the people in her family that had been killed, and she just kept going. She ran out of fingers on both hands. She started off naming them with a calm voice, but by the time she reached the last finger on the second hand, she was trembling, and I had tears forming in my eyes. The loss was staggering. The place might as well be a combat zone.

One family came to me precisely because they believed their son was a target of the gangs. They lived in fear for his life. It was depressing, and at the same time they were angry at the young man for getting himself in such a mess. They took my suggestion of inviting the young man to a session. He came and at first was quite resistant, being quiet and not saying much, but he decided he would come back. The next time he came with the whole family, and he looked more animated, and he was wearing a nice-looking shirt that everyone complimented him about. He was quite verbal, and the whole session was about what possible solutions to his problem might be utilized. He was looking to get off the island and to go to school, to better himself. The next week he was dead. When I met with his sister, she was extremely distraught with her grief.

What kind of explanation for such tragedy could possibly be given? I had nothing that would take away her pain. I had no answer that seemed to satisfy. It reminded me of a time riding in the car with an elderly man who had just left his dead mother at the rest home. She had been there suffering with a long illness, and then she finally died, and we were coming back from the last "visit" with her. He looked my way in the car and said, "Why? And don't tell me it's just part of God's grand design."

Well, such things *are* part of God's grand design, but that doesn't comfort. It doesn't make sense that a loving God would put up with such suffering, and people struggle with that (see Chapter 14).

Now that grief is considered a psychological disorder by the *Diagnostic and Statistical Manual of Mental Disorders*, 5th edition (*DSM-V*), it poses a problem for psychotherapists. Do you work to reduce the symptoms of grief, or do you work to promote more grieving? When Jesus entered into the mourning of people, He cried. When people lose someone important to them, they grieve. It's a normal process and a needed process, or else the person gets stuck and cannot put the loss to rest. It becomes an incomplete gestalt that sits on the street of that person's life and begs to each passing setback.

When I am with a grieving person, I attempt to provide support, to make sure they sense my presence with them. Related to that, if it fits, if I actually do grieve the loss, I allow myself to enter into it and share the grieving with the client. I mourn with them. I promote grieving by asking them to tell me stories about the person who has died, especially stories about times they have enjoyed being with that person and what that person has meant to them. I ask to see pictures.

In more quiet moments, I inquire into what the person believes about death, about life after death, and so also about the current condition of the deceased.

1. Do you believe in life after death?
2. Where do you believe your loved one is right now?
3. Do you think he/she can see and hear you?
4. Do you believe you will see that person again?
5. What makes you believe these things?

It is bad enough to lose a child to death, but when one believes she has killed her own baby, that can be quite rough. The issue of abortion is one that divides families; I bring it up here simply because I have met with women who have had to deal with the guilt of having had an abortion. In such cases, the grief is compounded by guilt. One woman, in particular, had had two children and then gotten pregnant outside of her marriage. Feeling trapped, she decided to have an abortion, but she felt guilty afterward; she felt she had committed murder. When her two daughters grew into adolescence, one of them became pregnant. The young girl did not want to have an abortion, but her mother thought she would be throwing away her opportunities in life if she didn't have one. Still, once again she felt horribly guilty to be contemplating what she regarded as murder. Eventually, the daughter did have an abortion, the daughter felt guilty, and the mother grieved heavily.

How any particular spiritual system handles what might be called a transgression is relevant to how a follower of that system regards his or her standing before God or the universe. In Christianity, the transgression is covered by the propitiation of Christ's atonement and the application of grace (see Chapter 15). One's standing with regard to one's failures in life are a concern for the person contemplating his or her own death and also the death of a loved one.

I have a friend and colleague who believes that when a person dies, he or she just ceases. There is no continuing consciousness, and so no regret, no awareness of being dead or of anything else. It's just over. The personal eschatology in such a case is just about what kind of ending the deceased endured, or about what kind of ending one wants for him- or herself. However, for other people, personal eschatology is not just about what kind of ending a person has, but what kind of transition a person experiences moving from this life to the life after death. The differing religious systems have various takes on this issue, for death and what happens to a person when death comes is one of those ultimate issues Paul Tillich referred to. It's one of those things covered in any given spiritual worldview, and that is because we all have to face our own inevitable ending.

NOTES

1. They are called "near-death" experiences, giving the implication that what is taking place is not death itself.

Conclusion

The writing of many books is endless, and excessive devotion to books is wearying to the body.

—Kohelet, Ecclesiastes 12:12

My wife hates to see me write. What she sees is the struggle with the self-discipline necessary to devote time to writing, the agony of feeling stuck and unable to get momentum going in order to make progress, and the manifestations of stress from approaching deadlines. She knows what it's like to be alone when I have to spend my "free" time writing instead of doing something with her. At the same time, we believe this is what I am supposed to be doing. Perhaps I could be doing it better, but this is what I am supposed to be doing.

Amy Tan (2003) said that she preferred to refer to herself as a writer. "A writer writes–she writes in the present progressive tense. Whereas an author, unless she is clearly said to be 'contemporary,' is in the past tense, someone who once wrote" (p. 7).

I am a writer. It's been a calling on my life since I was 10 years old. Writers write best when they write about what they know. James Michener (1992) said, "With my pen I have engraved warrants of citizenship in the most remote corners, for truly, the world has been my home" (p. 512). So I have written here about spirituality and the practice of psychotherapy, because for years now they have been my homes. More specifically, I have attempted to call attention to what makes for spiritual competence in the practice of psychotherapy, and I have used Christianity (something I know) in order to illustrate various dynamics and situations that I believe will show up in the lives of spiritual people, whether they be Christian, Jewish, Islamic, spiritist, Buddhist, Hindu, or Native American. There is not, of course, a hard parallel so that the doctrines line up with balance and symmetry. But there is community in all groups of spiritual people attempting to encourage one another in the practices of their respective religions. There are rigid and legalistic people in these communities, and there are those with more compassion, even if "grace" has a decidedly specific meaning in Christianity that is lost when one leaves behind the propitiation of sins in the death of Christ. There is still the potential of grace in common among human beings.

Competence is knowledge, ability, and the results of their application over time. It is not necessary to know everything about all kinds of spirituality in order to work with people, but it is necessary to know something. It is also necessary to have an open mind and the attitude of a respectful learner in working with spiritual people, because a therapist has to entertain the possibility that what his or her clients are saying is true—not just phenomenologically true. This respectful openness to the experience of the client allows the therapist to learn specific features about the client's spiritual world. My hope is that peering into my spiritual world will have contributed to the reader's knowledge and will affect the way in which psychotherapists approach spirituality in their practices of psychotherapy.

I believe that people come to us as situated beings and not as sets of symptoms like the check boxes on an Exner scoring sheet for the Rorschach. They overflow the categorical systems of the *Diagnostic and Statistical Manual of Mental Disorders* (DSM). They defy reduction. They make contact with us, and before you know it, we have become part of their complex situations. These people are spiritual to some degree, and so we cannot escape spirituality as an important aspect of the overall situation of which they make us a part. Furthermore, we are spiritual to some degree, and so we afflict them with our own religious contagion.

In all these various situations, there is spirituality as relationship and there is spirituality as process—the what and how of religious significance. These things appear in the ultimate concerns people contemplate, discuss, and ruminate over in the company of others.

References

Ambrose, K. (2012). *Spirits of New Orleans: Voodoo curses, vampire legends, and cities of the dead*. Covington, KY: Clerisy Press.

American Psychological Association. (2003). Guidelines on multicultural education, training, research, practice, and organizational change for psychologists. *American Psychologist, 58*, 377–402. doi:10.1037/0003-066X.58.5.377

American Psychological Association. (2010, June 1). *Ethical principles of psychologists and code of conduct* (Amendments to the 2002 Ethics Code). Retrieved from http://www.apa.org/ethics/code/index.aspx

Archer, M. (1982). Morphogenesis versus structuration: On combining structure and action. *British Journal of Sociology, 33*(4), 455–483.

Archer, M. (2007). The trajectory of the morphogenetic approach: An account in the first-person. *Sociologia, Problemas e Práticas, 54*, 35–47.

Archer, M. (2010). Morphogenesis versus structuration: On combining structure and action. *British Journal of Sociology, 61*(Suppl. s1), 225–252.

Archer, M., Collier, A., & Porpora, D. (2004). *Transcendence: Critical realism and God*. New York, NY: Routledge.

Aristotle. (2006). *De anima* (R. D. Hicks, Trans., with an introduction by W. Ott). New York, NY: Barnes and Noble.

Aten, J., O'Grady, K., & Worthington, E., Jr. (Eds.). (2012). *The psychology of religion and spirituality for clinicians: Using research in your practice*. New York, NY: Routledge.

Bankart, C. P. (1996). *Talking cures: A history of western and eastern psychotherapies*. Belmont, CA: Wadsworth.

Bartz, J. (2009). Theistic existential psychotherapy. *Psychology of Religion and Spirituality, 1*(2), 69–80.

Batchelor, M. (2010). *The spirit of the Buddha*. New Haven, CT: Sacred Literature Series/Yale University Press.

Bauer, W., Arndt, W., & Gingrich, F. W. (1957). *A Greek-English lexicon of the New Testament and other early Christian literature*. Chicago, IL: University of Chicago Press.

Beck, J., & Demarest, B. (2006). *The human person in theology and psychology: A Biblical anthropology for the twenty-first century*. Grand Rapids, MI: Kregel.

Bennett-Levy, J., Butler, G., Fennell, M., Hackman, A., Mueller, M., & Westbrook, D. (2004). *Oxford guide to behavioural experiments in cognitive therapy*. New York, NY: Oxford University Press.

Berger, P., & Luckmann, T. (2011). *The social construction of reality: A treatise in the sociology of knowledge.* New York, NY: Open Road Integrated Media. (Original work published 1967).

Bhagavad Gita. (n.d.). Chapter 2: The philosophy of discrimination (Shri Purohit Swami, Trans.).

Bloesche, D. (2007). *Spirituality old & new: Recovering authentic spiritual life.* Downer's Gove, IL: IVP Academic.

Bloom, D. (2013). Situated ethics and the ethical world of gestalt therapy. In G. Francesetti, M. Gecele, & J. Roubal (Eds.), *Gestalt therapy in clinical practice: From psychopathology to the aesthetics of contact.* Milano, Italy: FrancoAngeli.

Blue, K. (1993). *Healing spiritual abuse: How to break free from bad church experiences.* Downers Grove, IL: InterVarsity Press.

Bonhoeffer, D. (1995). *Ethics.* New York, NY: Touchstone/Simon & Schuster. (Original work published 1949)

Bounds, E. M. (1997). *Purpose in prayer.* New Kensington, PA: Whitaker House.

Bradstreet, A. (2006). Sage. In H. Nichols (Ed.), *Anne Bradstreet: A guided tour of the life and thought of a Puritan poet* (pp. 153–179). Phillipsburgh, NJ: P&R.

Bragdon, E. (2013). *Kardec's spiritism: A home for healing and spiritual evolution.* Woodstock, VT: Lightening Up Press (Original work published 2004).

Brennan, B. (1987). *Hands of light: A guide to healing through the human energy field.* New York, NY: Bantam Books.

Brawer, P. A., Handal, P. J., Fabricatore, A. N., Roberts, R., & Wajda-Johnston, V. A. (2002). Training and education in religion/spirituality within APA-accredited clinical psychology programs. *Professional Psychology: Research and Practice, 33,* 203–206. doi:10.1037/0735-7028.33.2.203

Brown, C. (1976). *Dictionary of New Testament theology* (Vols. 1–3). Grand Rapids, MI: Zondervan.

Brown, C. (1978). Spirit. In C. Brown (Ed.), *New international dictionary of New Testament theology* (Vol. 3, pp. 693–708). Grand Rapids, MI: Zondervan.

Brown, F., Driver, S., & Briggs, C. (1978). *A Hebrew and English lexicon of the Old Testament.* Oxford, UK: Oxford University Press. (Original work published 1907)

Brownell, P. (2008). Faith: An existential, phenomenological, and Biblical integration. In J. H. Ellens (Ed.), *Miracles: God, science, and psychology in the paranormal, vol. 2, medical and therapeutic events* (pp. 213–234). Westport, CT: Praeger.

Brownell, P. (2010a). *Gestalt therapy: A guide to contemporary practice.* New York, NY: Springer Publishing Company.

Brownell, P. (2010b). The healing potential of religious community. In J. H. Ellens (Ed.), *The healing power of spirituality: How faith helps humans thrive, vol. 2, religion* (pp. 1–22). Santa Barbara, CA: Praeger/ABC-CLIO.

Brownell, P. (2012a). *Gestalt therapy for addictive and self-medicating behaviors.* New York, NY: Springer Publishing Company.

Brownell, P. (2012b). Spirituality in gestalt therapy. In T. B.-Y. Levine (Ed.), *Gestalt therapy: Advances in theory and practice* (pp. 93–103). New York, NY: Routledge.

Buber, M. (1958). *I and thou* (2nd ed.). Edinburgh, UK: T & T Clark. (Original work published 1923)

Buber, M. (2002). *Between man and man*. New York, NY: Routledge. (Original work published 1947)

Buber, M. (1988). *Eclipse of God: Studies in the relation between religion and philosophy*. Amherst, NY: Humanity Books. (Original work published 1952)

Burkitt, I. (2013). Self and others in the field of perception: The role of micro-dialogue, feeling, and emotion in perception. *Journal of Theoretical and Philosophical Psychology, 33*(4), 267–279. doi:10.1037/a0030255

Burr, V. (2003). *Social constructionism* (2nd ed.). New York, NY: Routledge.

Canda, E. R., & Furman, L. D. (1999). *Spiritual diversity in social work practice: The heart of helping*. New York, NY: Free Press.

Capra, F. (1976). Modern physics and Eastern mysticism. *Journal of Transpersonal Psychology, 8*(1), 20–40.

Carpenter-Song, E., Hipolito, M., & Whitely, R. (2012). Right here is an oasis: How "recovery communities" contribute to recovery for people with serious mental illnesses. *Psychiatric Rehabilitation Journal, 35*(6), 435–440.

Chrétien, J.-L. (2004). *The call and the response*. New York, NY: Fordham University Press.

Clark, A. (2011). *Supersizing the mind: Embodiment, action, and cognitive extension*. New York, NY: Oxford University Press.

Cole, P. (2013). In the shadow of the leader: Power, reflection, and dialogue in gestalt group therapy. *Gestalt Review, 17*(2), 178–189.

Coles, R. (1990). *The spiritual life of children*. Boston, MA: Houghton Mifflin.

Comas-Diaz, L. (2006). Cultural variation in the therapeutic relationship. In C. D. Goodheart, A. E. Kazdin, & R. J. Sternberg (Eds.), *Evidence-based psychotherapy: Where practice and research meet* (pp. 81–105). Washington, DC: American Psychological Association.

Consoli, A., Tzaquitzal, M., & González, A. (2013). Mayan cosmovision and integrative counseling: A case study from Guatemala. In S. Poyrazli & C. Thompson (Eds.), *International case studies in mental health* (pp. 141–153). Thousand Oaks, CA: SAGE.

Corey, G. (2013). *Theory and practice of counseling and psychotherapy* (9th ed.). Belmont, CA: Brooks/Cole, Cengage Learning.

Corsini, R., & Wedding, D. (Eds.). (2007). *Current psychotherapies* (8th ed.). Florence, KY: Cengage.

Cory, G. (2000). *Toward consilience: The bioneurological basis of behavior, thought, experience, and language*. New York, NY: Springer Science+Business Media.

Cosmelli, D., & Thompson, E. (2011). Brain in a vat or body in a world? Brain-bound versus enactive views of experience. *Philosophical Topics, 39*(1), 163–180.

Critchley, S., & Bernasconi, R. (2002). *The Cambridge companion to Levinas.* Cambridge, UK: Cambridge University Press.

Crocker, S. (1999). *A well-lived life: Essays in gestalt therapy.* Cambridge, MA: GestaltPress.

Crook-Lyon, R. E., O'Grady, K. A., Smith, T. B., Jensen, D. R., Golightly, T., & Potkar, K. A. (2012). Addressing religious and spiritual diversity in graduate training and multicultural education for professional psychologists. *Psychology of Religion and Spirituality, 4*(3), 169–181. doi:10.1037/a0026403

Crowell, S. (2010). Existentialism. In E. Zalta (Ed.), *The Stanford encyclopedia of philosophy.* Retrieved from http://plato.stanford.edu/entries/existentialism

Cushman, P. (1992). Psychotherapy to 1992: A historically situated interpretation. In D. K. Freedheim, H. Freudenberger, J. Kessler, S. Messer, D. Peterson, & H. Strupp (Eds.), *History of psychotherapy: A century of change* (pp. 21–64). Washington, DC: American Psychological Association.

Culp, J. (2013, Spring). Panentheism. In E. Zalta (Ed.), *The Stanford encyclopedia of philosophy.* Retrieved from http://plato.stanford.edu/archives/spr2013/entries/panentheism

Dalai Lama. (1999). *Ethics for a new millenium.* New York, NY: Riverhead Books.

Damasio, A. (1999). *The feeling of what happens: Body and emotion in the making of consciousness.* New York, NY: Harcourt.

Dana, H. E., & Mantey, J. R. (1955). *A manual grammar of the Greek New Testament.* Toronto, CA: Macmillan. (Original work published 1927)

Davis, A. (1999). The experimental methodology in psychology. In G. Breakwell, S. Hammond, & C. Fife-Shaw (Eds.), *Research methods in psychology.* Santa Barbara, CA: SAGE.

Davis, W. (2008). *Wade Davis: The worldwide web of belief and ritual.* Retrieved from http://www.ted.com/talks/wade_davis_on_the_worldwide_web_of_belief_and_ritual.html

Dawkins, R. (2006). *The God delusion.* New York, NY: Houghton Mifflin.

de Saint-Exupery, A. (1942). *Night flight.* New York, NY: Harcourt, Brace & World, Inc.

DeRobertis, E. (2011). Prolegomena to a Thomistic child psychology. *Journal of Theoretical and Philosophical Psychology, 31*(3), 151–164.

Derrett, J. (1986). Hinduism. In C. Jones, G. Wainwright, & E. Yarnold (Eds.), *The study of spirituality* (pp. 504–509). New York, NY: Oxford University Press.

Diaz, J., & Schneider, R. (2012). Globalization as re-traumatization: Rebuilding Haiti from the spirit up (*Pwogwam Santé Mantal Jeremie Haiti*). *Journal of Social Issues, 68*(3), 493–513.

Duncan, B., & Miller, S. (2000). *The heroic client: A revolutionary way to improve effectiveness through client-directed, outcome-informed therapy.* San Francisco, CA: Jossey-Bass.

Edwards, J. (2011). *A treatise concerning religious affections in three parts.* Amazon Digital Services. (Original work published 1746)

Elder-Vass, D. (2007). For emergence: Refining Archer's account of social structure. *Journal for the Theory of Social Behavior, 37*(1), 25–44.

Epstein, R. M., & Hundert, E. M. (2002). Defining and assessing professional competence. *JAMA: Journal of the American Medical Association, 287,* 226–235.

Falb, M., & Pargament, K. (2012). Relational mindfulness, spirituality, and the therapeutic bond. *Asian Journal of Psychiatry, 5*(4), 351–354.

Field, T. (2009). *Complementary and alternative therapies research.* Washington, DC: American Psychological Association.

Flew, A. (2007). *There is a God: How the world's most notorious atheist changed his mind.* New York, NY: HarperCollins.

Flynn, B. (2004). Maurice Merleau-Ponty. In E. N. Zalta (Ed.), *The Stanford encyclopedia of philosophy* (Fall 2011 ed.). Retrieved from http://plato.stanford .edu/archives/fall2011/entries/merleau-ponty

Foster, R. (1978). *Celebration of discipline.* New York, NY: HarperCollins.

Fowler, J. (1996). *Faithful change: The personal and public challenges of postmodern life.* Nashville, TN: Abingdon Press.

Francesetti, G. (2012). Pain and beauty: From the psychopathology to the aesthetics of contact. *British Gestalt Journal, 21*(2), 4–18.

Frankl, V. (2000). *Man's search for ultimate meaning.* New York, NY: Basic Books.

Friedman, M. (2000). Existentialism. In A. Kazdin (Ed.), *Encyclopedia of psychology* (Vol. 3, pp. 290–294). Washington, DC: American Psychological Association.

Fries, G. (1978). Logos. In C. Brown (Ed.), *The new international dictionary of New Testament theology* (Vol. 3, Pri-Z). Grand Rapids, MI: Zondervan.

Gant, E. (1994). Truth, freedom and responsibility in the dialogues of psychotherapy. *Journal of Theoretical and Philosophical Psychology, 14*(2), 146–158.

Gartner, R. (2004). Predatory priests: Sexually abusing fathers. *Studies in Gender and Sexuality, 5*(1), 31056.

Geek New Testament. (1983). Atlanta, GA: Society of Biblical Literature. Retrieved from http://www.biblegateway.com/passage/?search=Romans%208:28-30& version=NASB

Geller, S., & Greenberg, L. (2012). *Therapeutic presence: A mindful approach to effective therapy.* Washington, DC: American Psychological Association.

Gockel, A. (2011). Client perspectives on spirituality in the therapeutic relationship. *The Humanistic Psychologist, 39*(2), 154–168.

Goldstein, K. (1995). *The organism.* New York, NY: Urzone.

Gonsiorek, J., Richards, C., Pargament, K., & McMinn, M. (2009). Ethical challenges and opportunities at the edge: Incorporating spirituality and religion into psychotherapy. *Professional Psychology: Research and Practice, 40*(4), 385–395.

Graumann, C. (1995). Commonality, mutuality, reciprocity: A conceptual introduction. In I. Marková, C. Graumann, & K. Foppa (Eds.), *Mutualities in dialogue* (pp. 1–24). Cambridge, UK: Cambridge University Press.

Greer, J., & Warnock, C. (2010–2011). *The complete Picatrix: The occult classic of astrological magic liber atratus edition.* Phoenix, AZ: Adocentyn Press.

Guinness, O. (1976). *In two minds: The dilemma of doubt & how to resolve it.* Downers Grove, IL: InterVarsity Press.

Gunaratana, B. (2002). *Mindfulness in plain English.* Somerville, MA: Wisdom.

Hage, S. (2006). A closer look at the role of spirituality in psychology training programs. *Professional Psychology: Research and Practice, 37*(3), 303–310.

Hanson, S., Kerkhoff, T., & Bush, S. (2005). *Health care ethics for psychologists: A casebook.* Washington, DC: American Psychological Association.

Harris, S. (2005). *The end of faith: Religion, terror, and the future of reason.* New York, NY: W. W. Norton.

Hass, L. (2008). *Merleau-Ponty's philosophy.* Bloomington: Indiana University Press.

Hill, P., Pargamet, K., Hood, R., McCullough, J., Swyers, J., Larson, D., & Zinnbauer, B. (2001). Conceptualizing religion and spirituality: Points of commonality, points of departure. *Journal for the Theory of Social Behaviour, 30*(1), 51–77.

Hindu Online. (n.d.). *Hindu ethics.* Retrieved from http://hinduonline.co/HinduReligion/AllAboutHinduism3.html#_VPID_34

Hirsch, I. (1996). Observing-participation, mutual enactment, and the new classical models. *Contemporary Psychoanalysis, 32*(3), 359–383.

Horton, M. (2011). *The Christian faith: A systematic theology for pilgrims on the way.* Grand Rapids, MI: Zondervan.

James, W. (2003). *Pragmatism.* New York, NY: Barnes & Noble. (Original work published 1907)

Jacobs, L. (1986). Judaism. In C. Jones, G. Wainwright, & E. Yarnold (Eds.), *The study of spirituality* (pp. 491–497). New York, NY: Oxford University Press.

Johnson, A. (2012). Naming chaos: Accident, precariousness, and the spirits of wildness in urban Thai spirit cults. *American Ethnologist, 39*(4), 766–778.

Johnson, D., & VanVonderen, J. (1991). *The subtle power of spiritual abuse.* Minneapolis, MN: Bethany House/Baker.

Johnson, M. (1990). *The body in the mind: The bodily basis of meaning, imagination, and reason.* Chicago, IL: University of Chicago Press.

Johnson, M. (2007). *The meaning of the body: Aesthetics of human understanding.* Chicago, IL: University of Chicago Press.

Johnson, W. B., Barnett, J., Elman, N., Forrest, L., & Kaslow, N. (2012). The competent community: Toward a vital reformulation of professional ethics. *American Psychologist, 67,* 557–569.

Kamlah, E. (1971). Spirit. In C. Brown (Ed.), *New international dictionary of New Testament theology* (Vol. 3, pp. 689–693). Grand Rapids, MI: Zondervan.

Kassis, H. (1983). *A concordance of the Qur'an.* Berkeley: University of California Press.

Keeling, M., Dolbin-MacNab, M., Ford, J., & Perkins, S. (2010). Partners in the spiritual dance: Learning clients' steps while minding all our toes. *Journal of Marital and Family Therapy, 36*(2), 229–243.

Keller, N. H. M. (2002). *Al-Maqasid: Nawawi's manual of Islam.* Beltsville, MD: Amana.

Kepner, J. (1999). *Body process: A gestalt approach to working with the body in psychotherapy.* Cambridge, MA: GestaltPress.

Keshavan, M. (2012). Spirituality and positive mental health. *Asian Journal of Psychiatry, 5*(4), 289.

Kevern, P., Walsh, J., & McSherry, W. (2013). The representation of service users' religious and spiritual concerns in care plans. *Journal of Public Mental Health, 12*(3), 153–164.

Kim, U., Yang, K.-S., & Hwang, K. K. (Eds.). (2006). *Indigenous and cultural psychology: Understanding people in context.* New York, NY: Springer Science+Business Media.

King, L. (2012). Meaning: Ubiquitous and effortless. In P. Shaver & M. Mikulincer (Eds.), *Meaning, mortality, and choice: The social psychology of existential concerns* (pp. 129–144). Washington, DC: American Psychological Association.

Krumrei, E., & Rosmarin, D. (2012). Processes of religious and spiritual coping. In J. Aten, K. O'Grady, & E. Worthington, Jr. (Eds.), *The psychology of religion and spirituality for clinicians: Using research in your practice* (pp. 245–273). New York, NY: Routledge.

Kübler-Ross, E. (1997). *On death and dying.* New York, NY: Scribner. (Original work published 1969)

Lake-Thom, B. (1997). *Spirits of the earth: A guide to Native American nature symbols, stories and symbols.* New York, NY: Plume/Penguin.

Lao-tzu. (1995). Tao te ching (S. Mitchell, Trans.). Retrieved from http://acc6.its.brooklyn.cuny.edu/~ phalsall/texts/taote-v3.html

Lee, G., & Wheeler, G. (2003). *The voice of shame: Silence and connection in psychotherapy.* Cambridge, MA: GestaltPress.

Lesser, E. (1999). *The seeker's guide: Making your life a spiritual adventure.* New York, NY: Villard Books/Random House.

Levinas, E. (1969). *Totality and infinity* (A. Lingis, Trans.). Pittsburgh, PA: Duquesne University Press.

Levinas, E. (1999). *Alterity & transcendence.* New York, NY: Columbia University Press.

Lewin, K. (1935). The conflict between Aristotelian and Galileian modes of thought in contemporary psychology. In *A dynamic theory of personality: Selected papers of Kurt Lewin* (pp. 1–42). New York, NY: McGraw-Hill. (Reprinted from *Journal of General Psychology, 5,* 141–177, by C. Murchison, Ed., 1931)

Lewin, K. (1940). Review of explorations in personality. *Journal of Abnormal and Social Psychology, 35*(2), 283–285.

Lewin, K. (1943). Defining the "field at a given time." *Psychological Review, 50*(3), 292–310.

Lewin, K. (1951). *Field theory in social science: Selected theoretical papers* (D. Cartwright, Ed.). New York, NY: Harper.

Lewis, M. (1997). *Altering fate: Why the past does not predict the future.* New York, NY: Guilford.

Limberg, B. (2013). Religion, spirituality and secularism in multicultural contexts. In R. Lowman (Ed.), *Internationalizing multiculturalism: Expanding professional competencies in a globalized world* (pp. 143–170). Washington, DC: American Psychological Association.

Lindsey, H. (1970). *The late great planet earth.* Grand Rapids, MI: Zondervan.

Lucas, J. (2003). *Knowing the unknowable God: How faith thrives on divine mystery.* Colorado Springs, CO: WaterBrook Press.

Macdonald, D. B. (1932). The development of the idea of spirit in Islam. *The Muslim World, 22*(1), 24–42.

Mann, D. (2010). *Gestalt therapy: 100 key points & techniques.* New York, NY: Routledge.

Marion, J.-L. (2000). Saturated phenomenon. In D. Janicaud (Ed.), *Phenomenology and the "theological turn"* (pp. 177–216). New York, NY: Fordham University Press.

Marion, J.-L. (2002). *Being given: Toward a phenomenology of givenness.* Stanford, CA: Stanford University Press.

McGrath, A. (1999). *Christian spirituality.* Oxford, UK: Blackwell.

Melchizedek, D. (1998). *The ancient secret of the flower of life* (Vol. 1). Flagstaff, AZ: Light Technology.

Merleau-Ponty, M. (1968). *The visible and the invisible.* Evanston, IL: Northwestern University Press.

Metaxas, E. (2010). *Bonhoeffer: Pastor, martyr, prophet, spy.* Nashville, TN: Thomas Nelson.

Meyerstein, I. (2006). Spiritually sensitive counseling with Jewish clients and families. In K. Helmeke & C. Sori (Eds.), *The therapist's notebook for integrating spirituality in counseling II: Homework, handouts and activities for use in psychotherapy. Haworth practice in mental health* (pp. 141–155). New York, NY: Haworth Press.

Michener, J. A. (1992). *The world is my home: A memoir.* New York, NY: Random House.

Moltu, C., Binder, P.-E., & Stige, B. (2012). Collaborating with the client: Skilled psychotherapists' experiences of the client's agency as a premise for their own contribution in difficult therapies ending well. *Journal of Psychotherapy Integration, 22*(2), 85–108.

Moriarty, G., & Davis, E. (2012). Client God images: Theory, research, and clinical practice. In J. Aten, K. O'Grady, & E. Worthington, Jr. (Eds.), *The psychology of religion and spirituality for clinicians: Using research in your practice* (pp. 131–160). New York, NY: Routledge.

Moriarty, G., & Hoffman, L. (Eds.). (2007). *God image handbook for spiritual counseling and psychotherapy: Research, theory, and practice.* Binghamton, NY: Haworth/Routledge.

Mounce, W. (2003). *Basics of Biblical Greek grammar* (2nd ed.). Grand Rapids, MI: Zondervan.

Muhammad Ali, M. (2002). *The holy Qur'an: Arabic text with English translation and commentary.* Dublin, OH: Ahmadiyya Anjuman Isha' at Islam Lahore.

Murphy, G. (1947). Field theory. In *Personality: A biosocial approach to origins and structure* (pp. 880–902). New York, NY: Harper.

Murphy, N. (2006). *Bodies and souls, or spirited bodies? (Current issues in theology).* Cambridge, UK: Cambridge University Press.

Murphy, N., & Brown, W. (2009). *Did my neurons make me do it?: Philosophical and neurobiological perspectives on moral responsibility and free will.* New York, NY: Oxford University Press.

Murray, H. (1938). *Explorations in personality.* New York, NY: Oxford University Press.

Nelson, J. (2009). *Psychology, religion, and spirituality.* New York, NY: Springer Science+Business Media.

Nerburn, K. (1999). *The wisdom of the Native Americans: Including the soul of an Indian, and other writings of Ohiyesa and the great speeches of Red Jacket, Chief Joseph, and Chief Seattle.* Novato, CA: New World Library.

Norcross, J., & Lambert, M. (2011). Psychotherapy relationships that work II. *Psychotherapy, 48*(1), 4–8.

Norcross, J., & Wampold, B. (2011). Evidence-based therapy relationships: Research conclusions and clinical practices. *Psychotherapy, 48*(1), 98–102.

Norcross, J. (Ed.). (2011). *Psychotherapy relationships that work.* New York, NY: Oxford University Press.

O'Conner, T., & Wong, H. Y. (2006). Emergent properties. In E. N. Zalta (Ed.), *The Stanford encyclopedia of philosophy.* Retrieved from http://plato.stanford .edu/entries/properties-emergent

O'Grady, K., & Bartz, J. (2012). Addressing spiritually transcendent experiences in psychotherapy. In J. Atan, K. O'Grady, & E. Worthington, Jr. (Eds.), *The psychology of religion and spirituality for clinicians: Using research in your practice* (pp. 161–188). New York, NY: Routledge.

O'Laoghaire, D. (1986). Celtic spirituality. In C. Jones, G. Wainwright, & E. Yarnold (Eds.), *The study of spirituality* (pp. 216–225). New York, NY: Oxford University Press.

Otto, R. (1950). *The idea of the holy.* Oxford, UK: Oxford University Press. (Original work published 1923)

Oxford Islamic Studies Online. (n.d.-a). *Nafs.* Oxford, UK: Oxford University Press. Retrieved from http://www.oxfordislamicstudies.com/article/opr/t125/e1690?_hi=4&_pos=1

Oxford Islamic Studies Online. (n.d.-b). *Ruh*. Oxford, UK: Oxford University Press. Retrieved from http://www.oxfordislamicstudies.com/article/opr/t125/e2027?_hi=3&_pos=1

PACFA. (2011). *Code of ethics: The ethical framework for best practice in counseling and psychotherapy*. Retrieved from http://www.pacfa.org.au/sitebuilder/aboutus/knowledge/asset/files/4/2012pacfacodeofethics.pdf

Packer, J. I. (1973). *Knowing god*. Downer's Grove, IL: InterVarsity Press.

Park, C., & Edmondson, D. (2012). Religion as a source of meaning. In P. Shaver & M. Mikulincer (Eds.), *Meaning, mortality, and choice: The social psychology of existential concerns* (pp. 145–162). Washington, DC: American Psychological Association.

Peng, Y. (2010). When formal laws and informal norms collide: Lineage networks versus birth control policy in China. *American Journal of Sociology, 116*(3), 770–805.

Perls, F., Hefferline, R., & Goodman, P. (1972). *Gestalt therapy: Excitement and growth in the human personality*. London, UK: Souvenir Press. (Original work published 1951)

Peters, F. E. (2004). *The children of Abraham: Judaism, Christianity, Islam*. Princeton, NJ: Princeton University Press.

Phillips, J. B. (1967). *Your God is too small*. New York, NY: Macmillan.

Polster, E. (2006). *Uncommon ground: Harmonizing psychotherapy and community to enhance everyday living*. Phoenix, AZ: Zeig, Tucker, & Theisen.

Polster, E. (2009a). A next giant step for psychotherapy. In B. O'Neill (Ed.), *Community, psychotherapy, and life focus: A gestalt anthology of the history, theory, and practice of living in community* (pp. 45–62). Wollongong East, Australia: Ravenwood Press.

Polster, E. (2009b). From the supernatural to the human. In B. O'Neill (Ed.), *Community, psychotherapy, and life focus: A gestalt anthology of the history, theory, and practice of living in community* (pp. 63–72). Wollongong East, Australia: Ravenwood Press.

Post, B. C., Wade, N. G., & Cornish, M. A. (2013, November 4). Religion and spirituality in group counseling: Beliefs and preferences of university counseling center clients. *Group Dynamics: Theory, Research, and Practice*. Advance online publication. doi:10.1037/a0034759

Quellette, P., Kaplan, R., & Kaplan, S. (2005). The monastery as a restorative environment. *Journal of Environmental Psychology, 25*(2), 175–188.

Quinte, W. V., & Ullian, J. S. (1978). *The web of belief* (2nd ed.). New York, NY: Random House.

Repcheck, J. (2007). *Copernicus' secret: How the scientific revolution began*. New York, NY: Simon & Schuster.

Richmond, L. (1999). *Work as a spiritual practice: A practical Buddhist approach to inner growth and satisfaction on the job*. New York, NY: Broadway Books/Random House.

Robinson, H. (2007). Dualism. In E. N. Zalta (Ed.), *The Stanford encyclopedia of philosophy*. Retrieved from http://plato.stanford.edu/entries/dualism

Rodolfa, E., Bent, R., Eisman, E., Nelson, P., Rehm, L., & Ritchie, P. (2005). A cube model for competency development: Implications for psychology educators and regulators. *Professional Psychology: Research and Practice, 36*(4), 347–354.

Rosenfeld, G. (2011). Contributions from ethics and research that guide integrating religion into psychotherapy. *Professional Psychology: Research and Practice, 42*(2), 192–199.

Roubal, J. (2009). Experiment: A creative phenomenon of the field. *Gestalt Review, 13*(3), 263–276.

Russell, S. R., & Yarhouse, M. A. (2006). Training in religion/spirituality within APA-accredited psychology predoctoral internships. *Professional Psychology: Research and Practice, 37*, 430–436. doi:10.1037/0735-7028.37.4.430

Salih Al-Munajjid, S. M. Who is the Holy Spirit? *Islam Q & A.* Retrieved from http://islamqa.info/en/ref/14403

Saunders, S., Miller, M., & Bright, M. (2010). Spiritually conscious psychological care. *Professional Psychology: Research and Practice, 41*(5), 355–362.

Schaeffer, F. (1971). *True spirituality: How to live for Jesus moment by moment.* Carol Stream, IL: Tyndale House.

Schilbrack, K. (2012). The social construction of "religion" and its limits: A critical reading of Timothy Fitzgerald. *Method and Theory in the Study of Religion, 24*, 97–117.

Shafranske, E., & Cummings, J. (2013). Religious and spiritual beliefs, affiliations, and practices of psychologists. In K. Pargement, A. Mahoney, & E. Shafranske (Eds.), *APA handbook of psychology, religion, and spirituality, vol. 2: An applied psychology of religion and spirituality. APA handbooks in psychology* (pp. 23–41). Washington, DC: American Psychological Association.

Sheldrake, P. (2012). *Spirituality: A very short introduction.* Oxford, UK: Oxford University Press.

Shellabear, W. G. (1932). The meaning of the word "spirit" as used in the Koran. *The Muslim World, 22*(4), 355–360.

Shi, L., & Zhang, C. (2012). Spirituality in traditional Chinese medicine. *Pastoral Psychology, 61*(5–6), 959–974.

Shiah, Y.-J., Chang, F., Tam, W.-C. C., Chuang, S.-F., & Yeh, L.-C. (2013). I don't believe but I pray: Spirituality, instrumentality, or paranormal belief? *Journal of Applied Social Psychology, 43*(8), 1704–1716.

Shults, F., & Sandage, S. (2006). *Transforming spirituality: Integrating theology and psychology.* Grand Rapids, MI: Baker Academic.

Singer, I. B. (1973). The bishop's robe. In I. B. Singer (Ed.), *A crown of feathers* (pp. 137–148). New York, NY: Fawcett Crest.

Singh, G., & Cowden, S. (2011). Multiculturalism's new fault lines: Religious fundamentalisms and public policy. *Critical Social Policy, 31*(3), 343–364.

Sittser, G. (2007). *Water from a deep well: Christian spirituality from early martyrs to modern missionaries*. Downer's Gove, IL: InterVarsity Press.

Smith, J. K. A. (2010). *Thinking in tongues: Pentecostal contributions to Christian philosophy*. Grand Rapids, MI: William B. Eerdman's.

Smith, W. C. (1962). *The meaning and end of religion*. Minneapolis, MN: Fortress.

Spinelli, E. (2005). *The interpreted world: An introduction to phenomenological psychology* (2nd ed.). Thousand Oaks, CA: SAGE.

Stein, E. (2009). *Potency and act: Studies toward a philosophy of being, volume XI in the collected works of Edith Stein*. Washington, DC: ICS. (Original work published 1931)

Stein, E. (2002). *Finite and eternal being: An attempt at an ascent to the meaning of being, volume IX in the collected works of Edith Stein*. Washington, DC: ICS.

Steiner, R. (2013). *An outline of occult science*. New York, NY: Start Publishing.

Stoeger, W. (2002). The mind-brain problem, the laws of nature, and constitutive relationships. In R. Russel, N. Murphy, T. Meyering, & M. Arbib (Eds.), *Neuroscience and the person: Scientific perspectives on divine action* (pp. 129–146). Vatican City State: Vatican Observatory/Center for Theology and the Natural Sciences.

Sue, D. W., Bingham, R. P., Porche-Burke, L., & Vasquez, M. (1999). The diversification of psychology: A multicultural revolution. *American Psychologist, 54*, 1061–1069.

Tan, A. (2003). *The opposite of fate: Memories of a writing life*. New York, NY: Penguin.

Tangney, J., & Fischer, K. (1995). *Self-conscious emotions: The psychology of shame, guilt, embarrassment, and pride*. New York, NY: Guilford Press.

Taylor, D. (1992). *The myth of certainty: The reflective Christian & the risk of commitment*. Downers Grove, IL: InterVarsity Press.

Tertin, B. (2013, November). When pot is legal, what do we say. Leadership Journal. Retrieved from http://www.christianitytoday.com/le/2013/november-online-only/what-would-jesus-smoke.html

Thomas, L. (2013). Research report: Spatial working memory is necessary for actions to guide thought. *Journal of Experimental Psychology: Learning, Memory, and Cognition, 39*(6), 1974–1981.

Tillich, P. (1959). *Theology of culture*. New York, NY: Oxford University Press.

Tolle, E. (2005). *A new earth: Awakening to your life's purpose*. New York, NY: Penguin Group.

Torrey, R. A. (2000). *The power of prayer*. New Kensington, PA: Whitaker House.

Tougas, C. (2013). *The phenomena of awareness: Husserl, Cantor, Jung*. New York, NY: Routledge/Taylor & Francis Group.

Tracy, J., Robins, R., & Tangney, J. (2007). *The self-conscious emotions: Theory and research*. New York, NY: Guilford Press.

Truscott, D. (2010). Existential. In D. Truscott (Ed.), *Becoming an effective psychotherapist: Adopting a theory of psychotherapy that's right for you and your client* (pp. 53–66). Washington, DC: American Psychological Association.

Turel, O., & Connelly, C. (2012). Team spirit: The influence of psychological collectivism on the usage of E-collaboration tools. *Group Decision and Negotiation, 21*(5), 703–725.

Vieten, C., Scammell, S., Pilato, R., Ammondson, I., Pargament, K., & Lukoff, D. (2013). Spiritual and religious competencies for psychologists. *Psychology of Religion and Spirituality, 5*(3), 129–144.

Viney, D. (2008). Process theism. In E. Zalta (Ed.), *The Stanford encyclopedia of philosophy,* np. Retrieved from http://plato.stanford.edu/archives/win2008/entries/process-theism

Walker, D. F., Gorsuch, R. L., & Tan, S. (2004). Therapists' integration of religion and spirituality in counseling: A meta-analysis. *Counseling and Values, 49,* 69–80.

Wedel, J. (2012). Involuntary mass spirit possession among the Miskitu. *Anthropology & Medicine, 19*(3), 303–314.

Weller, P. (2010). Lost in translation: Human rights and mental health law. In B. McSherry & P. Weller (Eds.), *Rethinking rights-based mental health law* (pp. 51–72). Portland, OR: Hart.

Wells, H. G. (2013). *The time machine.* USA: SoHo Books. (Original work published 1895)

Wiesel, E. (2006). *Night.* New York, NY: Hill and Wang. (Original work published 1985)

Willard, D. (1988). *The spirit of the disciplines: Understanding how God changes lives.* New York, NY: HarperCollins.

Willard, D. (1998). *The divine conspiracy: Rediscovering our hidden life in God.* New York, NY: HarperSanFranciso/HarperCollins.

Willard, D. (1999). *Hearing God: Developing a conversational relationship with God.* Downer's Grove, IL: InterVarsity Press.

Williams, M., Teasdale, J., Segal, Z., & Kabat-Zinn, J. (2007). *The mindful way through depression: Freeing yourself from chronic unhappiness.* New York, NY: The Guilford Press.

Wilson, D. (2011). *Spiritualist mediums and other traditional shamans: Towards an apprenticeship model of shamanic practice.* (Doctoral dissertation). School of Divinity, College of Humanities and Social Science, University of Edinburgh. Printed in *Redefining shamanisms: Spiritualist mediums and other traditional shamans as apprenticeship outcomes.* (2013). New York, NY: Bloomsbury Academic/Bloomsbury.

Wink, P., Adler, J., & Dillon, M. (2012). Developmental and narrative perspectives on religious and spiritual identity for clinicians. In J. Aten, K. O'Grady, & E. Worthington (Eds.), *The psychology of religion and spirituality for clinicians: Using research in your practice* (pp. 39–67). New York, NY: Routledge.

Winick, B. J. (1997). *The right to refuse mental health treatment.* Washington, DC: American Psychological Association.

Witesman, E., & Wise, C. (2012). The reformer's spirit: How public administrators fuel training in the skills of good governance. *Public Administration Review, 72*(5), 710–725.

Wojtyla, K. (1979). *The acting person: Analecta Husserliana, the yearbook of phenomenological research* (Vol. X). Dordrecht, The Netherlands: D. Reidel.

Wolterstorff, N. (1995). *Divine discourse: Philosophical reflections on the claim that God speaks.* New York, NY: Cambridge University Press.

Wright, N. T. (1992). *The New Testament and the people of God.* Minneapolis, MN: Fortress Press.

Yancey, P. (2003). *Rumours of another world: What on earth are we missing?* Grand Rapids, MI: Zondervan.

Yontef, G. (1997). Relationship and sense of self in gestalt therapy training. *Gestalt Journal, 20*(1), 17–48.

Yontef, G., & Bar-Yoseph, T. L. (2008). Dialogical relationship. In P. Brownell (Ed.), *Handbook for theory, research, and practice in gestalt therapy* (pp. 184–197). Newcastle, UK: Cambridge Scholars.

Young, J. S., Wiggins-Frame, M., & Cashwell, C. S. (2007). Spirituality and counselor competence: A national survey of American Counseling Association members. *Journal of Counseling and Development, 85*, 47–85.

Žižek, S. (2003). *The puppet and the dwarf: The perverse core of Christianity.* Cambridge, MA: MIT Press.

Zukov, G. (1989). *The seat of the soul.* New York, NY: Fireside/Simon & Schuster.

Index